THE EMPEROR'S CLOTHES

To

ROBERT NEUMANN

CONTENTS

Chap.		Page
I.	The Landlady's Ornaments	1
II.	The Dogma in the Manger	31
III.	Mr. Hulme's Sloppy Dregs	56
IV.	Mr. Eliot's Liberal Worms	105
V.	Mr. Willey's Lunar Spots	140
VI.	Old Puritan Writ Large	159
VII.	Poetry and Truth	194
VIII.	Poetry and Truth (cont.): Romanticism and Classicism	233
IX.	Lord Peter Views the Soul	253
X.	Augustinian Novelists	299
XI.	The New Philistinism	312
ACKNOWLEDGEMENTS		325
INDEX		326

CHAPTER I

The Landlady's Ornaments

NOWADAYS we are very commonly told that the Age lacks Faith. When this statement is made from pulpits, it means that the churches lack congregations, and that too is what it usually means when it is given as a conclusion to public opinion surveys. On the other hand, we are also very commonly told that Reason has failed. These statements might lead to the simple and melancholy belief that the majority of us at present has neither reason nor faith, not even faith in reason. I think there is a certain sense in which each statement can be taken, if not as true, at least as a warrantable generalisation. But that sense would depend on a careful definition of what the users mean by those rather vague expressions 'Faith' and 'Reason'. If we adopt both statements as true, it looks as if we shall have to account for the present uncomfortable state of the world by the theory that what used to be called our faculties are simply exhausted.

I do not wish to deny that the world is in a bad way. But I must add that there is no bad time like the present. Any extension of our knowledge, either of ourselves or of history, confirms this opinion. I would even agree that more faith, in something or the other, makes it easier for people to live their lives, at some level or the other. But my interest, with which the whole of this book is connected, is rather with the other statement—that Reason has failed.

There are many different tones of voice in which this statement can be made. During and before the last war, many speakers made it in connection with the condition of Germany, in a tone of alarm and regret. Those who spoke with any precision usually meant that 'reasoning has failed', that people who were still able

1

to see a reasonable point of view, one based on real experience of human needs and circumstances, were not strong enough to put this point of view to Hitler and his colleagues.

But the statement, in one form of words or another, is now being put forward by a different kind of proponent, who also means something quite different by it, though he is not always clear what he does mean; and he says it in quite a different tone of voice. The commonest member of this class is a literary critic who is attracted toward general ideas, although he is not always skilled in dealing with them. Under the decent tone of mourning with which he celebrates the obsequies of Reason, one can often detect a faint note of satisfaction. This can only be explained by supposing that he believes that, if Reason has indeed failed, we have something better to put in its place. That is what the literary critics or the writers about literature, with which this book is largely concerned, do mean. They mean that something which they call Reason has failed to provide us with an explanation or a way of life, and that therefore something else called Faith can come into its own.

Basil Willey* shows that many seventeenth-century anti-rationalists thought that to discard superstition, including the belief in witches, might be the first step towards atheism. It was better to believe anything than nothing. With the exception of C. S. Lewis, whose interest in the Devil plumbs unusual depths, most of the writers with whom I shall deal are not so conventionally anti-rationalist as this. They merely claim to represent orthodox Christian theology and a higher kind of reason.

Anyone who writes about literature ought to have cultivated a sense of history, including the history of philosophy and its terms. If he has done so, he will have involved himself in some attempt at understanding how philosophy and the meaning of the terms it uses have been affected by the development of the sciences. The sciences show men at work employing, among other mental capacities, their reasoning power. There is no sign that Reason, in this sense, has so far failed mankind. One of my

*The Seventeenth Century Background.

motives in writing this book has been the realisation that the thinkers whom I discuss do not find this fact, if indeed they grasp it, as consolatory as they should.

Philosophers themselves have been considerably responsible, by using the term in a variety of ways which are sometimes inconsistent, for the confusion which is so common to the literary. They have been fond of distinguishing what they call *a priori* modes of thought, for instance the particular kinds of abstraction which we employ in the mathematical sciences and in formal logic, from our other powers of obtaining knowledge by inference. What has impressed the philosophers about mathematical knowledge has been its certainty. They attributed this certainty to the fact that the mathematician or logician extracted truth by analysing the implications of the propositions or statements with which he dealt. How far such propositions were applicable to the reality of experience was not relevant.

Every philosopher building a system of the universe has had a hankering for a like certainty. Philosophers infect the literary and make them yearn too, if indeed the yearning is not what makes every man a philosopher at heart. But our ability to reason is based on inference, on our attachment to human experience, and this can never give us more than a high approximation to certainty. Our world is probability. This was grasped by philosophers such as Hume and Kant; but even these two, to a different degree, by their attitudes toward mathematical reasoning, have misled those whose emotional hunger for certainty is so great that they choose intellectual starvation if they cannot have their preferred diet. If by Reason we mean reasoning-power, our capacity for inference and thus for increase of real knowledge, we can say that Reason has not failed.

To many people, however, Reason stands only for our capacity for forming abstractions and deductive systems without the check or even the stimulus of experience. This is what passes for thought at many very different levels of learning. One of the main tasks of genuine thinking is to make sure that 'Reason' in this sense, does fail.

An opinion which is at least implied by a great many of the writers whom I shall discuss is that during the seventeenth century, because of the scientific and philosophical developments which took place, a valuable tradition was broken which should have remained dominant. In so far as these writers refer solely to the tradition of poetry, I agree that they have some justification for this opinion. But I shall propose a quite different set of causes, and I shall contradict the assumption, which lives like a gollywog in most of their ink-wells, that it would be a good thing if we were able to wish out of the way the dominant achievements of the eighteenth and nineteenth centuries.

The eighteenth century is often called The Age of Reason; and what is commonly complained of nowadays in the nineteenth century is less the aggressiveness and irrationality of its sexual and industrial relations (which however the lapse of time has not cured) than the rationalism of many of its leading writers and thinkers.

When we use the words 'century' or 'age' we mean in practice the intellectual attitude which was dominant and generally accepted as normal by two or three generations of people. In a certain sense we can describe the eighteenth century as the Age of Reason and we can also say that the nineteenth century was marked by an increase of rationalism. But it is as well to remember that in those ages, as at all times, most people, including those people who lived by employing one or more of their mental capacities, were governed at the best by feeling, and at the worst by prejudice, rather than by the results of the deliberate exercise of their reasoning power. This meant, then as always, that the majority of people were dominated by various abstractions. This realisation may help us to examine our own dominant abstractions and prevent us from absolutely preferring them.

Many of our contemporary writers and critics, especially those whom I call neo-scholastic, dislike the rationalism, liberalism and humanism which became dominant intellectual attitudes after the seventeenth century. But what is important, now as then, about these attitudes, is how far they can be described as true or false.

If they were merely abstractions, deductive systems of thought, and were not continually controlled by an ever-developing human experience, they were so far false. In so far as they sprang from the same experimental method which gives us a correct history, psychology and anthropology, they were true. What the neo-scholastic critics of those abstractions fail to observe is that, in advocating a return to dogmatic theology, to ecclesiastical 'orthodoxy', they themselves show that they are governed by a much falser and more obstinate abstraction. For there is no experimental check on theology.

Chief among those abstractions of previous history which are attacked by neo-scholastic literary critics today is the idea of inevitable progress, which is always linked by them with rationalism. I suggest that the cause for the failure of this idea, for our inability to believe in it any longer, is the same that we constantly discover in other generalisations and ideals which seem promising but which somehow fail to guide our lives—that it is a false abstraction. In other words, this idea was based on insufficient experience. That means that men were using their reasoning power, their capacity for inference, incorrectly or not enough. For reasoning or being rational is simply making logical inferences, examining experience impartially and returning to the check of experience. In so far as we use our reasoning power upon our experience we always make some progress in the direction we are exploring. Progress for the whole human race would be, if not inevitable, at least highly probable, if a sufficient majority of people were trained to use their reasoning power on their general experience, as a scientist is trained to use his reasoning power on his special experiences.

There were, no doubt, some excellent or exciting manifestations of the human spirit in the seventeenth century and before, which were set aside by the preoccupations of the eighteenth and nineteenth centuries. But, on the other hand, we can justly say that both these ages did much to establish a tradition which had become, and ought to have become, dominant in the seventeenth century, the tradition of experimentalism, of the correct use of reasoning power. The fact that, in this tradition, some people have now begun, however insufficiently, to reason about themselves, to apply scientific methods of inquiry to what, too often with unwarrantable implications of absolutism, we call human *nature*, is one of the main causes for the contemporary dislike of scientific method among influential literary men, and for their attempt to lump the scientific approach with all the other outworn and ultramontane abstractions.

The fact remains that, though there is no such thing as 'Inevitable Progress', by using our reasoning power upon our experience we do progress, and only so. If you will not allow that it is our human obligation to increase knowledge, and that the use of reason in the sense which I have defined it is an essential part of this work, you have no alternative save to build your intellectual framework out of dogma, abstractions whose analysis is forbidden. The writers whom I discuss and whom I call neo-scholastic, because they are reverting, at various speeds and from various directions, to a pre-scientific philosophy, try to do just this. Chief among the dogmas which they try to import into our intellectual outlook is the dogma of Original Sin, which is certainly the psychological foundation of Christian orthodoxy. This dogma implies, not that we do not or are unwilling to use our reasoning powers upon our own natures, but that we are incapable of doing so. Most of the people I discuss live by or on the use of imagination. That may make it excusable for them to cherish a mystery. But they ought not to foster mystification.

On all counts, Mr. T. S. Eliot is probably the most significant of the neo-scholastic writers in England today. This is partly because he is really distinguished as a poet and literary critic; partly because his reputation as an orthodox Christian became general only shortly after his reputation as a poet; partly because he has thus had nearly twenty years to establish his views in works which are always sure to be received with interest and respect; and partly because the method he uses to establish them is insidious.

In 1934 T. S. Eliot published his *After Strange Gods*. Its subtitle was 'A primer of orthodoxy'. This was not the first indication which he had given, either in prose or verse, of his theological views and intentions. There had been, for example, the collection of essays at first called *For Lancelot Andrewes*, later revised and re-issued as *Essays Ancient and Modern*; while in *Ash Wednesday* and some of the Ariel poems his conversion had already reached poetic expression. Nevertheless, I see *After Strange Gods* as a landmark, in the particular and remarkable sense which is implied in its sub-title.

The book consists of three lectures delivered to the University of Virginia. It is about orthodoxy and heresy as qualities which can be discovered and for which we ought to seek in contemporary literature. I do not think that Mr. Eliot fully succeeds either in defining or isolating these qualities. What he has in mind seems to be something closely in conformity with the theology of the Catholic Church, although even this is not categorically stated. But the kind of evaluation which he is attempting in this book certainly calls for such an arbiter. We have to conclude from this book that Mr. Eliot thinks that the Church ought to be the arbiter, not only of human but of literary values. In fact, he makes a curious distinction between literary and theological evaluations of merit: but I hope to show that from his own point of view this distinction is untenable. He made it perhaps because an excellent literary taste, acquired from learning to discriminate the best rather than the orthodox, was for the moment stronger than theological discipline.

For Mr. Eliot himself the book would probably lose its point if he were able to define its two main terms more precisely. Certainly for those who cannot help believing that the prime qualities of literature are something more interesting, important and indeed universal than orthodoxy and heresy, the book would lose most of its curious significance. For Mr. Eliot's quiet and really unargued reinstatement of these and other dogmatic terms is in itself a method. When first realised, its effect on a mind which cannot regard the liberal and humanistic tradition of free inquiry as dead is disquieting. Mr. Eliot reminds me of a dignified landlady who without a word retrieves the tribal ornaments from the cupboard where the guest has hidden them, and puts them back on the mantelpiece. The 'orthodox' or neo-scholastic literary movement of our time has had champions far more explicit, aggressive or naïve. Among writers who are mainly or solely creative, there are for instance Mauriac or Graham Greene, who express their orthodox theology through the colour of their imaginations. In explicit philosophy, between such extremes of dignity as Maritain on the one side, and C. S. Lewis or Miss Sayers on the other, we have T. E. Hulme, who was ready to tackle most of the tougher issues and whose baseless assumptions were few, if essential to his argument. But nothing has been more valuable to the scholastic reaction than Mr. Eliot's decorous though unlegitimised reoccupation of a territory which many of us had thought already subject to reason. Perhaps he soothes many whom he does not convince. People who care for literature and particularly for poetry would always sooner be reminded of the seventeenth-century pulpit in the golden age of tough-minded bishops, than of the soap-box. Those who, like C. S. Lewis and Miss Sayers, never shirk any theological issue, pay for their earnestness and temerity with a certain vulgarity, like the Salvation Army.

In any case, Mr. Eliot's approach is disturbing. He makes his critics feel ungentlemanly, not only because he has thus reticently identified his whole life with a point of view, but because no one can seriously question his importance as a poet and critic. As far as England in the twentieth century is concerned, it was his sensibility which restored poetry to itself. His apparent 'modernity' was not merely a reaction to Victorianism and Georgianism, to the work of Tennyson in decay, to Swinburne obsessed with verbalism, or to Drinkwater and the Squirearchy. It was a successful attempt to restore the true tradition of English poetry, the direction which it had lost since the seventeenth century. In this attempt to restore the English tradition, his instinct to use large transfusions of the European and the strictly contemporary was a sound and true one. Moreover his selection of the moment and even, in a partial sense, of the cause of the deviation from the true poetic apperception was also precise. In the seventeenth century, there did develop a 'split in sensibility', a dissociation between intellect and emotion which did not completely heal in poetry, until our day. One can however agree in part with the diagnosis and the treatment, while still questioning the pathology. The split in sensibility is, either openly or by implication, the foundation of much of Eliot's critical opinion. Implicitly his diagnosis has been that poetry was dying because of liberal humanism. Liberal humanism was based on free or scientific inquiry, which has shown itself as continually in conflict with the philosophy of the Church. The cure is 'orthodoxy'; submission to dogma, to authoritarian belief. If thought and emotion are split, if scientific inquiry conflicts with the world-view of the Church, then we must give up science. Though Eliot never, as far as I know, makes a definite pronouncement of this kind, it is implied in his use of the word 'orthodoxy'. In *After Strange Gods* we are told that there is an orthodox Christian sensibility which authors ought to exemplify. Mr. James Joyce did eminently exemplify this (the evidence is one short story, 'The Dead'). Lawrence and Katherine Mansfield, who often describe wanton cruelty and insensibility, and moreover express no moral disapproval of what they describe, did the opposite. Mr. Eliot ignores the rather commonplace explanation that both these authors may have felt it to be their first business to put down what they saw. Nor does he pay any attention to the fact that Lawrence's whole work was an express reaction against what he regarded as romantic falsifications of emotion. I do not think Lawrence was interested in cruelty as such. He was simply trying, often mistakenly, to get down to the truth about human sexual relationships. This of course left no room for any kind of 'orthodoxy' in his sensibility.

Mr. Eliot however thinks that such an orthodoxy of sensibility is possible and desirable. If we fit *After Strange Gods* into the implications of his work as a whole, we shall see that he follows T. E. Hulme in regarding the tradition of science and of liberal humanism as mainly responsible, not only for heresy or un-orthodoxy of sensibility, but for the 'split' which took place in the seventeenth century. But since his method is so rarely explicit, we shall have to examine the whole body of his critical and social writings. With many of his followers who have committed themselves more openly, if not more rashly, this will not be necessary.

I shall not only discuss the neo-scholastic movement in modern English criticism, the contemporary attempt to find a continuity with the world-view which existed before the Renaissance, when the method of scientific inquiry became dominant. I shall also attempt to provide some opinion on what the relations between literary, particularly poetic, apperception and scientific inquiry, that is, any free inquiry which aims at knowledge, ought reasonably to be. The very assumption that such relations can and ought to be found is an implicit claim that 'orthodoxy' is of its nature a bar to creative and critical development. I am saying therefore, among other things, that whatever went wrong with poetry after the seventeenth century, it was not 'science'; not, that is, the kind of inquiry which is free from regard for authoritarian beliefs. That Mr. Eliot is so important as a creator and critic, and continues to be so; that orthodoxy has not sterilised his production or his critical sensibility (although in my view it has weakened them), is the reason why he receives a large share of attention in this book. To most of the purely literary critics who have come after him, the fact that 'orthodoxy' has seemed to work; that, in competent hands, it has produced some interesting poetry and literature, has been perhaps of excessive importance. Orthodoxy or something like it has certainly provided a good many poets and some novelists with something to write about, but this fact does not justify us in making any assumptions about the value either of their work or of orthodoxy.

Writers who concern themselves with this problem of the split in sensibility, of the seventeenth-century impingement of scientific method and discovery upon the literary imagination, and who think that our present troubles have arisen because men then 'chose' a humanistic instead of a theological world-view, are fond of saying that 'Science' or 'Scientists' need only be accepted as talking sense inside their own fields; outside, their pronouncements are no more valid than anyone else's (unless, oddly enough, their religious and philosophical views happen to be 'orthodox', as they sometimes are). Mr. Basil Willey is a good example of this. The type of statement which he and his kind make is important for my purpose because of the way in which it is generally worded. It is not of course 'Science' which makes pronouncements: and the expression 'Scientist' as it is invariably used in this conjunction is in fact a similar piece of hypostasis. I mean that, when they refer to 'Science' or 'Scientists', Mr. Willey and those who agree with him create fictional entities to which they attribute objective substance. But a scientist's pronouncements are valid when they result from the application of scientific method. What this is can be discussed later on. The point is that there are no 'fields' which can be marked as out of bounds to scientific method, and this is true even though the results of inquiry may be negative. Similarly there is no abstract entity called Science, and no person who is wholly described as The Scientist. To those who hold that The Butcher is still The Butcher even when strolling out on early-closing day in a bowler hat and striped trousers instead of a striped apron, I should reply that when we are considering the butcher's field and the validity of his theory and practice, we are concerned with his actual selection, dissection, handling and delivery of joints. To many people, including myself, his butchery may be not only an influence upon his whole personality, but a symptom of it; but that is beside the point. We are talking of the application of a technique or a method and the validity of its results. What was rediscovered in the seventeenth century was the method by which we obtain and can hope to obtain knowledge.

To many of the writers I have quoted and intend to quote, for instance Willey, and in particular T. E. Hulme, with his philosophy of 'intuition' based on Bergson and opposing itself to the abstractive intellect, my analogy of The Butcher would probably be only too welcome. Hulme had a great part in the invention of the literary man's bogey of The Scientist dissecting a dead universe and delivering the ever more disjointed pieces. It is true that anyone using the method of science, the method of obtaining knowledge, has to spend part of his time generalising, forming hypotheses, and that this is a kind of 'abstraction'. But that it 'kills' anything is a mere metaphor from anatomical and botanical techniques. Whatever 'killed' poetry, or rather whatever weakened and impoverished poetic imagination from the seventeenth century onwards, it was not scientific method as such. Anyone engaged in scientific inquiry has to spend a great deal of his time in a learning passivity which differs from the poet's chiefly in its objects, which are those of direct external perception rather than those which have been selected by or subjected to internal emotion. Science is essentially the method by which we obtain knowledge. We therefore cannot say that there exist 'fields' in which The Scientist has nothing to tell us. (*A fortiori* we cannot say that we can obtain another kind of 'knowledge' in those fields, by other methods.)

It is worth noting that contemporary scholastic and theological thinkers are glad to invoke the authority of The Scientist who does make statements outside the 'field' of his speciality, provided that these confirm or can be interpreted as confirming the limitations of the scientific method of obtaining knowledge. Welcome also as equally authoritative are the interpretations, given by philosophers, of recent scientific discoveries or principles which can also be taken as meaning that our pursuit of knowledge is inherently limited. I should be surprised and dismayed at this common human wish for intellectual self-castration if I did not see that there was always in these cases a further intention of substituting a different kind of knowledge or 'truth', coupled with a sense of relief that the way to do this had apparently been left open. One must grasp that not to know something does not mean the same as to know something quite different.

'Scientists' as respectable as Eddington are joyfully invoked as theologians by the neo-scholastics. The word 'Scientists' is in inverted commas here because Eddington and others who apply scientific method and technique in a special field are in fact invoked by the neo-scholastics simply for the authority of that method and technique, not at all for its application: and also because it has been found in practice that they leave it behind, like everyone else, when they enter the field of theology and the supernatural.

This metaphysical use of the words Science and Scientist is typical of neo-scholasticism and is in fact made by all the writers criticised in this book. The practical purpose is to enable them to equate science with the quantitative sciences and thus to insinuate an unnecessary limitation into our human capacity for knowledge. Our inevitable errors and ignorance can then be attributed to the inadequacy of the human mind and of human intellectual procedure, while a different, divine and presumably perfect kind of knowledge can be posited on the other side of an impenetrable curtain. It is necessary therefore to state here that, in the usage of this book, and I believe in fact, a scientist is someone in the process of applying the scientific method of inquiry in no matter what field; while science is the accumulated and progressively organised body of results from such applications. Like the butcher, the scientist will take a day off, though less regularly, and stroll out in flannels instead of a white coat. Both of them are liable to become churchwardens. Both of them on their days off will be willing to chat and even to argue on a great variety of subjects which have nothing to do with the laboratory or the refrigerator. For both of them there will be an inevitable danger in this. On this day neither will be formed and circumscribed by the material in which both normally work, and which by its very nature largely accounts for the neatness and inevitability of their execution and for the chief value and further productivity of their results—that a structure of nature is revealed and that a community continues to be nourished on mental or physical meat. A butcher, though he may go to Smithfield and there take a shrewd interest in the operations of the wholesale market, let alone criticise the Government for bulk-buying, may be excused for a certain passivity toward the provenance of his material. Division of function is a principle at least of second nature. Similarly the scientist does not have to discuss ultimates in order to do some good precise work with his given material. He will, for example, discuss whether it exists or not, when he is being an amateur philosopher, on his day off. As an amateur philosopher, however, he has one great advantage over his fellow-churchwarden, the butcher, that his *expertise* is of much wider application. It is capable of exhibiting the structure of any material and predicting the future behaviour of any similar agglomeration or organisation of that material. The scientist, that is, can generally think correctly as a philosopher; because the philosopher, when he is thinking correctly, is thinking as a scientist, in relation to his particular material. The butcher has perhaps one advantage over both of them, at least as far as his working week is concerned; that when he has no carcase, he is not tempted to display any chops.

Whatever the butcher may think or not think about his whole-sale supplies, the scientist generally gets his working material from unimpeachable sources: from predecessors in the special field with a tradition which includes the view that they would not be paid by monkeying about with the facts and records; from instrument-makers with a tradition of accuracy which is priceless to themselves; and also from direct observation individually and in a team whose work is mutually corrective.

Unless a scientist is thus working in a given material, that is, with phenomena which force themselves on him as existing quite apart from his own personal and mental activity, and which he tries to account for by a recording and comparative technique, his views are no more interesting and conclusive than those of the butcher who is chatting of something other than chops; although they may be expressed with more literary grace.

It will be said that the material of theology, questions of the human being's feeling of guilt and responsibility, his sense of something outside himself at once supporting and punitive and therefore his capacity for love and dependence, his hopes and fears about death, are precisely something that does exist and force itself upon the attention of all of us, including scientists. In my sense of the word, none of these is a 'given' material. They are certainly just as much a material for scientific inquiry as anything else in the world; but, as one of its first tasks, such an inquiry has to try and isolate what is pure and spontaneous in such feelings, from what is the result of particular education and communal habit; to try and get down in fact to the 'given' material. In this field scientists are welcomed by the neo-scholastics only as theologians, not as scientists. Conversely, theological dogma is implicitly a refusal to admit that scientific inquiry can have any authoritative pronouncements to make about human responses.

It is significant that the scientists who have been promoted from churchwardens to deacons are usually physicists or astronomers, workers whose interests are most remote from the professional study of psychology, other people's and probably also their own. But we must remember that they are being invoked on their day off. Eddington, who is frequently thus invoked by literary men, and who answers, I must repeat, not as a scientist but as a theologian, so that his views carry no special scientific weight, has also been responsible for an excellent definition of scientific method. "Physical knowledge," he says, "is hypothetico-observational," and adds: "This means knowledge of the results of a hypothetical observation, not hypothetical interpretation of the result of an actual observation." This means that generalisation and experiment cannot be separated. The generalisation is already implied to some extent in the experiment which the scientific observer makes. But it is also the experiment, the operations which the scientist performs, which state the actual meaning of the generalisation. Neo-scholastic thinking, on the contrary, is always an attempt to force generalisation and experiment apart. It is common practice for all neo-scholastics and for those who dislike and fear science to try to identify scientific method with measuring techniques which are supposed to produce exact results; the implication is that where the material does not allow for exact calculations arising from the use of instruments, there can be no science.

Bertrand Russell, on the other hand, said that scientific method implied great boldness in the framing of hypotheses coupled with great patience in collecting facts. This agrees with Eddington's view but says nothing about calculating instruments. I mention this here because I want to make it clear at an early stage that what happened in the seventeenth century was the establishment of the recognition of the way in which we actually obtain knowledge, if at all. Men did not begin—far from it—by becoming materialists, or denying God; even less, as Mr. Willey suggests, did they suffer a mysterious change in their taste for 'explanations'. Simply it became visible beyond reasonable dispute, over a number of fields, that if we wish to know, observation is an essential part of expressing our ideas in meaningful form. This does not mean that we must have no general views in mind while we observe. Quite the contrary. But our ideas, our general views, are ideas of what we are looking for.

This hypothetico-observational principle, however, is a general one. It is an attitude of mind, or has to become one. In so far as it did become so, it probably made the biggest intellectual contribution to the liberal humanism which developed in Europe after the seventeenth century. The obsequies of this liberal humanism are now constantly—I hope prematurely—being celebrated by our neo-scholastics. Mr. Eliot and others condemn liberalism— by which they mean just this attitude to experience. It is a general principle, as I have said. One wonders therefore what neo-scholastics who use trains, steamships, aeroplanes, and are motored from stations and airports to give their international lectures, would put in its place. I do not say that these mechanical objects embody moral worth, only that they are inevitable long-term products of the hypothetico-observational approach. Many of our neo-scholastics, I am sure, are logical enough to be Luddites. They would give up their air passages if they could only have the medieval scholastic system undamaged by Galileo. But that is the least they must learn to ask. If men learn to think consistently in the direction that leads to aeroplanes, they will also think in the direction away from authoritarianism and therefore theology. Moreover, they will learn to think in a direction which leads to classifying all phenomena as objects of study, therefore we can say, as examples, toward psychology and anthropology and away from Sin and the Church. Those who blame 'Science' and

'Scientists' for our misfortunes would speak more accurately if they blamed scientists for not thinking consistently, for not applying their method to all the phenomena they meet, for having too many days off. If scientific workers were in fact consistent, they would realise and also demonstrate that their method is a unifying principle. It is useless to say for instance that you cannot 'measure' the mind. You can observe it. Mechanical materialism and mechanical idealism no more and no less than modern scholasticism are all, as philosophies, forms of hypostasis, of attributing existence to the unknowable. They are therefore essentially attempts to deny this principle of the unity of knowledge which we should have learned and accepted in the seventeenth century.

One of the main theses of this book is that the growing body of knowledge is thus unified; that we know, if at all, in one way, not two. Another main theme is a question which I shall make some attempt to answer: If we assume that there is this unity, a growing unity of a growing body of knowledge, what relations ought to exist between it and the human mind in its imaginative and creative functions? I find it impossible to believe that no such relations need exist, that ascertainable truth is of no importance to an imaginative or indeed a critical writer. On the other hand I see that an important and vocal section of our literary life both in England and Europe does, implicitly at least, assume that there are two ways of attaining to truth, the one scientific and presumably inductive—this is lightly treated as a rule—and the other theological. To this section any admission of limitation in the applicability of scientific method, any suggestion that there are fields in which our hypothetico-observational principle cannot achieve any results, is a kind of victory. They are often misled by philosophers; and often also scientists themselves do not bother to make themselves plain enough. The propaganda-value and the comfort provided by these 'victories', these triumphs of a certain kind of 'invincible ignorance', are so great however that perhaps no explanation can ever be plain enough. The so-called Indeterminacy Principle is a case in point (the Principle of Uncertainty associated with Heisenberg). This has been and still is continually referred to as something which undermines causality, and so leaves the door open for Free Will and the Spiritual. Bertrand Russell however has stated quite clearly what the Principle is really about and what conclusions we are or are not justified in drawing from it.* In *The Scientific Outlook* he writes:

"The Principle of Indeterminacy states that it is impossible to determine with precision both the position and the momentum of a particle; there will be a margin of error in each, and the product of the two errors is constant. That is to say, the more accurately we determine the one, the less accurately we shall be determining the other . . . the Principle of Indeterminacy has to do with measurement *not* with causation. . . . [The Indeterminacy] is a physical fact causally connected with the fact that the measuring is a physical process which has a physical effect upon what is measured. There is nothing whatever in the Principle of Indeterminacy to show that any physical event is uncaused."

This should be plain enough. That it is not is shown—among a host of examples—by a reputable literary critic, Mr. Walter Allen commenting on a reputable scientist's opinions (Dr. J. Bronowski: *The Common Sense of Science*).

"Indeed, so far from the universe and nature being governed by immutable laws, it now appears that what lies at the heart of the universe and nature is—uncertainty. The future of the electron cannot be predicted with complete certainty because we can never be completely certain of its present. Heisenberg's principle of uncertainty refers to very small particles and events, but, as Dr. Bronowski comments:

" 'These small events are not by any means unimportant. They are just the sorts of events which go on in the nerves and the brain and in the giant molecules which determine the qualities we inherit.' (By the time we have inherited them they are not uncertain.)

*And see p. 270.

"This revolution Dr. Bronowski summarises:

" '(The notion of uncertainty) replaces the concept of the inevitable effect by that of the probable trend . . . the uncertainty *is* the world. The future does not already exist; it can only be predicted. . . . History is neither determined nor random. At any moment it moves forward into an area whose general shape is known, but whose boundaries are uncertain in a calculable way. . . . The will on the one hand and the compulsion on the other exist and play within these boundaries.' "

From all this Mr. Allen proceeds to draw the conclusion:

"If statistical probabilities have taken the place of immutable laws and if it is the essence of statistical probabilities that they can tell us how often, in a given series, the coin will fall heads and how often tails, but can never tell us the sequence in which they will fall heads or tails, then once again the onus for the future is thrown upon individual choice and action." (He finds a reflection of this in literary existentialism.)

I should say, on the other hand, that there was nothing in the Heisenberg Uncertainty Principle and indeed nothing in Dr. Bronowski's remarks to justify any statements at all about the freedom of the will (individual choice and action). The Uncertainty Principle, as Russell says, tells us about physical measurements, not about hypostatical entities such as Will and Freedom. As Dr. Bronowski says—"History is neither determined nor random. At any moment it moves forward into an area whose general shape is known, but whose boundaries are uncertain *in a calculable way*." (Not in an incalculable one.)

It is true that we have now to accept a philosophy based on statistical probabilities rather than detailed and strict determination. But I think that Mr. Allen's misunderstanding arises from an old confusion between determinism and predictability which was one of the errors of nineteenth-century billiard-ball mechanism. This confused view is the one which can be stated as:

if we knew all causes we should know all events. This view, if it is to have verifiable meaning, posits an All-Knower, a concept which is itself unverifiable in experience. The confusion is one which, says Russell, speaking of Bergson, "vitiates . . . a great deal of the thought of most modern philosophers—I mean the confusion between an act of knowing and that which is known."

Bronowski, it seems to me, has the distinction clear, for he says: "The future does not already exist; it can only be *predicted*." Mr. Allen ought to note that he says "It *can* be predicted."

What Dr. Bronowski's book is about is the improvement of the understanding of the sciences by poets and artists. As Mr. Allen goes on to comment:

"What one dreams of, of course, is that poets and men of letters should be as much at home in the ideas *that have made their world* as Dante and Chaucer were in theirs and Dryden in his. Perhaps it is no longer possible. But if that is so, science, to go back to Wordsworth, will never put on form of flesh and blood and take its place as a dear and genuine inmate of the household of man. In which case, we may expect the 'loss of nerve' that according to Dr. Bronowski has befallen us as a *result of the shattering of the unity of knowledge* to be progressive."

These comments seem to me instructive and just. In particular it seems to me that poets ought to grasp not only what ideas have made their world but that these ideas have really done so; and that first of all they ought to grasp what it is that constitutes the unity of knowledge. If they do not grasp that this unity in fact consists in the method by which we obtain knowledge and that this method is the essential characteristic of science, it is certain, so it seems to me, that the assumption that knowledge is not essentially unified will take over and dominate them, as it is already beginning to do. This means further that the only intellectual system which they can adopt will be one based on authority, not on inquiry. We all of course believe much on mere 'authority' and, to live, we are obliged to do so. The important thing is that nothing should prevent us, poets or citizens, from using our minds if we have the will and ability to use them.

This is not abstract 'Liberalism' (with which Mr. Eliot says our society is 'worm-eaten'); it is the principle of biological survival. That free inquiry often produces fear and repugnance, as well as enlightenment and liberation, is not an argument against it, although it is true that these emotions always have that apparent force in the minds of those who prefer some other system, and account for much of the reaction against 'liberalism'. Intellectually, as I have already tried to show, nothing has changed in a way which justifies the reaction, between the seventeenth century and our day. This means that, in spite of the ill-founded philosophical contributions of some scientists, there really has been no new development in science and critical philosophy which justifies a departure, in any branch of thought, from what Eddington himself called the hypothetico-observational method of obtaining knowledge. What our age may have to content itself with learning is that we *know* not so much and may not soon know very much more, even of what it seems biologically imperative for us to know. On the other hand, to depart from the method which leads us to knowledge will not make us any less ignorant.

What Eddington called the hypothetico-observational method has throughout history been the method, and the only method by which men have arrived at what real knowledge they have. This means that in so far as the method has been applied, there has been a certain *progress*. A 'belief in progress' became dogmatic (and was thus of course mistaken), during the nineteenth century, as a result of the very successful application of the method in physical and mechanical fields. Historically, the contemporary development of a counter-philosophy, based on scholasticism and theology, can best be understood as a reaction against this 'belief in progress'.

Certainly, the neo-scholastics can point to insecurity, war, destruction and a refusal to go to church, wherever they look; but to blame these on to science, on to the desire, the possibility and the method to know more, seems to be a clear case of *post hoc, propter hoc*. The disparagement of scientific method, and the refusal to admit that its applicability is potentially unlimited, express themselves among those who are not yet wholly convinced by dogma in general statements of the type—"Our moral progress has not kept pace with our material progress"; and among those who have become converted, in statements about Original Sin. The belief in Original Sin, the belief that human beings are born essentially 'bad' and cannot become 'good', except through supernatural assistance, generally implies in practice that we cannot become better by knowing more about ourselves and about the nature which we share with others.

The belief in progress did in fact, as I have said, become dogmatic in the nineteenth century, therefore uncritical; and, in so far as uncritical, false. But it is useless and senseless to base dislike of scientific method upon the beliefs and conduct of people who merely saw its achievements in the limited physical field but who made no attempt to apply it in their own private lives, nor in their public activities and relationships, and who indeed did not begin to understand that it was possible to make such an application. By the beginning of the twentieth century the collection of the data of observation of human mental life and human social relations had hardly begun, and we are only now in the stage of framing some of the most important hypotheses.

However anti-Pelagian* your view of 'progress', it is in fact fairly useless to deny that 'knowledge' does, within the limitations of its own method, 'progress'. That a large number of contemporary critics and polemicists who refer to the idea of progress do not accept this meaningful limitation of the word partly accounts—very largely so, in my opinion—for their contempt of mankind, and enables them to enjoy, as cheerfully and unctuously as they do, the race's bad health. There are a great many reasons, no doubt—some of them connected with emotional, intellectual or social vested interests, all of them of

*See p. 70.

profound psychological importance—why so many people do not wish to believe that any of us can learn to behave better, without supernatural aid. It is a sad fact that the anti-Pelagians, or the Augustinians, as Mr. Walter Allen calls them—especially those whose belief in Original Sin is dogmatic—do not always behave better, but often worse. This may suggest that morality in behaviour is after all intimately connected with one's intellectual outlook, and may actually depend on whether that outlook is true or false. There are many examples of this connection and I shall refer to others in the course of this book; but as an illustration I summarise an article in *The Times Literary Supplement* of June 8th, 1951.

This was a review of a book by John Nef, called *War and Human Progress*. With some justification, it seems, in the substance of the book he is reviewing, the reviewer tries to place the responsibility for total war on contemporary scientists and on "the corrosion of faith and the corruption of moral standards by modern philosophy". . . . "The roots of war lie in those qualities of human nature which earlier ages described as sinfulness. But the interpretation of life which accepts the fact of sin also acknowledges the saving mercy of grace—the possibility, that is, that the spirit of man can discern the good and that the human will can strive to attain it. Fulfilment of this possibility requires supernatural help . . ."

"Nothing," the reviewer says elsewhere, "is in deeper contrast with the attitude of many contemporary scientists than the sense of social responsibility and religious awe which restrained Napier . . . and Newton from recording clearly, even in secret notes, ideas which they knew could be turned to purposes of mass-destruction."

The facts behind this illustration are, on the contrary, that Napier described his 'engines of mass-destruction' as clearly, probably, as he thought them out—they were mostly pale shadows of Leonardo's speculations. However, Urquhart says that he built and tried one of them with complete success. Napier thought of them, not with shame, but as "proffitabill and necessary for . . . withstanding of strangers, *enemies of Gods truth and religion.*"*

The last quotation suggests that if Napier were or were likely to be restrained by anything, it would not be by religious awe. Examination and comparison of contemporary religious and scientific character seem to confirm this. Scientists are, as the worst you can in general say about them, anxious and half-hearted in their agreement about the necessity of mass-destruction, engined or otherwise. It was against the expressed prayer of the only scientists who knew what the results would be, that President Truman and Mr. Churchill persisted in their determination to drop the first atomic bomb. The real flame-throwers and fire-eaters are in the religious camp. Einstein in his moral views on war compares favourably with many Church leaders. A Commission appointed by the Federal Council of the Churches of Christ in America said:

"If, as we have felt bound to acknowledge, certain key industrial targets are inescapably involved in modern war, we find no moral distinction between destroying them by tons of TNT or by fire, as compared with an atomic bomb, save as greater precision is possible in one as compared with others. . . . We believe that American military strength, which must include atomic weapons, as long as any other nation may possess them, is an essential factor in the possibility of preventing both world war and tyranny."

I do not say that the practical view of this Church Commission, its evaluation of the moral distinction between various engines of mass-destruction, is necessarily incorrect. But one does not have to be a pacifist to think it both remarkable and significant that none of the Established Churches has ever declared uncom-promisingly that mass-destruction is morally wrong. Surely a

*As for Newton's military work, it was confined to some studies in ballistics, which he published immediately.

case could be made out for this view which would not be inconsistent with the teachings of Christ? Many scientists, on the other hand, have found themselves able to do so. Further it may be held that this American Church Commission (among other religious bodies) has given its blessing to 'totality' in a way which, for internal philosophical reasons, comes more easily to the religious than to the scientific mind. It is reasonable, I think, to conclude that, historically, war has been nearer to 'total', the more it has been religious and the less it has been scientific. The science of war itself, as treated from Clausewitz onwards, has directed itself toward destroying the enemy's military power and the springs of it. A strong religious motivation, as we can see from the Crusades against the Albigenses, is more likely to encourage the belief in the moral rightness of sacking, pillaging and total slaughter. We must firmly believe in the absolute wrongness of our adversaries, their 'sinfulness' as *The Times Literary Supplement* reviewer called it, before we can know that we are right in destroying them utterly. It is true that a totalitarian political system can also give something like this moral security to its devotees, but from history it seems obvious that they learnt this attitude more from the teachings of the Church, for so many centuries the guardian and teacher of all moral philosophy, than from the scientists, whose philosophy has not yet had time, either for good or bad, to be anything like so clearly formulated. The totally non-scientific concept of Original Sin, which is the essence both of Church theology and of neo-scholasticism, is also in fact the only belief which allows us to destroy babies and the unborn, in peace of conscience. It can do this because it enables us to act in peace of intellect. Behind the doctrine of Original Sin, behind also therefore the new militant theology and scholasticism, is the implication that scientific investigation, if and when it is carried over into the field of human mental life and human social behaviour, is not only fruitless, but wrong. This is the only logical conclusion of an authoritarianism which tries to claim finality for its view of human conduct and psychology.

I shall have a good deal more to say on the subject of Original

Sin. The example quoted here from a leading literary review is, however, a good and significant example of the kind of attack which is being made on the idea of the possibility of human moral progress. Moreover the attack in general on the concept of 'progress' illustrates clearly the neo-scholastic way of thinking. We can call it the compulsion of hypostasis. Not only do these writers have to keep their own concepts at a high level of abstraction, but they prefer to tilt at the windmills of their adversaries, those generalisations often made by the ignorant; and always divorced from the field-work, the testing in experience, of any kind of scientific method: a method which is of course also applied in psychology and anthropology and on which any fruitfulness in their results must depend.

I think that it is reasonable to hold that every increase of knowledge is valuable, in however small a degree, and that in so far as the sum of knowledge in the world can be said to have increased, then the world can be said to have *progressed*. But any moral implication in the word progress must be carefully examined. The new anti-Pelagians, having an absolute standard of morality, do not regard morality as in any important sense dependent on knowledge. It is easy therefore for them to distinguish a duality in human history, to admit the advance of physical knowledge, while discerning stasis or decline in morality, which for them should arise from faith. Hence it is easy too, for them to condemn, for misinterpretation and false optimism, those Victorians who based a belief in total progress on the doctrine of evolution, and on material and scientific successes.

The Victorians, however—not least those who had the most earnest moral hope about culture, enlightenment and unending advance upon this planet—were personally often far from optimistic. Yet an eschatological gloom did not prevent the best of them, for example Matthew Arnold, from examining the clearly visible cultural, intellectual and social changes around them in the spirit of liberal and humanistic inquiry, rather than of Church orthodoxy; although Arnold may be said to have been the inheritor of both traditions. The humanistic, heretical or inquiring spirit, the

essentially scientific, was still the stronger. No one can say that
Arnold's judgment of the contemporary state of culture was
flattering, or anything but critical. His views on keeping the study
of science in its educational place, as compared with the classics,
were not perhaps very different from Mr. Eliot's own. Mr. Eliot
writes much of tradition, especially of tradition as the basis of
orthodoxy, and by tradition he means our dual European inheritance, from the Greek and Latin classics on the one hand, and
from Christianity on the other. Where Arnold differed and where
he was, I think, representative of the best of his time, was in the
fact that tradition, primarily if in the main unconsciously, meant
for him the tradition of liberal humanism, just that spirit of
unimpeded inquiry which begets both intellectual (and hence
material) progress and a humanitarian morality.

Arnold and his sad, serious and honest like were the heirs of a
tradition, the tradition of free inquiry, which in spite of all
contrary appearances, is our oldest; and which had maintained its
dominance in Europe, with whatever difficulties, since the
struggles of the seventeenth century. (Can we not even say that
the tradition, in the manifestation of a Protestant conscience, has
had the larger share in conditioning and capacitating Mr. Eliot—
the Pilgrim Fathers have done more for him than the Church
Fathers?) One of the main intellectual fruits of the tradition for
Arnold and his like was that knowledge was still indivisible. For
them it was perfectly possible to conceive of moral progress for
mankind as a whole, just because knowledge was really conceived
of as the essential instrument of any progress. In so far as the
Victorians meant this, and this is what those who cared about
culture, tradition, the mind and its freedom did mean, I do not see
that the idea is ridiculous nor that it has been shown to be wrong
or even extremely improbable.

If, for the sake of theoretical clarification, we can separate the
intellectual interest of human beings from their more self-
interested passions, particularly fear and greed, we can see that,
left to itself, the development of knowledge would be a natural
process. Knowledge naturally and inevitably increases among

men unless men themselves do something to stop it, either by removing the tools of knowledge or by denaturing its receptacle. If the growth of knowledge is not actively impeded, by amputation or perversion, its mere quantitative and departmental increase will gradually bring about a qualitative change in the whole body of knowledge, will beget a world-view which will always be approximating to the truth. That this gradual change and approximation to a true world-view cannot be said ever to have been observed on a large scale in human history is only a reflection of the violence with which usurping world-views have maintained themselves. They are usurpers, because they are not, as they should be, abstracts of growing knowledge, but the symptoms of the self-interested passions, in particular of fear and greed. The anti-Pelagians, the believers in Original or absolute Sin, certainly recognise that evil has its roots in these passions, but ignore or deny the fact that the first manifestation of their evil is in the tainting of our intellects, the distortion of our capacity for receiving truth. That Catholic orthodoxy locates sin in the *mind*, not primarily in conduct, does not imply a recognition of the way in which these passions in fact operate. On the contrary it implies a refusal to recognise that these passions can be understood and criticised intellectually, even by those who suffer from them, and that thus, and thus only, their effects on conduct can be controlled. I do not deny that this requires a different social climate and that we must then become acclimatised to it. But the first step is that human beings should not be discouraged in discovering that such self-understanding is possible and desirable. One of the chief ends of Catholic orthodoxy, however, in its mental location of sin, is to make a prime sin out of heresy, which in order to pursue inquiry in peace and freedom has to shut the door on authority.

Because these self-interested passions are omnipresent, it remains purely hypothetical to talk of an unimpeded advance, or preferably, process, of knowledge. Such a process however was what was implied by those Victorians who, in the second half of the nineteenth century, reached some insight into the material and philosophical changes around them, but by continuing in the tradition of liberal inquiry were able to see a future as well as a past for moral and cultural life. Matthew Arnold in particular saw the functions of the literary man and the poet alike as critical. Sweetness and light never meant a 'belief in enlightenment'. They were, on the contrary, only potential products of continuing a method which so far had brought us all our valuable results in any field.

For two centuries there had been an intellectual preparation for a new cosmology, which did not become conscious and formulated, in the literary mind at least, until about half-way through the nineteenth century. Apart from the fact that at this time there were revolutionary contributions to the science of man as well as to the science of nature, there were a number of other practical reasons why the 'split in sensibility', which we date to the seventeenth century, was less clearly manifest and effectual before about Arnold's day. For one, poets are good at finding for themselves naturalistic substitutes for mysticism, as we see from the different cases of Wordsworth and Shelley. For another, the literary mind continued to be able to find an intellectual sustenance in the classics, though, naturally and rightly, of a concrete and imaginative kind. The possession of literary sensibility does not always imply much power of abstract thought or even much interest in philosophy. One of the contributory causes of the novel's rise to dominance may indeed have been the necessary limitation of its imaginative field to the concrete and the naturalistic. For many reasons, it has been possible and comparatively easy for novelists to pay no precise philosophical attention to theology. But by about the middle of the century, those whose temperament and training obliged them to pay this attention—for example, George Eliot—also found themselves obliged to choose between the intellectual claims of theology and the method and outlook which had produced the undeniable achievements of science, while making them what they were themselves and endowing them with their standard of truth.

It is easy to put a wrong satirical emphasis on Miss Macaulay's story* of the Victorian clergyman who lost his faith as regularly as his collar-stud. The charge of an arbitrary and even a fashionable reaction is easy to make, and is also often convenient to our contemporary neo-scholastics. But there was nothing arbitrary about Arnold's *Literature and Dogma* and *God and the Bible*. They were the result of continuing logic and impartiality. What has happened between our day and the late middle of the nineteenth century, when a literary man and critic, conservative, religious, without specialised scientific training, and perhaps indeed with some anti-scientific bias, with strong interest in the humanities and more importantly with a respect and understanding of our main intellectual tradition in Europe, could accept the ordinary realistic scientific world-picture and celebrate the obsequies of dogma? Certainly not a different and improved logic nor contradictory factual observations. But these would be needed to deflect the process of knowledge in the direction of the new theological outlook. Anything else, as I have said, can only be an amputation or perversion of knowledge. Many of our poets and critics, the very people who would still perhaps agree with Arnold that their proper business is to distribute the "best that has been known and thought in the world", are today most deeply engaged, sometimes unconsciously, but often consciously, in this amputation and perversion.

* *Told by an Idiot.*

CHAPTER II

The Dogma in the Manger

WHEN I said that many of our poets and critics who have attached themselves more or less firmly to the cause of dogmatic theology were engaged in the amputation and perversion of knowledge, I did not mean to imply of all or even of most of them that this was a direct or a willing aim. Their aim is in most cases, I should say, emotional, not intellectual. Because their attitude embodies a natural emotional outlook, of fear in the face of inevitable nescience, one can feel a natural sympathy with it, without taking the further step of attaching oneself to an intellectual system which attempts to counter and thus console it with false positive claims. Though the cosmology which present knowledge allows us to hold is not a comfortable one for suffering human beings, the neo-scholastics, by drawing unwarrantable moral conclusions from the decline of dogmatic religion, make our mortal state more miserable than it need be. Among them it is more common than not to stress the moral rather than the cosmological and eschatological grounds for a revival of dogmatic Christianity, to fix their attention on the state of this world, rather than on their hopes for a next and better one.

"The Christian thinker," says Mr. Eliot . . . "proceeds by rejection and elimination. He finds the world to be so and so; he finds its character inexplicable by any non-religious theory; among religions he finds Christianity, and Catholic Christianity, to account most satisfactorily for the world, and especially for the moral world within; and thus, by what Newman calls 'powerful and concurrent' reasons, he finds himself inexorably committed to the dogma of the Incarnation. To the unbeliever, this method seems disingenuous and perverse: for the unbeliever is, as a rule, not so greatly troubled to explain the world to himself, nor so greatly distressed by its disorder: nor is he generally concerned (in modern terms) to 'preserve values'." (From The *Pensées* of Pascal.)

We may set against this another quotation, this time from *The Idea of a Christian Society*:

"To justify Christianity because it provides a foundation of morality, instead of showing the necessity of Christian morality from the truth of Christianity, is a very dangerous inversion: and we may reflect, that a good deal of the attention of totalitarian states has been devoted, with a steadiness of purpose not always found in democracies, to providing their national lives with a foundation of morality—the wrong kind perhaps, but a good deal more of it. It is not enthusiasm, but dogma, that differentiates a Christian from a pagan society."

We need not for the moment consider the ambiguities of Mr. Eliot's use of the words 'disorder', 'values' and 'morality', nor the substitution of the word 'enthusiasm' for some such expression as 'moral earnestness', 'conscience' or 'Christian morality', which would be more natural and less tendencious here. What is significant and typical in these paragraphs, in my opinion, is the kind of distinction which is drawn between the believer and the unbeliever, in their relation to morality. The most interesting thing about it is that it is a distinction with very little difference.

One of the commonplaces of observation is that what we may call dogmatic, or even systematic, unbelievers are much more concerned about social or objective morality, the state of the world, than the general Lacedæmonian (we can allow this to be partially covered by Mr. Eliot's remarks about the totalitarian states); and that they are often deeply troubled about the morality of private relations.

Unbelievers, when they are dogmatic, share an important fault with the dogmatic believer, as defined, at least in implication, by Mr. Eliot. They have missed the point of the genuinely Christian contribution to moral experience and growth. They too begin with the state of the world instead of the state of their own hearts. They are Marthas, troubled about many things. They have not understood Blake's account of moral *process*—"No man ever did good except in minute particulars."

Dogma, on the other hand, never made any of us Maries. I know only one place, at least in his expositive writings, where Mr. Eliot shows even faintly that he has grasped the observational fact that morality, however it is learnt, operates only through feeling. This is in *After Strange Gods* where he discusses Christian sensibility in relation to various authors, and I have already referred to it. There he is far from clear and we must not forget that because he is discussing heresy and dogma, his main concern, even in this book, is with conformative conduct rather than with the morality of feeling. We may already have some idea what Mr. Eliot means when he writes of 'disorder' and 'values'. We can say at least that 'order' has more connection with the imposed system of an authoritarian Church, and 'value' more to do with privilege, than either has with the original Christian conception of charity.

To try, as the neo-scholastics do, to make morality depend on the metaphysical dogma and the authority of the Church means the death of morality. Matthew Arnold's account of religion in *God and the Bible* and *Literature and Dogma* deserves renewed interest because he saw that this would be so, and was concerned to amputate dogma and metaphysics from the main body of moral feeling while there was time to save its life. In opposition to the neo-scholastics, his conception of the Christian faith is specially important and interesting because he claims to do exactly what the neo-scholastics say cannot be done, as they are most concerned of all to show. Mr. Eliot and those who share his opinions do not want people to be moral except as the Church prescribes. Mr. Eliot sometimes refers adversely to 'private morality'—for example, as of George Eliot. This is only a way of stigmatising all ethical standpoints which are not strictly that of the Church; although, apart from having been individually tested, they may represent a human and traditional co-operative effort which lies anywhere between Protestantism and free thought. I do not believe that even Mr. Eliot could say that Matthew Arnold's morality was 'private'. It was based on the perennial Protestant return to the Bible, a procedure always disliked by the metaphysical and dogmatic Church. Arnold saw that the metaphysics and dogma of the Church have really nothing to add to the traditional religion which we have received from the Old and New Testaments and which he considers as a developing and complementary body of moral experience. Israel, as he says, was not a metaphysical philosopher, and a right knowledge of the Godhead was never prescribed for salvation, until after the lifetime of Christ. With a negative view of metaphysics, Arnold perhaps allows himself to be too cheerfully, even if indefinitely, positive in his working references to the ultimate objects of religion—"the Something not ourselves, the Eternal that makes for righteousness".

This philosophic heedlessness has been seized upon by F. H. Bradley, whom Mr. Eliot quotes with approval (see this chapter p. 41). Perhaps Arnold could not at that time have thought differently. In any case, the "Eternal Something, not ourselves" is not a Something which we can know 'in itself' or indeed know at all. For Arnold to have said less was impossible. To have said more would have been to enter into a counter-metaphysics, as usual of the unknowable. What both books are about is what we *can* know, the developing body of moral experience. But there is no need to gloss over the fact that, in taking this historical and empirical viewpoint, Arnold overtly precluded the whole of metaphysics and dogma as well as the supernatural, including all the miracles, from verifiable meaning. And more: "The Church is necessary, the clergy are necessary," said Arnold, but this seems to be a kind of axiom, or a demarcation of critical theory, rather as the concept of the Eternal making for righteousness is. If the intellectual honesty of Arnold's general position has moved us to any kind of sympathy, we may accept both the Eternal and the Church as working propositions because the absolute content has been pumped out of both of them. I do not wish to deny that for the orthodox this removes also their significance.

To Arnold, religion was 'morality touched with emotion'. Attachment to the traditional Church was one of the emotions which touched Arnold's moral experience into religion.

Within the limits of these two attachments, to the Bible and the Church, which provided him with that minimum of belief which would distinguish his religion from ethics, Arnold made a plain statement of the rational and critical view. It seems to me to be for its time, the year 1876, both honest and correct. But if I single out Arnold's date, with the comment that it is remarkable that what was plain enough to one of the best and most thoughtful critics of his day has in three-quarters of a century become obscure, forgotten or unacceptable to many of his successors, although there has been nothing in between to justify a reaction, I do so in the awareness that Arnold's was not the only representative 'Victorian view'. His work was a landmark as a plain statement of empirical morality, which was not opposed to the development of knowledge as a whole. But dogma has had its own continuity, and it looks as if Newman has been more influential than Arnold. Arnold of course was hampered by the need to refer to a framework of logic, science and history, while Newman could speak straight to the heart and imagination. Indeed we can say that Newman clarified the rational situation by effectually removing belief from the sphere of argument. Since his day, the most persuasive religious propaganda has based itself on the admission that:

"faith was indeed incapable of rational 'proof', but that on that very account it was unassailable by the 'mere' reason; a faith which rested on demonstration would be either compulsory and mechanical, or would be exposed to disproof by other demonstrations." (From Basil Willey: The Seventeenth Century Background. Nineteenth Century Studies.)

No one can say, however, that this admission leads to intellectual satisfaction, nor can it indeed be the official standpoint of Catholicism, which seems rather to 'solve' the difficulty by implying that knowledge is hierarchical, a matter of intellectual 'class'.

I choose Arnold because he puts the theoretical position sufficiently plainly to provide a background for literary men; because his literary rank and insight still demand the highest respect, and because he has received adverse attention from our leading neo-scholastic, Mr. Eliot.

This adverse critical attention is interesting further for the typical obliqueness of its method. Eliot attacks Arnold either by applauding Bradley: "Those who have read through (Bradley's) *Ethical Studies* will be ready with the remark that it was Bradley in this book and in the year 1876 who knocked the bottom out of *Literature and Dogma*," or by pretending that as a serious, intelligible and well-considered contribution to the theological controversy, *Literature and Dogma* is no longer of importance or even of interest:

"*Literature and Dogma, God and the Bible*, and *Last Essays on Church and Religion* have served their turn and can hardly be read through. In these books he attempts something which must be austerely impersonal: in them reasoning power matters, and it fails him."

This is simply untrue.

There were a great many other writers in the nineteenth century and onwards, many of them of distinction, who 'lost their faith', whose conclusions, that is, about dogmatic theology were adverse. Mr. Eliot's basis for choosing those he will study, which is necessarily here my own, is again interesting. It is brought out clearly in his remarks on humanism (The Humanism of Irving Babbitt and Second Thoughts on Humanism), and the quotations which follow contain or imply all that is important, for present purposes, for us to know of Mr. Eliot's conception of religion, and of his reasons for choosing certain subjects to attack rather than others.

"Mr. Babbitt makes it very clear . . . that he is unable to take the religious view—that is to say that he cannot accept any dogma or revelation: and that humanism is the *alternative* to religion. And this brings up the question: is this alternative more than a *substitute*. . . ? Is it, in the end, a view of life which will work by itself, or is it a derivative of religion which will work only for a short time in history, and only for a few highly cultivated persons like Mr. Babbitt—whose ancestral traditions furthermore are Christian and who is, like many, at the distance of a generation or so from definite Christian belief? Is it in other words durable beyond one or two generations?"

"The religious habits of the race are still very strong, in all places, and at all times, and for all people. There is no humanistic habit: humanism is, I think, merely the state of mind of a few persons in a few places at a few times."

"The humanistic point of view is auxiliary to and dependent upon the religious point of view. For us, religion is Christianity and Christianity implies, I think, the conception of the Church.

"Mr. (Norman) Foerster finds that 'the essential reality of experience is ethical'. For the person with a definite religious faith, such a statement has one meaning: for the positivistic humanist, who repudiates religion, it must have another. And that meaning seems to rest upon obscurities and confusions. I can understand, though I do not approve, the naturalistic systems of morals founded upon biological and analytical psychology (what is valid in these consists largely of things that were always known)*, but I cannot understand a system of morals which seems to be founded on nothing but itself—which exists, I suspect, only by illicit relations with either psychology or religion or both, according to the bias of mind of the individual humanist."

*I find it impossible to understand, and therefore to approve, this parenthesis.

Finally:

"Professor Babbitt knows too much . . . too many religions and philosophies, has assimilated their spirit too thoroughly . . . to be able to give himself to any. The result is humanism."

These quotations remind us forcibly that for Mr. Eliot it is not ethical meaning, but dogma, by which he means authoritarian statements by the Church about belief, which is the essential part of religion. Further, if there is any consistency at all among these quotations, we must suppose that he wishes to separate dogma as finally as possible from any rational system of ethics. How otherwise is it possible for him to reach the conclusion, which for many people in his situation would be despairing, that Professor Babbitt 'knows too much'? Too much, one must suppose, to assent to any dogma, not too much to extract the common ethical basis from his exhaustive religious study? But Mr. Eliot has stated his election of dogma, sometimes guardedly and elliptically but, here and there, even in so many unamplified words. What one ought not to miss is the fact that, to be logical, Mr. Eliot would not be thankful to anyone who could show that the Christian ethic was self-evident. This was indeed the dominant and pious intention of many of the Victorians who either 'lost their faith' or who arrived at conclusions resembling humanism, whether they had been more influenced by German higher criticism or by Comtean positivism. George Eliot's serious and well-trained intellect found it necessary to sacrifice dogma and the supernatural, but to her, as to Mr. Norman Foerster, 'the essential reality of experience (remained) ethical'. And the meaningful content of Arnold's 'Eternal that makes for righteousness' is hardly different from this. But Mr. Eliot will have nothing to do with the empirical except to stand it firmly on its head. We see now on what grounds he chooses his opponents. The extremist in religion is perhaps like the extremist in politics— his worst foe is what we may call a Third Force. If a principle is chosen pragmatically, there is an obvious danger that it will really work. Mr. Eliot is trying to put the Church, from the moral point of view, in the position of the Dog in the Manger—saying in effect that men shall not be moral except after the Church's dogmatic formula. I should be quoting him unfairly out of his context if I did not add that Mr. Eliot in these essays (written round about 1928) sees a philosophical and practical value in humanism, but as culture, not as ethics. His main anxieties on its behalf are those already quoted: that it is a *state of mind* of a few persons in a few places at a few times, and that, as a derivative of Christianity and of definite Christian belief, it cannot be expected to be durable for more than one or two generations.

One may ask whether Mr. Eliot is not putting the cart before the horse. One does not need to have Professor Babbitt's knowledge of the world's religions and philosophies, to know that, in attributing the moral understanding of Arnold and George Eliot, and subsequent 'humanists' up to Babbitt, to the cause that they were living on Christian capital, and to claim that any ethic which is still valid for us today has no important source but Christianity, is not only to beg the question, but to distort history.

I suppose this is where Mr. Eliot's distinction between the cultural and the ethical comes in. But I should say on the contrary that Matthew Arnold, to give only one example, was powerfully *and directly* affected by the ethical meanings of both the Old Testament and of classical teaching, not merely as both were subsumed and developed in the Christian tradition.

But neither Mr. Eliot, nor any of the writers in any of the quarterlies and weeklies and even dailies, where I have so often seen it referred to, really justify this idea about living on Christian capital, nor the accompanying fear that that moral capital may be exhausted, as Mr. Eliot, for one, suggests, 'in one or two generations'.

This strikes me as implicitly an example of the gross materialism which always sooner or later infects philosophies in proportion as they aim at substantialising the spiritual: morality, like oil or gold, is a quantitative resource and may be exhausted. One sees the same quantitative anxiety in Mr. Eliot's other fear about the 'too few humanists in too few places at too few times'. What he means, I suppose, is something not unlike the Comtean view that, to be effectual, humanists also need the binding traditions and observances of a Church. And yet dogmatic Christianity has had the services of a Church since its early days, and still the truly religious within the Church—those who attempt to love their neighbours as themselves—are, like the humanists, too few, too scattered, too intermittent.

Moreover, Mr. Eliot is surely too convinced an anti-Pelagian to wish or to expect anyone to say that religion, even orthodox Christianity, has made the actual world very much better than it otherwise would have been. The reason for the moral in-effectuality of both humanism and religion is the same—that we are not so very easily convinced of the truth of the basic moral observations, especially in our young and formative years, and that even when we are, they are very difficult to apply. But humanism encourages us to look for the empirical and rational steps towards moral conduct, as dogmatic religion does not and cannot.

The point about the religious humanists, of whom Matthew Arnold is an example, is that they have a strong yearning for the empirical. The main intellectual drive of such typical Protestants is to show that the ethics of Christianity are verifiable, demon-strably true, and that its moral essence consists just in this, the freedom of intellectual assent. This search for verifiability followed a typical course in Arnold, it led to the 'documents', that is, to the Bible. The nearer to the Bible, the further away from the Church. The historical Protestant path, which is still continually followed by individual moralists, must lead to absolute freedom for all inquiry, and so to the separation of morals from any dogma, including that of the Church. This is why Eliot is more hostile to Arnold for his empirical morality than if he had had none at all.

The attack on the moral views of the humanists is expressed, as one might expect, as an attack on their Pelagianism. I quote this as it is interesting for later chapters of this book:

"For it is not enough to chastise the romantic visions of perfectibility—the modern humanistic view implies that man is either perfectible or capable of indefinite improvement—because from that point of view the only difference is a difference of degree. . . . It is to the immense credit of Hulme that he found out for himself that there is an *Absolute* to which Man can *never* attain."

This then is the hypostatical shape of the mind which attacks Arnold, particularly through Bradley, whose mental framework is similar. The real enemy is Arnold's view that we cannot find in experience, and also do not require, any such Absolute: God is known only as moral experience, and since this is discovered, not revealed, moral progress is possible, the transition from the morality of the Old Testament to that of the New being one such advance in the race's moral apperception.

The paragraph which Eliot quotes from Bradley's *Ethical Studies* is cleverly chosen:

" 'Is there a God?' asks the reader. 'Oh yes,' replies Mr. Arnold, 'and I can verify him in experience.' 'And what is he then?' cries the reader. 'Be virtuous, and as a rule you will be happy,' is the answer. 'Well, and God?' 'That is God,' says Arnold, 'there is no deception, and what more do you want?' I suppose we do want a good deal more. Most of us, certainly the public which Mr. Arnold addresses, want something they can worship; and they will not find that in an hypostasized copybook heading, which is not much more adorable than 'Honesty is the best policy', 'Handsome is that handsome does', or various other edifying maxims which have not yet come to an apotheosis."

"Such criticism," comments Eliot, "is final. It is patently a great triumph of wit and a great delight to watch when a man's methods, almost his tricks of speech, are thus turned against himself. But if we look more closely into these words and into the whole chapter from which they are taken, we find Bradley to have been not only triumphant in polemic but right in reason."

It is interesting but perhaps here not strictly relevant, to ask whether one can really be 'triumphant in polemic' unless one is 'right in reason'. But it must be admitted that Bradley has picked on the most serious inconsistency of Arnold's position: God is a metaphysical concept and, since Arnold will have nothing to do with metaphysics, the name is used by him in fact only as an emotional invocation and, thus retained without any content, is a weakness not strength in his argument. But Arnold was not and probably could not be prepared for complete agnosticism. Religion for him was morality tinged with emotion and if 'The Eternal', whether making for righteousness or not, is a concept difficult to verify in experience, Arnold meant a *feeling*, not an intellectual experience, the experience of a tradition whose main significance was that it was continuous and did not either begin or end with ourselves.

It is perfectly true, as Bradley says, that people *want* something more: they want assurances about the supernatural, especially about the economics of the supernatural, the system of payments and penalties which might be conjectured to counterbalance the moral experiences of earthly life. This no kind of intellectual analysis, whether it calls itself philosophical or theological, can give them. That is the point of Arnold's work, to remind us that we know nothing of the supernatural and that the validity of moral experience remains, as it always was, unaffected by the existence or non-existence of the supernatural. *Literature and Dogma* and *God and the Bible* are the literary man's handbooks of negative theology. I do not see how Mr. Eliot can so easily dismiss Arnold as 'weak in philosophy' or 'reasoning power'. His philosophical arguments are not original, nor intended to be, and that is their strength. They are essentially Kant's critical arguments, which have never been given a satisfactory metaphysical answer, and they simply remind us of what we ought not to forget. Mr. Eliot and his kind sometimes seem to imply that a philosophical argument dies if it is not repeated every few years, like a kind of claim. This may be true and I think it is so of merely metaphysical or dogmatic philosophical structures which live only in words. But a sound philosophical argument is an analysis of some sort of experience, it is not merely a legal claim upon our understanding which has to be made annually in order to preserve its validity.

Some such assumption is behind Mr. Eliot's references to the 'unreadability' of these books of Arnold. They are only unreadable to eyes and minds already firmly closed. But to anyone, however familiar with the philosophical arguments, who wishes to see how the controversial climate has changed between Arnold's day and ours, they make extremely interesting reading. For in the pages of the neo-scholastics, whether they are suave like Mr. Eliot's or something between apocalyptic and tub-thumping like Mr. Lewis's or Miss Sayers's, free controversy, so much alive among the Victorians, has been stifled. In one way or another, they all behave as if their chief adversary, the continuity of historical and scientific experience and discussion, just were not there.

The last paragraph may make it appear as if my selection of writers to lump together as neo-scholastic, is indiscriminate or even careless in its literary evaluation. This is not so. I am well aware that the perceptions of Mr. Lewis and Miss Sayers, either of life or literature, are immeasurably coarser than Mr. Eliot's, who is in any case probably the most distinguished critical and creative mind to be discussed in this book. But Mr. Eliot, having a precise and profound sense of language, has only himself to blame, if he is mentioned in such a breath. He shares the vices for which I call them all 'neo-scholastic'. He also uses many words as if they were things, and with them gives a Name a Bad Dog, for example 'Liberalism', and 'Science' which he in general employs with a pejorative flavour. Mr. Eliot has said, a statement of profound importance for us in this book, that we must learn to scrutinise our reading of literature by precise Christian and theological standards, but perhaps first we should all scrutinise our reading of theology, especially of literary theology, by precise literary and semantic standards.

Arnold is interesting, especially for his time, because he had grasped the importance of the semantic principle that words are not things, and the philosophical arguments he selected should be taken as leading up to a special implication of this principle for literature and religion. It is remarkable that a man so exceptionally and significantly sensitive to the motive power of the language of great literary and religious writing, to the seemingly independent existence which all good poetry attains, should have been so clear about the distinction between that and the kind of 'existence' which can be discussed with philosophical meaning.

Basically, as I have said, Arnold's arguments are those of post-Kantian critical philosophy. It seems doubtful that the purely critical side of Kant's philosophy has ever since been set aside by any more positive view. These arguments are set out by Arnold in *God and the Bible*, a sequel to *Literature and Dogma*, particularly in the chapter called 'The God of Metaphysics'. There he begins with a criticism of Descartes:

"Everyone knows," says Arnold, "that Descartes, looking about him . . . for a firm ground whereon he might take his stand and begin to operate, for one single thing which was clearly certain and indubitable, found it in the famous '*Cogito, ergo sum*, I think therefore I am'. Thinker after thinker has paid his tribute of admiration to the axiom; it is called the foundation of modern philosophy. Now we shall confess with shame . . . that from this fundamental axiom of Descartes we were never able to derive that light and satisfaction which others have derived from it. And for the following reason. The philosopher omits to tell us what he exactly means by to *be*, to exist. . . . Perhaps he really does mean something more by the words, something that we fail to grasp. We say so, because we find him, like philosophers in general, often speaking of essence, existence and substance, and in speaking of them he lays down as certain and evident many propositions which we cannot follow. For instance, he says: We have the idea of an infinite substance, eternal, all-knowing, all-powerful, the creator of all things, and with every possible perfection. . . .' All this, I say, our guide finds certain and not admitting of the least doubt. It is part of the things which we conceive with clearness and distinctness and, of which, therefore, we can be persuaded thoroughly. Man is a finite substance, that is, he has but a limited degree of being, or perfection. God is an infinite substance, that is, he has an unlimited degree of being, or perfection. Existence is a perfection, therefore God exists; thinking and loving are perfections and therefore God thinks and loves. . . . Not Descartes only, but every philosopher who attempts a metaphysical demonstration of God, will be found to proceed in this fashion, and to appeal at last to our conception of *being, existing*."

Arnold deals with these concepts of being or existing, semantically, in a way which anticipates certain twentieth-century attitudes and shows that it is not unreasonable to place him in the succession which leads to Ogden and Richards. Being and Existing, when they mean anything at all, must be conceived in a way which derives from their original etymology, roots which mean 'breathing' and 'growing', but the certainty in the Cartesian metaphysician's mind is about something which thinks and loves without breathing and growing.

"Let us take the grand argument from design," says Arnold. "Design, people say, implies a designer. The ambiguity lies in the little termination, *er*, by which we mean a *being* who designed. We talk of a being, an *être*, and we imagine that the word gives us conscious intelligence, thinking and loving, without bodily organisation. . . . Design implies a designer? Human design does; it implies the presence of a being who breathes and thinks . . ."

What Arnold calls the 'grand argument from design', Kant calls the 'physico-theological proof'. This is one of three to which he reduced all the purely metaphysical proofs of the existence of God, claiming to have demolished them all. The ontological proof, originated by Anselm, is the one to which Arnold refers in his discussion of Descartes, with its conclusion that God must exist, since existence is a perfection which God could not conceivably lack. Kant pointed out that existence is not a predicate, it is not an implication or quality of any subject, or on the other hand something that must be affirmed or denied about any given subject:

"A hundred thalers that I merely imagine may have all the same predicates as a hundred real thalers," he says.

By Aquinas, whose philosophy is now regarded as the intellectual groundwork of Catholic orthodoxy, the ontological proof was set aside in favour of the cosmological proof, which states that if anything exists (as for instance I know myself to exist), then an absolutely necessary Being exists, and this must be the Ens Realissimum, that being which has the greatest possible reality. Kant said that this was only the ontological argument over again, since the Ens Realissimum is claimed as the subject of all possible predicates which belong to being absolutely. If Aquinas's favourite proof can thus be reduced to one on which orthodoxy does not pretend to build, it looks as if the intellectual foundation which he provides to neo-scholasticism might be shaky.

Of the physico-theological argument, or argument from design, which maintains that the universe exhibits an order which is evidence of purpose, Kant says that at best this proves only an architect, not a creator, and therefore cannot give an adequate conception of God. By this he seems to mean the same as Arnold, that the order of the universe, if it is indeed visible, still implies nothing whatsoever about the being who thinks and loves.

His practical conclusion is again like Arnold's—that the only theology of reason which is possible is that which is based upon moral laws or seeks guidance from them. Like Arnold, he is not out to deny the existence of God, merely to purify conception from conclusions which are without intellectual warrant.

These references are not intended to be more than a reminder that there is a historical philosophical sequence, at least from Kant, in which Arnold may be found. There has been a negative progress of knowledge. We know that we cannot *know* the existence of God. If people are to believe in the existence of God they must do so on other than intellectual grounds. The logical analysts in our own day have found additional negative arguments, summed up by Russell as his 'theory of descriptions', which claims that existence can only rightly be asserted of 'descriptions' or qualifications, and not of names, of the connotative and not the denotative; but that need not detain us. It is important to notice that scepticism, even if it appeals to logic and the demonstrable, is still a tradition—that is, it has a consolidated existence which goes far beyond our or any contemporary needs, wishes or ideas. Mr. Eliot, I know, 'will not argue' (*After Strange Gods*) with those who are in radical intellectual opposition, but they are, after all, in this opposing *tradition*, a consolidated existence beyond immediate logomachies, which it is a tall order to ignore. But if you will not argue, what else can you do with it?

And if God's existence presents us with such grave philosophical difficulties, what are we to say of such dependent categories as the incarnate divine and the miraculous, which, as they are claimed to manifest themselves, do fall within the region of critical and historical experience? For those, who 'will not argue' about God's existence require that in the name of 'orthodoxy' we should assent to such dogmas as the Fall, the Incarnation, the Virgin Birth and, even more important and perhaps even more remarkably, Original Sin, which do fall within the empirical purview and the field of ordinary probability. One should keep it continually before one's eyes that when the neo-scholastics talk about these dogmas they are not speaking symbolically. In general, they mean exactly what they say in so far as they know what they mean. Mr. Eliot's foundation is and claims to be dogmatic (Original Sin, the theological dogma, must be admitted as a 'very real and terrible thing') and it may be said that the foundation of dogma, in turn, is faith and ecclesiastical authority. But if there were nothing but dogma and authority there would be no theology. I do not believe for one moment that Mr. Eliot would allow that the

Church's dogma is inconvertible. Somewhere in the vaults of history she keeps the intellectual gold to honour her dogmatic paper.

But not all the neo-scholastics are intellectually so reticent, nor perhaps so wise, as Mr. Eliot. They 'will argue'. I suspect that it is really because he knows a great deal more about theology and philosophy than, for instance, Mr. Lewis or Miss Sayers, that Mr. Eliot will not. They, however, are willing if not able to divide the philosophy and the psychology of the divine between them. Miss Sayers, in *The Mind of the Maker*, tells us exactly how God feels, and in particular how he would feel if he had written a detective story. (One of hers: he could have done no less.) Mr. Lewis, in *Miracles*, shows himself sufficiently impressed with Miss Sayers's understanding of creative and critical ability, her own and that of others, to use the gist of this analogy.

Both these writers could be described, not too metaphorically, as fundamentalists. They claim that all the answers which the human mind requires, to form an adequate picture of the universe it inhabits, are to be found in the Christian revelation, as interpreted by the Church; and this includes answers to those ætiological and eschatological questions which according to the empiricist are meaningless. One may perhaps admire the consistency of their determination more than that of their logic, but one should never forget that to be willing to answer all the ultimate questions does not imply that you are willing or able to answer all the intermediate ones. A psychological or anthropological study at any level, provided it is honest and objective, will provoke the observer to reflections which cannot be set aside by the doctrine of Original Sin, and this even if he comes to agree with Freud that human beings are radically aggressive. An answer may be framed much more to shut up an opponent than to satisfy him. Adults, when they have got themselves into the position of claiming omniscience, even a vicarious one, as the neo-scholastic apologists have done, are bound to try and treat their adversaries, or even their questioners, as children.

On these ultimates Miss Sayers and Mr. Lewis 'will argue',

whereas Mr. Eliot 'will not'. As a result his work reads far less condescendingly and more tentatively. The tone becomes different, as soon as he will argue, or at least quote argument, as in the paper on Bradley and Arnold, or indeed in the one on Babbitt. Here he himself shows signs of withdrawing behind the magisterial manner (with that worst of the master's mannerisms, playful sarcasm). Mr. Eliot's work is mostly staid, objective and critical, at least when its objects are literary. An emotional mannerism suggests that he is producing a case, rather than a study, and that he is not sure of it. And, indeed, it would surely have been better, from his own point of view as well as ours, if he had treated Arnold's religion of morality with more respect.

We may agree with Bradley that Arnold's 'Eternal making for righteousness' is not verifiable in the sense in which a scientist would be satisfied to use the word, and it seems obvious now that in basing his beliefs on the inductive and experimental Arnold dismissed theology and metaphysics quite as radically as, let us say, A. J. Ayer in our day. But the morality of experience, which he isolated as the essential of religion, seems to me to have at least the level of objectivity which we find in many of the social sciences, and certainly to record for us much more realistically and exactly than the neo-scholastics do, the nature of Christianity. Bradley makes too much of an implied utilitarianism in criticising Arnold, and this is also one of the stock ways in which the Pelagian classicists of our day try to make their opponents look ridiculous. The implication was that Arnold claimed that the Eternal, making for righteousness, also—at least in the long run—made for happiness and that this is not so very different from talking about the greatest good of the greatest number (and that this of course is damnable). Here I should like to draw attention to a common controversial habit (alluded to elsewhere as 'Giving a Name a Bad Dog') which comes into prominence whenever there has been a marked change in the philosophical climate, and which always affects worst those who have an emotional objection to an empirical attitude. There has been such a climatic change between the time of the Utilitarians and ourselves and now it seems very difficult to examine the value of their proposition objectively. The anti-Pelagians in particular are much inclined to believe that a change in the *fashion* of philosophy, which can certainly be induced, and can possibly be brought about by this system of pejorative reference, can, if it favours their beliefs, be rated as a kind of criticism. The basic utilitarian propositions are descriptive of human behaviour, and being descriptive, tied to the individual observation, are necessarily partial and open to contradiction. But it is not intrinsically absurd to seek happiness, one's own or that of other people, or that of as many people as possible, and we can hardly say that, even as a political philosophy, utilitarianism has failed, because it quite certainly has never and nowhere been thoroughly tried. What Arnold did say was that:

"To feel that one is fulfilling in *any* way the law of one's being, that one is succeeding and hitting the mark, brings us we know, happiness. . . . We have already had Quintilian's witness how right conduct gives joy. Who could value knowledge more than Goethe? but he marks it as being without question a lesser source of joy than conduct."

This certainly looks like utilitarianism—to say that men will not, and to imply that they ought not to, be expected to behave well without the promise of some reward, and that the reward is happiness and that happiness is worthy to be sought. But I am not so sure that this is unverifiable by ordinary common-sense observation, which we constantly use and must use, to continue living. I believe that the original object of the teaching of Christ was to show men how to be happy; that this is the meaning of the Christian concept of love or charity, and has always been, however dimly and imperfectly, the aim of any philosophy which has concerned itself with the laws of human life and behaviour on this planet; and that this concept, which we particularly associate with Christ, is what Arnold had in mind and what the neo-scholastics today have largely forgotten. Arnold's 'Eternal' and 'Righteousness' could no doubt do with more definition; they seem to be concepts poetically 'thrown out', as he would say, at an object only dimly perceived. But if his statements about the relation of happiness and morality are in a different class, as regards verifiability, from scientific statements, they are also in a different class from the statements of mystics. They are based on general and traditional human experience and the causal connections which it has noted, and there is a considerable question whether the experiences claimed by the mystic are of any meaning or value even to himself unless they are an extrapolation from these more common and naturalistic connections. We plain mortals can generally see well enough the causal connection between conduct and the happiness it brings, while we cannot see the causal connection between the inward experience of the mystic and the happiness that is supposed to bring, unless the mystic is also concerned with conduct: unless, in other words, he provides us with a human hypothesis as well as a mystical one, for the equilibrium and sense of significance, the fulfilment and peace which he in general claims to achieve. However true it may be that if you seek happiness you will not find it (surely because this is too abstract to be an occupation), if you despise it, either for yourself or—how much more easily this comes—for other people, if you try, that is, to cut yourself away from the texture of ordinary actual living, you will not find anything at all.

I intend no more than to suggest that Arnold's 'Eternal making for righteousness', if interpreted as what he would have called a symbol 'thrown out', is, whatever Bradley may say to the contrary, not without meaning. What seems to me altogether acceptable in Arnold, and what he largely if not entirely meant, is that morality is organically *human*, it is within the human race and develops with it. That it is not a dogma up in the sky must be plain to many of us beside the Existentialists, as it was already plain to Arnold. But since that fact is far from plain to our neo-scholastics, it has to be repeated here.

The subject-matter of religion, says Arnold, is *conduct*, and conduct, at a low estimate, is three-fourths of human life— "every impulse relating to temper, every impulse relating to sensuality—and we all know how much that is." And if morality is thus human, and indeed, we can say, what makes society organic, then it must develop or die. We have admitted that Arnold never makes clear, and perhaps did not know, what he means by the Eternal, but at least we can say that conduct, the moral law of human existence which is internal to society, is always concerned with what does not begin and end with our individual experience. Change, as in other evolutionary departments, may appear retrogressive, and even often is so. But the moral law is internal, not superimposed, it is like other natural laws, a generalisation which acts at the same time as a method of making discoveries—moral discoveries. This is the only way in which it can remain 'moral'. Christianity, then, as expounded by Christ, may be looked upon as a set of moral discoveries resulting from the application of the developing moral law as expounded by Israel.

We can comprehend, if not justify, the dogmatic claims of the neo-scholastics when we grasp that morality cannot be both relative and absolute. If it is based on the experiences of man, it not only does not require but cannot admit the sanctions of theology. The old distinction between natural and revealed religion was in this sense a valid one. Hence we can see light upon the depreciation and actual dislike of humanism which is felt and expressed by Mr. Eliot and others. We *must* believe, if we do, 'because it is impossible'. There is no other ground. Possibility means that which lies within experience. But Arnold was right that the Christianity of Christ, developing out of and criticising and interpreting the religion of Israel, did refer to experience, in particular to the basic experience of the need of charity.

It is interesting therefore to see where the practical moral preoccupations of the neo-scholastic literary philosophers lie, what aspects of human conduct and its implied scale of values they think worth notice or consideration, since their idea of morality, which is based on the theological doctrines of the Fall and of Original Sin, is fixed and extra-human. I shall make frequent references to other writers, but it is in Mr. Eliot's work that we find the clearest and most detailed picture, the nearest thing to a system, and also the most interesting omissions. Both in his prose and his poetry there are many references to Time, particularly to the Past; but in the poetry in general, references to the concept of love, Christian or secular, are rare, and in the later poetry any awareness of the immediate neighbour, in the Christian sense of that term, is lacking. There is a recognition of and a distaste for copulation. From the earlier poems we can remember *Sweeney Agonistes* and also the typist in *The Waste Land*. By the time we reach the *Four Quartets* the mainspring of human life has become a habit of peasants, remotely imagined. Spring is

> 'The time of the coupling of men and woman
> And that of beasts.'

We cannot blame Mr. Eliot for not being a poet of love, but we cannot call him a Divine Poet in the suffering, concrete way of Dante or Donne. As he says to his soul,

> 'Wait without love,
> For love would be love of the wrong thing.'

In one of the late scenes of *The Cocktail Party* he seems to allow Edward and Lavinia the faint warmth of a dismal companionship in inadequacy. There is more in human love than this and most dramatic poets, Christian or not, have been aware of it. Even if the ecstasies sometimes prove to be illusions, it is the natural task of the dramatic poet to make us feel the force and indeed the creative stimulus of the illusion upon its victims. Mr. Eliot's main interests now lie with a theory about human emotion and behaviour, rather than with the emotion and the behaviour themselves. But the dogma of Original Sin and of the Fall cannot serve him or anyone else dramatically or poetically. It cannot bridge the discrepancy between the abstract idea of Good and suffering humanity in need of charity. His characters are all in that state of passive suffering which Arnold, dramatically, saw and condemned in his own Empedocles. Beneath the large flat tombstone of unalterable, because abstract, guilt and sin which he has laid upon them, they squirm but they cannot act. And in his polemic and philosophical writing he has become obsessed with the bones of society, because the flesh has failed him. This is the necessary and evil result of hypostatical thinking.

In these prose works also, where he makes an attempt to sketch an ideal or improved order of living, his prime concern is never with the individual heart and its needs and capacities, nor indeed in any real sense at all with that 'freedom of personality' which Christian thinkers in general claim to hold sacred*, but with the order and structure of society.

But Mr. Eliot tries to base his Christian society upon an abstraction, the doctrine of the absolute and inherent imperfection of men and women, without reference to their real relationships or the world of real activity into which they are born, without reference, that is, either to experience or tradition. Christ never made this mistake. Can anything be more central to his teaching than the concept of charity, which refers to the individuals of flesh and blood with whom one is actually in touch? Whatever he has to say—and it is relatively little—about the possible order of society, springs only from this. And whatever we can apply of his teaching springs only from this. And from our failure to grasp this point springs also the badness of our present society and of all other societies. There never has been a Christian society, but to dwell continually and only on our incapacities, and to claim, as the dogmatists do, that because they are real, they are absolute, certainly means that we always shall miss the point, and that there never will be a society in which charity is more important than power. A good society must be a living organism, it must have vitality and growth, and this means that individuals must be so born and educated that they can perennially recognise something spontaneous and new as well as something ancient and common in the other individuals they meet. This is the meaning of love or charity. This kind of sharply individualised awareness is

---

*I am not under any liberal illusions about individualism; I refer strictly to personality, the entity with which these writers claim the state etc. ought not to interfere.

moreover an essential characteristic of the good artist and poet, to whom, therefore, dogmatic abstractions of any kind are special poison.

The goodness or badness of society does not consist in conformity or non-conformity with any imposed intellectual structure. To try and impose any intellectual dogma whatsoever on the growth of society, which is the growth of individuals, comes always in the end to an attempt to abstract and perpetuate what is old and bad in that society. Dramatically it means robotry or death in character and personality. Mr. Eliot is no better and no worse than Mr. Shaw in this respect.

Dogmatic theology, because it denies the goodness or badness taught to us by experience, is driven to make common front with the worst causes, which can still be recognised as such by any mere reader of the gospel. Mr. Eliot and his followers or supporters are at heart concerned not with charity but with power. Our deplorable society therefore should not hope or expect to get from them the succour that it needs. For all our genuine cultural impulses of whatever kind, even the lowest including the range of examples given by Mr. Eliot in *Notes Towards the Definition of Culture*, seem to spring from our need of charity rather than of power. At least we can say that culture originates in the urge to live together rather than in the urge to die together, for whatever cause. The Church, if it were to regain its ancient authority, would do so more than ever by imposition, and by alliance with corrupt and power-seeking forces, as we can observe wherever it has had the opportunity to advance of late years. The Church has never remembered for long how to rule men by their affections, and now, for obvious reasons, it can only intervene restrictively in their intellectual interests or in any but their simplest pastimes.

All dogma, in fact, including, and especially, the dogma of Original Sin, divorces us from real and natural morality, which can only be taught us by personal and individual love, generally experienced early and unconsciously. If we cannot learn our morality from that reality, we shall learn it from another: hate.

CHAPTER III

Mr. Hulme's Sloppy Dregs

IN his introduction to his *Notes Towards the Definition of Culture* Mr. Eliot says that "to rescue this word (Culture) is the extreme of my ambition." The semantic aim is stressed throughout the book and this, in a dogmatist, must draw our attention and perhaps arouse our suspicion. Can it be that Mr. Eliot detects a semantic abuse only on the part of those, the secularists, whom he must regard as the enemy? There are many hints throughout the book that the issue of the dependency of culture upon religion, or vice versa, was after all prejudged in Mr. Eliot's mind:

"The facile assumption of a relationship between culture and religion is perhaps the most fundamental weakness of Arnold's *Culture and Anarchy*. Arnold gives the impression that Culture (as he uses the term) is something more comprehensive than religion; that the latter is no more than a necessary element, supplying ethical formation and some emotional colour, to Culture which is the ultimate value."

It looks as if in rescuing the word Mr. Eliot has reserved it in his mind already for a higher fate than mere liberty.

One may limit one's aim to a semantic criticism, but I do not think it makes sense to limit one's semantic criticism. Apart from this one work Mr. Eliot is not more remarkable than anyone else for his interest in semantics, while the philosophy on which he now bases his life and work abounds in terms which have to be believed before they can be understood: for so I interpret Mr. Eliot's studied refusal to analyse these basic concepts of his faith which he says are of the greatest importance for the rest of us.

But for those of us for whom belief is still not a mere surrender of intelligence, but something connected with at least the possibility of discussion; who cannot, with Tertullian or Sir Thomas Browne, believe the more, and even the more virtuously, 'because it is impossible'; nor even, with the Queen in *Alice in Wonderland*, perform our spiritual exercises before breakfast, by believing six impossible things, there is only one way in which we can give scholasticism, old or new, any meaning, and that is by trying to investigate its terms.

Most of these words and conceptions have already been mentioned—Original Sin, the Fall, the Incarnation. Moreover it has already been said that these ideas immediately involve us with other conceptions which are necessary to give them some appearance of objective validity: the dual conception, for instance, of the words 'truth' and 'knowledge', the implication that these have, each of them, two distinct and opposed applications, one in the field of science and one in the field of religion.

These words and conceptions may be said to provide the new scholasticism with its basic stock-in-trade, but it will be necessary to investigate other terms which are common in wider fields, particularly in literature and criticism. The changes in the use of the words Romanticism and Classicism, for instance, will illustrate what happens when notions of heresy or orthodoxy get loose in literary criticism or in the philosophy of art.

These words, which throughout their history have always been remarkable for semantic abuse, are important as they are used by the neo-scholastic literary school, because they stand in a special relation to the Pelagian heresy, which is a denial of the strict dogma of Original Sin. The Romantic, according to the neo-scholastics, is someone who bases all his thinking and writing on the assumption that man is only corrupted by society, that he is born 'good' and, perhaps more importantly, is perfectible by his own efforts. It is important to notice that the possibility that

natural 'goodness' or natural 'badness' do not have any very
precise meaning is never taken into account.

All these words and conceptions are manifestations of a single
attempt to reassert a world-view, that of theological scholasticism,
which is in absolute contradiction to the philosophy, the implications and the practice which derive inevitably from the
scientific approach to the world. I have adopted Eddington's
term—hypothetico-observational—to define this. Whether or not
your emotional or impulsive reaction to the idea of science is
favourable, it is advisable, especially if you are a person dealing
with words, to make yourself aware that this absolute opposition
between science and scholasticism is a fact. There are many
people who are trying or will try to muddle you. Not all of them,
as we have already seen, are clerical or literary. Some of these
amateur theologians are men of science, for instance, Eddington
himself. Outside their own specialities, men of science do not
seem to treat words or conceptions more critically than anyone
else. Unless creative and critical writers themselves begin to find
out exactly what they are talking about, we may find ourselves
back in the Dark Ages sooner than even those who hanker for
them, as the source of all light, may like.

The commonest way of disguising this total opposition between
religious dogmatism and science would certainly often dismay the
more imaginative writers, if it were clearly grasped. In the face of
scientific argument, not all of them have the stamina of D. H.
Lawrence ('I don't feel it here,' i.e., in the solar plexus). The
disguise is the Two Truths theory, which I have already mentioned.
This is used by clerical and professional theologians, and we must
expect them to use it. Their position is by definition hypostatical,
and this is the only way they can keep it up.

But it is also used freely by literary men and critics who should,
one feels, have vested *their* interests in purifying the language of
the tribe, not in leaving it worse·confounded. Underneath, the
Two Truths theory is merely another form of hypostasis, an
unwarrantable attribution of substance to a mere concept. It
states that science, whose method has admittedly produced

verifiable results in its special fields, must stick to those fields. Religion on the other hand has its own special field of 'Truth'. This theory, in one form or another, has been prominent since the seventeenth century, when the results of the scientific, the hypothetico-observational, method became striking. In the seventeenth century, it received the support even of inductive or materialistic thinkers, such as Bacon, who were impatiently enthusiastic about the results of scientific method and did not want, for various reasons, to be bothered by the orthodox authorities. In our day, those thinkers who fear that materialism is necessarily hostile to poetry as well as to religion and who equate 'Science' with 'Materialism', and 'Materialism' with a universe of billard-ball atoms and no morals, use this theory as their chief intellectual basis. As usual we must except Mr. Eliot, who never argues but states. But the theory is present or implied not only in the professionally theological works, including those of Maritain, Demant and others, but in the theological applications to literature which Basil Willey has taken from T. E. Hulme, apart from the Hallelujah Chorus of C. S. Lewis and Miss Dorothy Sayers. Cleanth Brooks, a distinguished and penetrating literary critic, employs the theory in a secular form, but he has also marked hostility to science and does not grasp what science is. In passing, I must also give special mention to Mr. Norman Nicholson (*Man and Literature*), since his revelation of what he means by science puts this characteristic incomprehension in a handy and referable form:

"During the last few centuries there has developed a tendency to think that truth is only to be known in the sphere of science, and by science is meant the art of recording and measuring natural phenomena. Thus that a halfpenny is an inch across is 'true'; that the 'Mona Lisa' is beautiful is a 'matter of opinion'. The effect on the arts of this unconscious belief is clear; the concerns of poetry, religion and so on are not true. . . . The imaginative life of poetry became at best only a fairy tale to be indulged in for its own sake. Clearly such a mental atmosphere was not likely to be productive of great poetry, and there are no great poets among the realists. . . . The revolt against the confinement of thought within the limits of dry materialism was headed naturally enough by the poet and the metaphysician. *But later on they were joined by the scientists too* (my italics), for the development of psycho-analysis and anthropology shows that scientists were *beginning to realise* that there were more things in the universe than could be put in a test-tube or measured by calipers. *The cult of the irrational* took many forms, *some of which seem scarcely to deserve to be called irrational* (Note: Then why call them so?) There was surrealism and its allied -isms: dadaism, symbolism etc. There was psycho-analysis and the study of the unconscious mind and its symbols. (Note: How can such a *study* be irrational?) There was the revived interest in myth and folk-lore."

Unfortunately there is much that needs to be said further on the subject of the scientists who 'joined' and why they did so. But first I must point out the confusion which Mr. Nicholson makes between the knower and the thing known, typical, as I shall often show, of his fellow-thinkers; here between the scientist and his object of study, between the irrational phenomena and their rational and co-ordinated examination. Then there is the quaint implication that the scientists moved rather later than the average human being into the Horatian position about the contents of heaven and earth, and apologetically produced several new kinds of subject-matter which they could not put into their test-tubes or measure with their calipers. I suppose Mr. Nicholson may think that by the expression "the art of *recording* . . . natural phenomena", he protects himself from the accusation that he is living in a Dureresque dream of retorts and crucibles (and perhaps also in a fantasy of Black Magic and Auto-da-fé). But I think it is clear enough, from the context, that he is talking in terms of outworn materialism, which necessarily involves him in outworn idealism. It must constantly be repeated that these attitudes are counterparts. One deals in lumps of matter and the other deals in lumps of mind. 'Psycho-analysis' and 'anthropology', as he conceives them, are Mr. Nicholson's 'lumps of mind'.

For the scientist, phenomena must have a 'given' quality, even if he inseparably and concurrently sets about evolving a working theory to discover the next stage of the 'given'. This primarily has nothing to do with any substantial universe behind the given phenomena, any Reality behind Appearance. The characteristics essentially discovered in the universe by the scientific approach are three. First, givenness: this word is preferable to objectivity as it does not immediately involve us with epistemological philosophy, either idealism or materialism. The second characteristic is unity. Phenomena, that is, do not arbitrarily resist his patterns of investigation, there is continuity between those elements in a situation or event which are recognisable and those which are new and as yet not altogether connected; in other words, scientific investigation does not have to reckon on *meeting* with the *super*natural. The third characteristic is regularity or law, which is continuous with the conception of unity—the given will continue to be given.

It will be seen that all these are qualities of the scientist's experience, not of any 'substance' behind phenomena. But when any of our experiences are really experience, when they have been examined and related and have produced some understood alteration in our information or emotions or both, they are potentially scientific. When there are any phenomena at all, there is the possibility of scientific inquiry, with or without test-tubes and calipers. Indeed, because unity of investigation, the practice of asking questions in such a way that the possibility of an answer is implicit, is an essential of science, all phenomena whatsoever must at least theoretically demand scientific inquiry. This is implicit in the concept Phenomena. No supporter of the Two Truths theory, I am sure, would claim that religion has no phenomena. To all of us the universe asks for a meaning.

The assumption that nothing is scientific which is not quantitative and 'materialistic', in the narrowest and most rigidly mechanical sense, is not an accident, nor wholly due to ignorance of what scientists are really up to with their laboratories and notebooks. It is an integral part of the Two Truths theory, which depends, as Bertrand Russell says:

"on the time-honoured principle that anything which cannot be proved untrue may be assumed to be true, a principle whose falsehood is proved by the fortunes of bookmakers."

This theory provides all our neo-scholastics with their necessary field of nescience, over which they may assume the truth of their preferences. To limit science to what science can gropingly measure is automatically to exclude the social and non-quantitative sciences from scientific status, and this, as the typical quotation given above from Norman Nicholson will illustrate, is exactly what theological apologists wish to do. For psychology and anthropology claim to tell us something about the nature of 'Man', and it is only by an act of enclosure around this concept, which keeps it in the field of nescience, by definition not open to scientific survey, that many other basic concepts of theological and scholastic thinking—such as 'Freedom' in 'Freedom of the Will'—can be preserved. When science is merely measurement, ignorance can be not only bliss, but knowledge. But of course to say that test-tubes and calipers not only never did, but never can, tell us anything direct about the Nature of Man (if we can for purposes of discussion accept that abstraction) is, even if true, not the same as saying that observation and the hypotheses based upon observation cannot tell us anything about the subject.

Comparatively lately, the neo-scholastics have received a bonus from certain scientists, including Eddington, Sir James Jeans, and others who should know better, in the form of support for some of the more fundamental theological doctrines, including that of Free Will. The support has sometimes been based on an interpretation of Heisenberg's Uncertainty Principle (often misleadingly and tendenciously known as Heisenberg's Principle of Indeterminacy). Over the implications of this principle Eddington exhibited a curious conflict of mind. Within the framework of Newton's mechanics, which treated momentum and position as independent entities, it has proved impossible to pin down with infinite accuracy the behaviour of the minutest particles of matter. Such a discovery is a typical signal to scientists that the framework is due for revision; and in good part it has been revised. But in the interim, while the older mechanics strongly governed the mental habits of professional scientists, the discrepancy presented itself as a breach in causality, through which something like the personal caprice of an electron could insert itself. Eddington, whose scientific thinking was always liable to disturbance by his religious convictions, was fascinated by this paradox of misstatement. Whenever he faced the blunt question whether such play in the gears of the machine was quantitatively large enough to cover the 'choices' and 'actions' of a living being, he admitted it was not so. In fact he categorically stated that nothing he had said in his theoretical work could be justly so interpreted.

He believed in Free Will, as he made clear more than once in his scientific as well as his mystical writings, but claimed that he did so on grounds of intuition, not at all because of the 'indeterminacy' of ultimate particles of matter.

"If we could attribute," he writes in *New Pathways in Science*, "the large-scale movements of our bodies to the 'trigger action' of the unpredetermined behaviour of a few key atoms in our brain cells the problem would be simple; for individual atoms have wide indeterminacy of behaviour . . . (but) . . . I should conjecture that the smallest unit of structure in which the physical effects of volition have their origins contains many billions of atoms. If such a unit behaved like an inorganic system of similar mass the indeterminacy would be insufficient to allow appreciable freedom."

However, having snatched 'freedom' from the electron, he at once proceeds to bestow it upon another conception, the unitary consciousness, whose reality is not necessarily greater nor whose existence more assured than those of the electron, merely because people have been talking about it longer.

"My own tentative view," he continues, "is that this 'conscious unit' does in fact differ from an inorganic system in having a much higher indeterminacy of behaviour, simply because of the unitary nature of that which it represents—namely the Ego."

As far as I can see, what this all amounts to is the following:

"There is nothing whatsoever in the Heisenberg Uncertainty Principle which has any bearing on the problem of Free Will. Pursuing scientific standards of truth, I have nothing to add to the negative contribution of my scientific predecessors to theological beliefs. However, I believe not only in Free Will, but in an absolute, detached and unified consciousness, which is the same as 'mind' or 'soul', as those terms are used by theologians. I think there is another order of truth—other than the scientific, that is— because, as Mr. Willey would say, I do, or I wish to do so, not for any scientific reason."

Eddington was in other words a stout supporter of the Two Truths theory, but the general reader must understand that this was, as usual, as a layman, not as a scientist. Eddington wrote about his religious opinions, and about many of his philosophical ones, on his 'day off'.

Eddington's case illustrates a condition which is common to many scientists, and has recently been discussed in an interesting article in the *Journal of the Philosophy of Science* by Professor Herbert Dingle. Dingle points out that twentieth-century scientists in general have not grasped the philosophical implications of the technique of observation and experiment which became the groundwork of scientific method in the seventeenth century, and which they themselves continue to employ correctly and fruitfully. Most of them are very imperfect philosophers. Their philosophy in general is an unconscious hangover from that old conception of substance, that there is, behind phenomena, behind experience and experiment, a substantial Real Universe whose nature they are endeavouring to determine. Dingle makes a special onslaught on materialism. Applying his ideas to Eddington and others, we can see that, whatever their views about freedom and causality in connection with the atom and however much continuing scientific investigation breaks the atom down into electrons, protons, neutrons, positrons and so on, the conception of these scientists does tend toward an ultimate abstract atomicity whose nature it is to be inaccessible and ever beyond experience.

What Dingle should have said is that, from this point of view, Idealism or Materialism is merely a matter of verbal preference. What is science is continuing and related experience. Atomicity is a concept which either materialism or idealism might juggle with. But I am afraid that Professor Dingle's selective criticism of materialism is significant. He rightly states that science is about experiences and their relations, and that the rigid concept of an external world, to the total knowledge of which science was continually approximating, limited the scientist's field of inquiry and therefore of experience—meaning by this that an ultimate external world was in fact a concept making a specialised demand on *measurement*. But he is yet able to say that it should now be possible, although admittedly unlikely, for religion and science to "advance in harmony and even with mutual assistance".

Professor Dingle's reason for supposing such a possibility is at first sight one we can understand. It is that science has nothing to say about the intrinsic value of any experience, only about the relations between experiences, all of which are equally valid scientific material, at least potentially.

"Macbeth's dilemma about the reality of his dagger, which he could see but could not feel, was no dilemma to the nineteenth-century playgoer. If the dagger had been real he would have felt it: he didn't feel it, so it was not real, and could therefore be ignored. It didn't occur to the scientist of that time that, 'real' or not, Macbeth certainly had the experience of seeing it, and that experience called for scientific study just as much as one accompanied by the corresponding experience of touch."

But since Professor Dingle confesses that he is not 'optimistic' about the prospects of this harmony, we must conclude that he regards the harmony as desirable, and his reasons for this are less acceptable. There will, he thinks, be further conflicts between religion and science; the present philosophical honeymoon—or should one say courtship—is unstable because:

"Men with little scientific curiosity, to whom their religion is the most precious thing in life," will not view "without protest what they cannot but regard as a degradation of the highest they know" when "the scientific psychologist, inevitably seeking to correlate religious experience with other phenomena," brings it "into relation with psychological states, some of which are regarded as abnormal or even pathological."

When religion thus returns the ring, the situation, according to Dingle, will rest on a misunderstanding. This seems to me a most extraordinary statement. It is perfectly true that a scientist is not concerned with the intrinsic values of the experience which he may correlate, perfectly true also that the word 'pathological' has not for him the chief significance that it has for those with a preconception of what is to be regarded as a healthy state. But I do not see how Dingle can miss that the religious protest which he foresees is intrinsic to the religious view. Scientific curiosity must intrinsically seek to correlate all phenomena, and religious preconception must intrinsically seek to bar this all-reaching aim, to put forth a departmental resistance which, if allowed, frustrates correlation, and therefore precludes 'harmony'.

If 'delusions' such as Macbeth's dagger or the pink rats of an alcoholic are as worthy of scientific study as any other genuine experience, which no one wishes to deny, this is not because the examining scientist believes that there are no such things as delusions. By relating the pink rats or the dagger to other communicable, agreed, and probable experiences, the scientist comes to give meaning to the concept 'delusion'. I also say nothing either absolute or comparative about the intrinsic value of the experiences, Macbeth's, the alcoholic's or the communicant's. I only say they have a meaning and are part of knowledge only in so far as they are agreed, communicable and related to other experiences, which in fact determine their probability, their givenness.

Many concepts which theologians regard as the most essential part of religion are not experiences at all in the sense in which both Professor Dingle and I are here using the word, a sense in which we both admit a 'delusion' as an experience. Dogma for instance is not anybody's experience in this sense. I think that Professor Dingle has unconsciously misinterpreted his own statement about the scientist's indifference to the value of experience, to mean that all experiences whatsoever have in fact the same value. This is to ignore the binding and imposed quality of the relatedness of experiences, which gives us science and all its positive achievements. Describing, as an illustration of the progressive metaphysical emancipation of science, the way, for instance, that mass, 'the fundamental property of matter', has been removed from substantiality by the theory of relativity, he says that it is now entirely a matter of "your or my caprice which of two bodies contains the more of the eternal, independent, substantial reality of the universe." Of course, it is not a matter of my caprice, but of my relations to other events, which may be measuring instruments or positions in space or time, but which, in any case, are given experiences, experiences imposed on my passivity. The word *caprice* in fact introduces the idea of substantive mentality, and proves that Professor Dingle has jumped out of the frying-pan of materialism into the fire of idealism.

When we are able to observe facts and to form hypotheses which we can use to predict further relevant facts, we are behaving scientifically, whatever the subject-matter of our observations may be. It will certainly be pointed out by those who prefer that psychology and anthropology should never be sciences, for instance, by those who still claim that theology is a science, as well as by many less prejudiced critics, that the real difficulty in the case of these social studies is to decide what is a fact and what is not.

All sciences need this particular skill, but there is no reason to deny that the observation of the facts of human behaviour, whether they are those of activity and organisation or are introspective, needs exceptional skill and training in detachment. But it must be said that if we encourage the development of this skill in suitable people, we may come to know about ourselves and about the laws which govern our human behaviour on this planet, whereas if we continue to ratiocinate in the fixed hypostatical concepts which we have inherited from scholastic thinking, as in one form or another, and consciously or unconsciously, most of us still do, human nature, as it is vaguely called, will abide a mystery, and we shall never be less foolish than we are now. We know in one way or not at all.

Therefore it is interesting and important to examine those theological concepts to which our literary neo-scholastics give most attention, and which they are most anxious to revive. It will be said that these concepts are the central dogmas of the Christian faith, the *sine qua non* of orthodoxy. That is so. But if we compare the practice of Mr. Eliot, who is a first-rate literary mind and therefore not likely to be a fool in other fields, with, let us say, C. S. Lewis or Dorothy Sayers, we see that these two are game, as Mr. Eliot is not, to go out on all the street corners and among the booths and side-shows, and there if necessary strip to the waist and challenge all comers. Orthodox theology, for them, has an answer to everything, and they are ready to give it with all the aplomb of Datas. I know that they are braver and stupider than many of their orthodox literary fellows, but it is interesting to consider why an orthodoxy which is not only less muscular but less pinheaded than theirs should be relatively cautious in its minimal claims.

Mr. Eliot, we find, commits himself to the dogma of the Incarnation and also to that of Original Sin, commits himself, that is, in so far as he may be said to give a philosophical assent rather more discreetly than valorously.

The Incarnation is a special case. It is so central to Christian belief that, without it, there is really nothing which can be intelligibly described as Christian orthodoxy. We may set it aside for the present, because it is a doctrine which the orthodox cannot be expected to surrender—or, apparently, to discuss. Mr. Eliot does not discuss it, whatever the warrior caste of literary lay theologians feels called upon to do. It is a doctrine which affects epistemology, and though I do not find it possible or necessary to ignore epistemological matters, the prime concern of this book is not with metaphysics, but with that area of discussion where neo-scholastic claims conflict with observable experience, the subject-matter of science. We might hold that the doctrine of the Fall of Man, as an unverifiable hypothesis about history, is in itself outside this area. But it is interdependent with the doctrine of Original Sin. This is the basis of theological psychology and, since psychology is a scientific subject whose material consists of observable experience, it should be possible to reach a rational understanding of what the neo-scholastics mean by this concept.

Possible, but by no means easy. It is more commonly referred to than explained. And if we take the reference back as far as we are able, we are not much better off, since it is difficult to be certain exactly what is orthodox and what is not. The two most important branches of the Christian organisation, the Roman and Protestant Churches, are not in complete agreement. Indeed, when Mr. Eliot refers to the Church, it would often be helpful to know which one he means, for the dogma of Original Sin not only refers, through its connections with the Fall, to a palæology without field-work, but has had in comparatively recent historical times a schismatic development which is still unresolved. We know from Mr. Eliot that Original Sin is a very real and terrible thing, but he does not even tell us in what its terror, certainly not in what its reality, consists, and no other literary neo-scholastic seems to be able to tell us more, except that we must believe it.

There is the doctrine as stated by Augustine that all men have inherited from Adam the inability to abstain from sin which Adam showed when he ate the apple of the Tree of Knowledge of Good and Evil. Of themselves, men have for ever lost the power to be virtuous and they can attain this only by the grace of God: but agreement as to whether this first sin on the part of the Father of Mankind has its nature of sin from the fact of disobedience to God's command, or from the curiosity which led Adam to seek independent knowledge, or from the concupiscence which the eating awakened in him, seems never to have been finally reached among those who claim, however, to be orthodox.

In *Paradise Lost*—which because of its literary merit ought to speak to the literary orthodox with peculiar authority on all matters relating to the Fall and to Original Sin—Milton supports what we may call the 'Test' theory. This is that Adam was put to the test by God's command, and failed through his disobedience, the eating of the apple having no inherent significance. Unfortunately, as far as I know, Milton has never been taken as settling the question. The Churches themselves seem never to have made a precise and agreed decision among the three possible interpretations which I have mentioned above, as a brief reference to the history of the controversy will show. Pelagius, a British monk who, when he was in Palestine at the beginning of the fifth century A.D., was affected, it is believed, by a certain slackness in the monasteries, developed a theory of self-help, that men were not born inherently sinful, but in a neutral moral condition, and that grace, conceived as divine intervention to save each individual soul, was not necessary but was granted in the general form of freedom of the will so that men had the capacity to become free of sin by their own efforts. After Augustine, whose views, one must believe, were conditioned by his own psychological experiences, these propositions were condemned, and the conception that men were essentially helpless toward their own nature, particularly toward their own concupiscence, while only the individual intervention of divine grace could help them to conquer this sinful tendency which they had inherited from Adam, for a time prevailed. This was followed by what is known as the semi-Pelagian theory, which lays stress on the imperfection of human nature and the essentiality of divine help or grace, but otherwise softens or ignores the Augustinian implications of the immediate and apparent damnableness of the new-born, with their cradle concupiscence, and of the utter damnation of the un-baptised. Nevertheless, even within the Catholic Church, the more austere view was revived with bitter partisanship by the seven-teenth-century Jansenists, while Protestantism, at the Reforma-tion, took an Augustinian slant culminating in the Calvinist predestination, a ferociously repressive doctrine to which we can point whenever it is stated that the 'Protestant spirit' is inevitably allied with a belief in 'Progress'.

So far we can accept that Mr. Eliot, as a Catholic or Anglo-Catholic, is probably a semi-Pelagian, and even perhaps that in refraining from stating what Original Sin exactly is he has followed the highest orthodox example. Human beings are radically imperfect, and are so from birth, and need the actual intervention of the divine if they are to heal their imperfections. But if the imperfection is radical and inherited it must bear some resemblance at least of type to the First Sin, and one would like to know in what the sinfulness of this consisted. If, as it appears, neither the 'Test' theory nor the concupiscence theory is inherent in this imprecise term when it is used by literary theologians, nothing else remains but to suppose that Adam's sin, which we share and from which we also suffer, was curiosity, the mere wish to find out. If this is so, and it strikes me as analytically logical, this not only accounts for the contemporary literary antagonism to 'Science', but it also leads us back to the Two Truths theory. If wanting to find out for ourselves, either as individuals or as members of a secular organisation, is at least potentially sinful, in the sense that it can be so defined by an *ex cathedra* pronounce-ment, we cannot do anything else, if we wish to avoid sin, than believe what we are told by religious authority—that is, we must attribute a special and 'higher' order of truth to a certain body of deductive and hypostatical pronouncements.

This, in fact, is what we are asked to accept if any intellectual content whatsoever is to be granted to current revived theological orthodoxy among the literary; if that is not to be regarded solely as an attempt to rationalise the sense of guilt and inadequacy which is partly natural, and partly fostered in all of us, from our earliest moments.

During this century we have been asked to accept it, sometimes with diffidence and an apparent wish to 'reconcile' the 'truths' of science and of religion, but sometimes also with dogmatic and specious aplomb amounting to insolence. The diffident approach often gets support from the tender-minded, and also from the genuinely tender-hearted, therefore it is likely to commend itself to those whose interests are specialised in a literary or artistic direction. The bolder dogmatic approach is more characteristic of those whose interest, or custom, is, whether openly or not, polemic and aggressive, although it may partially disguise itself as a concern with literature or art. A certain kind of split character which couples dogmatic insolence, to the point of violence, with genuine critical or æsthetic ability is also possible, and appeared with T. E. Hulme.

Hulme's *Speculations*, edited from notes and scattered material by Herbert Read, appeared posthumously not long after the end of the First World War, in which Hulme had been killed at the age of thirty-four. This book is a manifesto against all the humanist philosophies since the Renaissance.* Hulme, making the humanist test the disbelief, implicit or expressed, in the dogma of Original Sin, classifies them all as essentially one philosophy. He is not more precise than any of the writers who have succeeded him about what he really means by Original Sin, nor, I should say, theologically more accurate. In general, he couples the rather wide interpretation that man is radically imperfect, and needs God to achieve any ethical standard whatsoever, with a rather more definite dogmatism about the nature of the divine, its complete separation from the sphere of ordinary knowledge by a real and, as it were, chasmic discontinuity. This might not call for any very active criticism, other than the observation that it is a rather flatly dogmatic example of the Two Truths theory, if Hulme had drawn the logical conclusion from this concept of absolute discontinuity

---

*It was the duty of every honest man to cleanse the world from these 'sloppy dregs' of the Renaissance, according to Hulme.

between the sphere of ethical and religious values, and that of scientific investigation—that there was no more therefore to be said, or known, about it. However, the bulk of Hulme's writings then follows, part of it æsthetic but most of it epistemological, which shows that Hulme himself did not allow the discontinuity, which he had posited, to trouble him and that the 'Keep Out' notice which this concept implied was meant only for humanistic, not for theological, reasoning. Hulme's æsthetic theory, particularly when it is about the nature of poetry, is acute though limited. It was part, I should say, of a then general valid reaction in the writing of poetry, and was therefore partly drawn from awareness of actual valuable practice among his contemporaries; while partly it gave them a reflective encouragement to continue in the same direction. This applies particularly to the Imagist poets with their insistence on concreteness and accuracy of description of the objects with which poetry deals, whether these objects are mental or physical. This, with its counterpart in Hulme, who narrows the æsthetic impulse to an urge for precision which can be said to have achieved its aim when we feel that the artist was actually and vividly in the presence of the object he describes, is true enough so far as it goes; and particularly in the case of poetry, which deals in words, it is a natural and healthy reaction when poets themselves have become infected by the historical tendency of language to become cloudy, hypostatised and meaningless—to detach itself, in short, from constant reference to experience. This means that in so far as Hulme and, for example, the Imagists were saying and doing anything valuable, they were simply reasserting the general nature of poetry, which of course has constantly to be reasserted, not only by movements or by critics, but by every poet, in so far as he is a poet, in his individual practice from day to day. It does not mean that the tissue of critical generalisation with which Hulme connected his æsthetic observations to his underlying philosophical concept was justified—any more than that the concept itself was verifiable. It was perfectly true that just before Hulme there was a confusion between poetry and mere emotion—perhaps partly due to 'War-

poetry', which needed cleaning up, and that what passed as poetry
was often vague, diffuse and sloppy, in short that verse-writers
were dealing in poetically and semantically diseased language;
but there is nothing in this to excuse a lot of critical language
about Classicism and Romanticism which is also made semantically sloppy by these hypostatised concepts. For Hulme simply
identifies Romanticism with the man-centred humanism which he
hates and whose universal rejection he prophesies, and Classicism
with the God-centred view of orthodox Christianity. This leads
him to some odd sorting of poets and to some perhaps anxious
subdivision of his own classes. Shakespeare, he says, for instance,
is classical, but with a *dynamic* classicism; he is a classic of motion.
Horace is still classical. This makes one wonder if there was also a
special Harrowing of Hell for otherwise deserving literary men
who were either pre-Christian or not clearly orthodox.

However, this view of the classical is the point of juncture
between his æsthetics and his main philosophy. Good poets have
throughout history practised in a way which agrees with Hulme's
limited æsthetic, whether he would have called them classical or
romantic. I have dealt with this at length in Chapter VIII. What I
wish to discuss here is Hulme's anti-humanistic contribution to
neo-scholastism.

T. E. Hulme's work stands on a dogmatic basis, as I have
indicated—the statement that man is a fallen and radically
imperfect creature. This he calls the doctrine of Original Sin and
characterises it as the central conception distinguishing the
medieval Christian attitude to life from the humanist attitude
which, so he says, has been dominant, to the point of completely
unconscious acceptance, ever since the Renaissance. His work is
also—with some striking variations which do not affect the underlying philosophical structure—based on the Two Truths theory.
His method is to divide knowledge into three spheres, claiming an
absolute discontinuity among them. The two extreme spheres are
those of religion and inorganic science, while the middle one
covers everything which we describe as biology or the social
sciences. He gives the extreme spheres a kind of polar absolute-

ness. The idea of discontinuity here is simply another way of stating that we have two ways of knowing, each absolutely and equally valid *in its own sphere*. But the idea of the third or intermediate sphere, and particularly of its separation from the sphere of normal science, is of special interest because it is an expression of Hulme's wish to keep biology and the study of social phenomena 'pure' from scientific method, to preserve, in fact, the whole content of 'Human Nature' for the field of nescience. This wish is at least implicit in all scholastic and neo-scholastic thinking, and seems to be also the only ground on which that philosophy can re-erect itself.

But this idea of the third sphere concerned with the vital or what Hulme calls the 'loose' sciences (it is a 'muddy mixed zone' between two absolutes: this seems an example of what Richards calls emotive language) has another and more particular use in Hulme. For though, as I have said, the fundamental concepts of this manifesto against humanism are stated as flat dogma, Hulme intended to be the philosopher of the reaction which he helped to inaugurate—to erect an intellectual system designed to be tight against the encroachments which, for example, physical and astronomical science had been making for quite a long time. To do this he was prepared to make at least some show of meeting critical philosophy on its own empirical ground. He thought he had discovered the technique and the empirical basis in the philosophy of Bergson. His reasons for isolating "the muddy mixed zone of the loose sciences" which are concerned with life (he refers to them also as 'vital' to distinguish them from physical or mechanical) become clear. Certain basic concepts of scholastic theology have to be saved at all costs. For example, the concept of a fixed 'Human Nature' and at the same time the contradictory concept of an absolute Free Will. For the dogma of Original Sin is not only inextricably involved with these two, but, in particular, without Free Will in the absolute, it becomes a doctrine of despair from which it is very difficult to keep out some kind of determinism. It is interesting that Hulme with his sharp separation of the spheres of knowledge should have felt so much eagerness to put up a rational dialectic in this 'vital' sphere. He was relatively young, as well as ardent and militaristic, and this may have brought out a special moral and intellectual pride. Certainly his zeal seems to have been in the first place philosophical rather than salvationist and, unlike for instance Mr. Lewis and Miss Sayers, to be more expressive of the study, or at least of the drawing-room, than of the soap-box. In any case, Bergson provided him with an imposing terminology for this effort, which was not less hypostatical in the original than in Hulme's interpretation.

Bergson, as we know, was centrally concerned to distinguish the 'vital' from the mechanical. I shall discuss Bergson's theories only in relation to Hulme's use of them, because it is only in this connection that they bear on the current situation in poetry and art. Apart from that their place seems to be in the history of philosophy.

I have referred to the fact that literary men who are Churchmen, and anti-humanist in the sense that Hulme defines it, in general take their thought back as far as the basic theological dogmas and attempt very little intellectual justification of their position. Their major premiss is Church Authority. This does not mean, however, that they admit, either to their readers or to themselves, that their beliefs are absolutely impossible to verify. In particular, T. S. Eliot, both in his poetry and in his prose, alludes to a whole corpus of ecclesiastical learning which, as I have said elsewhere, is a kind of bank where the intellectual gold is kept to honour all fiduciary issues, when the demand is made. On the other hand, it is not uncommon for literary theologians to suggest, as a kind of *tu quoque*, that as far as popular understanding and practical application are concerned, the average member of a democratic society is in the same intellectual position as the ordinary lay faithful—the 'metaphysic' of science, for him, is also based on Authority, and he has to accept conclusions based on a reasoning which he cannot possibly follow. ". . . A word half-understood, torn from its place in some alien or half-formed science, as of psychology," says Mr. Eliot in the essay on Lancelot Andrewes, "conceals from both writer and reader the utter meaninglessness of a statement . . . all dogma is in doubt except the dogma of sciences of which we have read in the newspapers . . ."*

This looks plausible enough; and no one deplores the inaccuracy and the wishful thinking of popular scientific journalism and of journalistic accounts of science, nor the hypostatisation which these share with scholastic thought, more than the respectable, hardworking scientific specialist. Of course the word 'dogma' is employed by Mr. Eliot in this one sentence, in two totally different senses, only the second, one can see, being loose, popular and pejorative. What is completely withheld from the average reader in this emotive aside is that the statements of scientists (it is only newspaper behaviour which turns them into 'dogma') have either a short-term or a long-term route towards verification: short-term towards their fellow-scientists who can understand the same technical language, and long-term towards their ordinary fellow-beings who can eventually see and judge of the predicted results. Theological dogma is never thus travel-stained, it remains always in the empyrean and never comes down to earth to be sullied by common use and proof.

Yet theological authority never ceases to imply that the arguments and proofs are available, although to find them we must leap over the history of the last three centuries—which has really been the history of the miserable passion for induction, for the forming of hypotheses on the basis of observation—and go back to the time when thought, as Mr. Eliot says, was "orderly, strong and beautiful"; was, in fact, a system of ideas about the unknowable which did very little to account for the known, and was largely based on unanalysed assumptions.

But it is true that not all writers who feel the need of a creed of a *Weltanschauung*, can be quite satisfied with the *feel* of the intellectual paper-money, even when they pass it. As writers, especially as good writers, they are perhaps more likely to be first impressed, especially in the psychological field with which they are so closely concerned, with a kind of faithfulness to law in the

*What does 'alien' mean in this context?

world around them, in particular to tragic law, than with its mystery as demanding an ætiological explanation. I do not think that Mr. Norman Nicholson (*Man and Literature*) is correct—at least I do not think that his statement means either very much or means what he says—when he says that few great poets are or have been materialists. Few great poets apart from Lucretius may have been materialists in the strict metaphysical sense. But few great poets have written about metaphysics in any form. It has been relatively common for them, as it were, to 'go to church on Sundays'—as in a way even Shakespeare did. But in fact they have mostly not wished to be bothered by any public or conventional creed at all, since all creeds become stereotyped and tend to stop them using their eyes, ears and other senses with fresh immediacy. It is quite likely that the present revival of scholasticism may help to produce good poetry in those poets whose gift lies in their sensuous immediacy or innocence and who are thereby saved from anxious or unskilled thought. However, we ought not in general to be in this state of primal intellectual innocency and, if we must think, it is better that we should think about something rather than nothing.

A shrewd sense of politics or perhaps of ecclesiastical policy is probably necessary to deflect a lively intellect, which often means an aggressive and argumentative intellect, from the discussion of metaphysical fundamentals. Hulme shows a mind of this quality even when discussing literature and art, but having chosen to be a philosopher he could, unlike Mr. Eliot, hardly do without a dialectic, although we can observe his natural preference for the aphoristic and the intuitive, the kind of philosophy which is really personal; not striving toward objectivity or even systematisation; more, let us say, of the type of Nietzsche, than of Aristotle or Kant.

Bergson was a godsend to him, for Bergson's philosophy appeared to give to intuition the kind of empirical status which every Englishman—even an Englishman of twentieth-century buccaneering type as Hulme was, intellectually—requires in order to philosophise comfortably. I am not myself taking here an æsthetic view of philosophies; I think that the English empirical tradition from David Hume onwards has given us our best approximation to 'general truth'. I only say that it is difficult for an Englishman wholly to ignore this tradition, whereas it is quite possible, for example, for a Frenchman to do so. I think that the famous French 'clarity' and 'logic' really amount to a certain linguistic structure, a prose shapeliness constructed out of words and concepts which are still implicitly 'classical' in the sense of Latinised, are scholastic and deductive and quite without density, floating detached both from emotion and experience. This linguistic structure gives the possibility of at least three attitudes toward empiricism, in France. It can be ignored as, let us say, Jacques Maritain largely ignores it. It can be discovered with rather naïve surprise and then clumsily translated into something very like scholastic terminology—this seems to be what the Existentialists are doing. Or it can be completely misappropriated in its psychological aspect and development, and used to give an appearance of verifiability to concepts which are really theological. This was what Bergson was doing. He was trying to save Free Will in the theological sense, by using an argument, an hypothesis, which referred to an apparent observation about the nature of human mental process, a piece of psychological empiricism. This was what Hulme seized on, because, whatever he might say about dogma, and about the separate spheres of 'knowledge', something in him could not be rationally satisfied with the idea of two equally valid (but often opposed) ways of knowing. He wanted one way of knowing, but he wanted that way—and this is a contradiction—to be a demonstration of the empirical truth of the dogmas which he had stated as unshakeable and indeed unapproachable postulates.

What Hulme set himself to attack was the world-view which he refers to as Huxley's Nightmare—"the certainty that nothing can exist outside the gigantic mechanism of causes and effects; necessity moves the stars in the sky, and necessity moves the emotions in my mind." As stated, this view certainly has a little too much of that self-complacency at his own cosmic heroism which was typical of the Great Victorian and which demanded an emotional counter-reaction. Probably it was quoted by Hulme partly because it is such a clear example of that picture-thinking of which, as we shall see, he accused intellectual, non-intuitional thinkers, because he himself was unable to conceive of any other way of thinking. This world-picture of Dame Necessity shoving us all, atoms and humans alike, ahead of her, till we all fall into the bottomless pit certainly calls for a natural rebellion, and that is what it gets from thinkers like Hulme and all those who feel, consciously or unconsciously, that 'the intellect'—and therefore the method of science—is some kind of wicked and wilful imposition upon the universe and not merely, when it is used correctly, the way in which we receive and classify our given experience. What was impossible for Hulme was to detect and demonstrate the real defect of such thinking—that it was only a form of hypostatsis, just as characteristic of materialistic philosophers as of idealistic. Necessity is thought of, although unconsciously, as a real entity distinct from the ordered events in which it reveals itself, and which are our experience.

According to Hulme, Bergson does deal successfully with Huxley's Nightmare. Bergson showed, he says, that the mechanistic theory of the universe is only a necessity of the intellect, not of the whole of nature. What the intellect requires, what satisfies it as an explanation of the universe, is 'explication'—'the unfolding of a tangled mass into an extensive manifold.' We must note here that Hulme had already staked a very subjectivist proviso about all philosophical explanations whatsoever—except, as far as I can see, those of theological philosophy—that they were all, at bottom, expressions of what the philosopher individually found satisfying. Any intellectual explanation of the universe—and this covers in fact all philosophies which are not opposed to science—seeks, he says, satisfaction through spatial unfolding. "It is not satisfied until it can see every part—it wants to form a picture."

Hulme continues "It is possible that there may be a method of knowledge which refrains from forming pictures . . . other methods . . . besides that of analysis. I may have a perfect knowledge of a friend's face . . . without being able to analyse it into parts."

Intellectual explanation, according to this, means visualisation or unfolding in space. Analysis means analysis into spatial parts. It is not only possible, one must reply, it is certain, that there are other methods of obtaining knowledge which are non-visual and therefore non-spatial, while still being analytic and representational. This geometric view of all logical thinking was possible to Hulme, and also to Bergson, because both men were acute visualisers. Visualisation is often a valuable habit, especially to poets; but in an attempt to obtain the clear and independent truth about the world of experience it is more of a nuisance, since it leads to argument by analogy, and to that particular erection of our own mental habits into laws and systems which I constantly refer to as hypostatisation.

Not only a great deal of mathematical thinking, but a great deal of common thinking on ordinary practical subjects, is non-visual and therefore non-spatial. Since Galton's *Inquiry into Human Faculty* it has been clear that there are a great many different types, between the almost hallucinative visualiser and the person who does not visualise at all. It might seem that Bergson and Hulme cannot be talking about anything so obvious as this, that they cannot really mean that intellectual analysis proceeds only by forming pictures. But Hulme, as far as his dialectic philosophy is concerned, is only an interpreter of Bergson, and Bergson's anti-intellectualist philosophy does seem to be built upon this simple misconception. He seems in fact to have no conception of the nature of abstract thinking, and therefore no belief in its existence. Russell makes this clear in his criticism of Bergson's account of number. Number, says Bergson, is "a collection of units", which we picture by having "recourse to an extended image in space". But actually by visualisation we cannot obtain a picture either of number in general or of any particular number. We may picture, say, a six at dice, but this is not the number six, and certainly it is not a picture of 'number'.

The intellect, then, in behaving abstractly, does not behave typically or efficiently as Hulme, after Bergson, claimed. We may agree that there are other methods of obtaining knowledge than the visual, or than spatial explication. But we mean something different from either Bergson or Hulme.

According to them, the intellect interprets, and distorts, reality as an 'extensive manifold', by unfolding it into parts and laying them out in space. If however there is, on the other hand, something which we can describe as an 'intensive manifold', something which cannot be analysed into parts but only seized as a whole, if there are cases of real interpenetration in the world, then, says Hulme, Bergson will have proved his point—there is another kind of knowledge than that which we obtain through the intellect.

Bergson considered that he had found this 'intensive manifold' in mental life itself. To account for the fact that our mental life, in so far as we are aware of it, certainly seems to consist of successive states and must therefore be said to be known by the intellect with its 'spatial' or explicatory analysis, Bergson formed the conception of two Selves, a more superficial self whose successive states can be thus intellectually analysed, and a more fundamental self whose states are totally interpenetrative, and can only be seized in flux by another mental faculty, a quite different way of knowing, which he called Intuition.

As Hulme says, "It is inconvenient that it is so difficult to convey what (Bergson) means by this fundamental self, because it is on the experiencing of this state that depends also what he means by an intuition. I said earlier that an intuition was the process of mind by which one obtained knowledge of an intensive manifold."

In short, intuition is what reveals the intensive manifold and the intensive manifold is what produces intuition. This argument certainly suggests a fundamental descent into the very narrowest circle of the mental underworld. Nothing could be further from an intellectual unfolding in space or daylight.

It is not necessary here to go into the question of how far Bergson was influenced by, or in practical agreement with, the conception of an unconscious Self which arose in the contemporary psychology of Freud and Janet and to which he refers in *Matter and Memory*, or how far this conception can be used to give meaning to his Fundamental Self. It is only Hulme's interpretation and its purposes which matter here. Hulme's purpose is to combat mechanistic determinism and to save the doctrine of Free Will and the conception of unpredictability in the universe. Therefore if we could suppose, perhaps charitably, that, in giving some sort of account of Intuition and of the Fundamental Self, Hulme was only referring to the way in which unconscious processes become conscious—and not only creative and mathematical thinkers but most people of ordinary education are now familiar with this—we should still not have got very far with understanding Hulme's philosophical intentions. He says himself that there is nothing mysterious, ineffable or infinite about either Intuition or the Fundamental Self. Intuition is a "perfectly normal and frequent phenomenon . . . in all probability any literary man or artist would understand—would grasp much more easily—what Bergson means by an intuition . . . nearly all of them constantly exercise the faculty." It is curious that Hulme did not observe that not only literary men and artists, but also intellectual and scientific thinkers, constantly exercise this faculty. In fact, the circulation between conscious and unconscious processes is characteristic of thinking of all kinds. We are all of us capable of a rapid, sometimes almost instantaneous, survey and summary of our mental events, in a direction in which we are practised, and have all of us experienced this. We can call this Intuition for conversational purposes, if we like, as long as we remember that it is indeed not a 'mysterious' or even a distinct 'faculty', nor one which peculiarly works on a material distinguishing itself from the rest of the circulation of mental life—what the Bergsonian Fundamental Self would have to be. It would perhaps be salutary to recall the expression 'A woman's intuition'. Surely this, if not totally 'mysterious'—let alone generally incompetent—clearly illustrates what I say: it is a quickening and sharpening of perceptiveness in a practised and interested direction.

I should say that, whether deliberately or not, Hulme leaves out the obvious fact that mental processes which he would describe as 'intellectual'—for example, analytical and scientific ones—work in the way I have discussed, exactly like creative or artistic ones, because he has to save Intuition and its counterpart, the Fundamental Self, so as to prevent the whole of Bergson's philosophy, and therefore the whole of the intellectual defence of dogmatism which he is trying to construct, from falling to pieces.

So this fundamental self has to exist and moreover it has to be free. To understand what Hulme means by freedom in the individual or unpredictability in the universe, we must go a little into the use he makes of Bergson's theory of time and change. The deterministic account of change, by which he means the mechanistic theory of the universe, that an infinite intelligence which knew all causes would be able to predict all effects, is only true, he says, if we admit that everything can really be analysed into separate elements so that change is only alteration in the position of particles. This applies if the knowing intellect is, as Hulme defines it, a faculty which operates only by 'spatial' unfolding. As already stated, this is a poor account of intellect and its operations.

"We have just seen," says Hulme, "that mental life at the level of the fundamental self cannot" be thus spatially analysed. We have just seen, on the contrary, I hope, that this Bergsonian concept has no apparent meaning, since the relationship of the Fundamental Self with the faculty of Intuition is the only evidence which Hulme has so far given for the existence of either. If Bergson was vaguely referring to what Freud and others have called the Unconscious, then it must be said that we only know about this at the level of the conscious (or Superficial) Self.

Nevertheless Hulme supposes that this Fundamental Self shows its freedom by changing in a way which will not fit in with the kind of conception the intellect forms of change. And "if we suppose," he says, "that free acts are possible, we are landed: it follows that real novelty is possible: that things can happen which could not have been foreseen even by an infinite intelligence." It may seem to be splitting hairs to say that the mere form of the last sentence is full of implication which is probably merely careless. But nothing whatsoever to do with real novelty, or things happening, can be said to follow from anything which 'we suppose' either about free acts on the part of the Fundamental Self, or indeed about infinite intelligence. But I believe that this construction, merely careless though it may be, is a minor illustration of the underlying confusion, which Hulme made equally with Bergson, between the totality of cause and effect, and an infinite intelligence which might be conceived to know that totality in an absolute sense.

The construction covers as usual a determination to attack the scientific method of understanding the universe. But the attack is not even well conceived. We have seen that the 'explicative' is not the sole or even the main way of knowing in the scientific sense. But it seems to be inexorably implied in both Hulme and Bergson that we are only free if we do not 'know' in this or indeed in any comprehensible sense. A free act is defined in effect as a non-intellectual and indeed unconscious act. The result is that Hulme's account of a determined universe lays altogether too much stress on the notion of an absolute predictability.

In scientific thinking this idea has much less practical bearing than Hulme understood. Philosophically it is a reaction to a doctrine of Free Will which is itself mechanistic, the notion of a separate faculty which consists of a capacity to shove without being shoved. Scientific thinking is concerned primarily with understanding necessary relations, not with producing effects. Similarly what we really mean by our will is a form of conscious understanding. The internal sensation of volition results from the adjustment of our emotions to our understood conditions. The sensation of frustration results from the failure of our fantasies of power, from the maladjustment to our conditions which is caused by imperfect understanding of them. The notion of an absolute predictability is a mechanistic one which troubles idealists much more than empiricists. It is interesting that this notion, whether it is employed by those who call themselves determinists or by idealists, is really inseparable from the notion of an infinite intelligence. To a scientific, or even to an ordinary human, intelligence actively engaged in seeking knowledge, it is not of much use.

Before the principle of Indeterminacy (better, Uncertainty) was propounded, a doctrine of science was that if *all* basic natural laws were correctly enunciated (basic laws being distinguished from others which could be derived from them by the exercise of reasoning), *and* if the state of the universe could be completely determined over a short interval of time, then the state of the universe could be determined at any other time, past or present.

It was also believed by scientists that there were no barriers to progress in the enunciation of natural laws; that increasing accuracy of apparatus and increasing accumulation of study would enable unlimited progress to be made in this direction.

No particular attention was paid to the possibility or otherwise of determining the state of a larger and larger volume of the universe; thus this doctrine resembled the statement of Archimedes that, given a sufficient lever and fulcrum, he could move the earth. This was a useful statement about levers; none but the shallowest mind looked forward to the day when the earth would thus be moved. The doctrine of determinism is a statement about the universe, that it is indefinitely amenable to prediction; nobody bothered himself about whether its entire state would in fact be predicted some day by scientists.

After the enunciation of the Uncertainty principle, it was agreed that on the ultra-microscopic scale the quantities of position and velocity could not be determined with unlimited accuracy at the same time. Other more complicated measurements, which could be determined with complete accuracy, took their place. Thus the expectation of being able to determine the state, not of a larger and larger, but of any smaller and smaller volume, of the universe, in the old terms, was disappointed. This is as if Archimedes had been forced to add: given any lever and fulcrum, he could not move a meson (which would still be a useful statement about the nature of levers).

I have indicated before, and shall say again, because in view of current literary, journalistic and theological misunderstandings it can hardly be over-emphasised, that the uncertainty is on an ultra-microscopic scale and shades into virtual determinacy at the level of practical life. The movement of a man's finger could not, under this principle, be indeterminate to the breadth of a hair, if it were watched for a lifetime.

In partial compensation for this loss of ground, the principle of relativity implies that it is now unnecessary to know the state of the whole universe in order to predict the behaviour of a part of it, over a certain range of time.

This doctrine of science, then, leaves no room for 'novelty' in the sense of being able to move a finger and thereby disturb the predictability of the surrounding universe. The novelty it admits is of a quite different kind: the statement of new and more nearly universally valid laws, and the registering of a somewhat larger store of facts about the state of the universe at given times.

Underneath the Hulme-Bergson ideas about predictability and novelty are all the usual misconceptions about the nature of knowledge—that it is not knowledge unless it is absolute, and that it is not scientific if it is not quantitative and dependent on measuring apparatus. He ignores the facts that science is a method of inquiry and that it refers to experience. There is an enormous range of scientific inquiry which produces an enormous body of verifiable information which is not affected, let alone invalidated, by the notion of universal predictability. The generalisations which result from scientific investigation into human life and behaviour on this planet, for instance in biology, medicine and psychology, are quite obviously verifiable or not. I mean that in these cases, as a mere minimum, it should be obvious to laymen, including Hulme, that the generalisations are verifiable or not, and claim to be knowledge only in so far as they are verifiable. If they are not verifiable, they can be, and are, continually set aside for others which are so.

The fundamental misconception is about the nature of intellectual process. According to Hulme, we cannot be said to 'know' anything in an intellectual sense, unless we know everything. We see now why the idea of infinite intelligence is really inseparable from that of an absolute predictability.

Hulme had put himself on an old and awkward spot. For in order to save the idea of 'novelty', of freedom in the universe, even an infinite intelligence would be liable to be suddenly caught out by arbitrary limitations. Anatole France (*Île des Penguins*) put it in the mouth of the Lord, and in a nutshell:

"In order not to impair human liberty, I will be ignorant of what I know, I will thicken upon my eyes the veils I have pierced, and in my blind clearsightedness I will let myself be surprised by what I have foreseen."

Hulme and Bergson have done nothing more than uncover, without solving, the old dilemma of God's omniscience versus our freedom. From Hulme as a convinced theist entering the arena of empirical discussion we might justly have expected more. But from his account we can only conclude that freedom in the universe is a form of ignorance, and that the reality or objectivity of the universe essentially depends on being unknowable by the ordinary human method.

Whatever his empirical claims, the Two Truths theory—the assumption that because we do not know something, and indeed cannot know it by our normal means of obtaining knowledge, we are therefore in a position to know something else by some other means—lurks at the back of all Hulme's work. What he means by 'real' or 'reality' is simply that which we do not 'know'.

The account of the difference between 'real' time (the Bergsonian *durée réelle*) and mathematical time is again cast in the superficially empirical form which was Hulme's chief debt to Bergson and most valuable instrument in trying to erect an anti-humanist and neo-scholastic philosophy. The illustrations all turn out however to be inapplicable, in general merely analogous, and in fact meaningless.

The distinction between the two times, says Hulme, is this:

"In the mechanical world . . . time might flow with an infinite rapidity, and the entire past, present and future be spread out all at once. But inside us, it is very different. In us time is undeniable fact. If I want to mix a glass of sugar and water I have to wait willy-nilly until the sugar melts. This is *real time:* it coincides with my impatience, that is with a certain portion of my duration which I cannot contract as I like."

This is an example of the curious spatial imagery which confirms that Hulme's view of the intellect was due to his inability to think outside his own visual habits. The distinction between mathematical and real time results from a confusion, not a clarification. The inhabitants of the 'mathematical world', as Hulme calls it—who include not only astronomers and the authors of *Bradshaw*, but all those less specialised citizens who keep a clock on the mantelpiece and regulate their engagements by it—would, according to Hulme's distinction between time calculated and time merely 'experienced', have a lesser reality in their experience than those who only vaguely look before and after: a tramp, let us say, who has never succeeded in stealing a watch, but knows he 'has been here before'. Yet, on the contrary, what is affirmed by the theory of relativity is that all measurers of time can be, and on occasion need to be, aware of abstracting from experience; but this again affirms the 'reality' of the experience.

That some of our experiences can be referred to conceptually, or in terms of measurement, is a necessity of communication. On the other hand, correct abstraction, or the forming of concepts, depends on awareness of concrete experience and reference to it. Failure to grasp this procedure and relationship causes the kind of confusion which results, in Hulme and others, in such false distinctions as his 'mathematical' and 'real' time. Incidentally this total incomprehension of the nature of normal abstraction results in a Platonic dualism, although again we must say it has been stood on its head: the concepts, 'the abstractions, the mathematical world are created by Hulme as bogus real entities, of a sort, inferior in his 'Platonism', to the entities of intuition and sensuous, but not over-conscious, experience. This does suggest, although one need not labour the point, an attribution to the normal intellectual processes of hostility or corruption; of actual ill-will or even Original Sin!

The quotation is important as an illustration of Hulme's confusion of subjective, or introspective, and objective experience, as well as of his dislike of an objectivity whose essential communicability takes the form of measurement.

How any temporal process taking place in a glass of sugar and water can be said to coincide with the emotional experience which I describe as impatience, or how that impatience can be identified with a *portion* of my duration, especially if I have not tried, by egg-boiler or stop-watch, to find out how long I felt impatient, is very difficult to understand. Hulme seems to have forgotten, too, that he can boil the water. The results of that, the speeding up of the 'real time' which he must also conceive as being present in the glass, will not be less apart from me or my time. The time taken will be the sugar's plus the water's plus the heat's time, not specially mine.

Hulme continues that "One could express the same idea in a different way which brings out better the causes of it and the more important consequences of it." Incidentally, the example brings out better Hulme's inverted Platonism which I have referred to above, as well as some of the consequences of that unconscious dualism.

"If a child has to fit together a jig-saw puzzle, it can learn to do it quicker and quicker. Theoretically . . . it requires no time to do it, because the result is already given. . . . The picture is already created and the work of recomposing it can be supposed going faster and faster up to the point of being instantaneous.

"But to the artist, time is no longer an interval that can be lengthened or shortened. To contract it would be to modify the invention itself. It is the actual living progress of the thought, a kind of vital process like *ripening*."

The word 'theoretically' covers an implied conception that mechanical or, let us say, inorganic reproduction, as opposed to living or artistic creation, is somehow 'unreal'. Hulme goes on:

"In the world of mechanism . . . there is no real creation of new things, there is merely a rearrangement of fixed elements in various positions. They can't be said to exist in time, because nothing *new* happens. . . . At a certain depth of mental life you experience real time because there is a real change. . . . In real time you get real creation and so real freedom . . ."

And further:

"Now here you get the essence of the thing. *Real duration, real time* is an absolute thing which cannot be contracted or hastened because in it *real work* is being done, really new things are appearing."

All this, reduced to its logical elements, reads as follows:

"Time is that which is produced by real change, and real change is produced by real work, and real work is that which embodies real time. So Time is produced by Time."

In fact, if we refer to the example of the jig-saw picture, there is no time distinction between the artist and the child, and it is striking that Hulme should leave out of account the movements of the child's hand and body, which, in however small a degree, must cause some chemical combustion and should therefore use 'real time' exactly as the glass of water and sugar does. Moreover, it is not possible that the operation should take no time at all. The finished picture which for the sake of discussion we may suppose to be in the child's imagination, or even another finished picture which he may have in front of him to copy, is a different or an ideal picture which must not be identified with the one on which his process of reproduction, mechanical or otherwise, is at work. Hulme merely has an unconscious preference for an ideal or mental process, and an unconscious wish to attribute a greater and substantive 'reality' to it than he is willing to attribute to one of which at least a partial mechanical materiality is obvious.

He might have confined himself to processes of living matter such as growth and gestation, and claimed that, because in general we cannot hasten these processes, they may be said to take place in 'real' rather than in 'mathematical' or mechanical time. Many of these processes can now be affected chemically, for instance the growth of plants and the rate of egg-production, which can be accelerated by heat and light, but on the Bergsonian definition it is difficult to say whether such over-time is real or mathematical. One cannot be sure from Hulme's account of Bergson's conception of the two times whether they are supposed or not to differ entirely *in kind*, yet it is difficult to give them any meaning at all, as distinct concepts, unless they are. The only distinction which Hulme illustrates concretely is the possibility of multiplication:

"In the case where you have a number of elements merely changing in position, time is not really involved at all, for time makes no difference to them. They never alter; they never grow old . . . If you doubled the speed at which the change of position took place it would make no difference at all to the system. Take any example of such a system, say the astronomical one. The planets following certain fixed laws follow certain fixed courses. It would make absolutely no difference to these courses if you supposed the speed doubled."

An impartial observer might be inclined to say that we know rather less about the practical possibilities of speeding up the cosmic processes than the vital ones and that, if anything, it is in the latter, as I have indicated above, that we can observe the effects of multiplication. We may therefore think that their time is no more and no less real than that of any other process in the universe.

It is Hulme's hope that we can "find the key to reality . . . in terms of mental life" because, he claims after Bergson, it is in mental life that we have an intuition of, we directly know, real time, real change, therefore real freedom and the possibility of new creation, as opposed to the 'fixed future' of a universe mechanically conceived. The main distinction between the mental life of which we have an intuition and the mechanical world which we know by the intellect, and can also foreknow to a greater or lesser extent, is that the first is *vital*. There are two further important distinctions between a vital process and a mechanical one. The first is that the vital cannot be "dissected and spread out, without losing its vitality at least in that form". The second is that we don't quite *know* what goes on in a vital process; while, as far as the mechanical view is concerned "whether the complexity of life comes as the result of the working out of certain mechanical laws, or whether it is following a plan laid down for it, in both cases the future is fixed and could be known to an infinite intelligence. That is 'they don't exist in real time at all.' " (Does this refer to the *concepts* of law formed by mechanists and finalists or to life as dissected by them?)

It is clear that the first of Hulme's distinctions here rests entirely on a confusion caused by his own purely metaphoric account of intellect. If he were being merely anatomical we might agree, although without much enlightenment, that the vital cannot be "dissected and spread out without losing its vitality". But in Hulme's context the reference is to the behaviour of the intellect—it is the intellect's act of *knowing* which dissects and spreads out the vital.

It is therefore not at all remarkable that we 'cannot quite know what goes on in a vital process'. Let us, however, notice that this very ignorance is equated by Hulme with our possibility of freedom. In other words the fact that we do not know something is taken to prove that we know something else. This, as I have remarked above, is the typical philosophical procedure of theological and scholastic apologists. Finally the same concept that ignorance is freedom is implied again in the last quotation, where the possibility of absolute foreknowledge is equated with complete determinism.

If there were an 'infinite intelligence' with 'absolute fore-knowledge' who had 'laid down a plan' for the universe to follow, I do not see how his plan could help taking real time. Surely Hulme's theology must have included the belief in some infinite intelligence of this sort? How is that to be saved from the fate of existing only in mechanical or mathematical time?

What Hulme has arrived at is that we know objective reality only through intuitive and unconscious processes (which I suppose would include some artistic ones). Intellectual, critical, scientific and conscious processes are subjective. By the time we can analyse our knowledge it has ceased to be knowledge. Knowledge would therefore, one supposes, be incommunicable and the intuitions of mystics are in the most favoured position. How much this resembles the anti-intellectualism of the Nazis and the 'knowing-together' of D. H. Lawrence, how redolent it is of blood and soil! How far from remarkable it is that Hulme was a professed militarist and that, for all his preferences for vital process he helped to inaugurate a cult for the non-vital in art! How unreason, in all its manifestations, yearns for death!

However, Hulme was not content to leave the world of apperception in the maya-like state to which he had reduced it. He was aware of his philosophical responsibilities and his duty to protect his intuitive pronouncements from too glaring a critical light, and so the verifying process of the intellect, its most important function, which had been thrown out like a bad angel, had to be summoned back to sign its own death warrant.

Hulme felt that, as far as the individual mind was concerned, he had 'refuted mechanism'. But on the other hand there might still be some people who would prefer to attribute subjectivity to our intuitive (or vital) processes, rather than to our intellectual awareness and analysis of the external world; who would still believe that that world could be most meaningfully and productively considered by intellectual methods, including the methods of calculation, as well as observation and generalisation; and who would claim that the 'feeling of free activity which you feel in a certain state of tension' tells us nothing positive or certain about the universe as a whole, nor indeed about anything external to the feeling, nor anything profoundly illuminating about the feeling itself.

"You now get the second passage to reality," says Hulme. "You have . . . still to prove that this state of flux . . . this feeling of a free activity . . . is not merely a subjective state of mind, but does give you real information about a reality which exists outside you": information, we must note, of a *superior* reality, whatever this may mean, to any which you obtain by observation, analysis or generalisation. I believe that, in his heart of hearts, what Hulme meant was that 'information' obtained in this way made you *feel* superior, although there was nothing at all implied about its actual value. I fear that all those who believe in a second (and superior) order of truth are imbued with this assurance, which is emotional, but not intellectual, and is based on a stock confusion of subjective with objective experience.

This question of 'intuitive' information about reality to which Bergson devoted his second book, *Matter and Memory*, "involves the relation of the mind to the body". It is interesting that Hulme himself thought that the novelty of Bergson's treatment of this question lay in the fact that he dealt with it "not as a mere matter of speculation but on the basis provided by an examination of a body of empirical observations". This sounds like a remarkable concession to the scientific attitude; but whether it is so or not becomes more doubtful when we examine the data which Hulme quotes from Bergson.

The 'body of facts' on which Bergson operates to support his theory of the relation of soul and body, and of the vitalistic current which carries a free and unpredictable creation through the material universe, "are those connected with aphasia, i.e., the various ways in which we lose our memory for words." It is not necessary to go into the modern psychological theories which among others attempt to account for this phenomenon, because Hulme ignores them; and though Bergson alludes to them, assuming their support, his proof is a metaphysical or philosophical one, and can be dealt with wholly within that category.

In Hulme's interpretation, at least, I myself cannot see what distinction he employs between aphasia and ordinary forgetfulness. He goes straight to the Bergsonian account of memory in which the account of non-remembering or forgetting is implicit. It is immensely difficult to escape from what I have elsewhere called 'the Topographical Illusion',* the tendency to think of the mind as if it were spatial, with floors and compartments. Much of the philosophical thought of Freud and Jung is vitiated by this habit. Therefore it is not surprising that Bergson and Hulme, those inveterate analogisers and visualisers, should fall straight into it.

"Just as many things exist in the next room," says Hulme, "of whose existence I am not conscious at this minute, so there exist trailed behind in me, as it were, a whole host of memories of my past of which I am at the present moment quite unconscious. It is then as if all our memories existed quietly in a kind of next room where one was not conscious of their existence; but that now and then one emerged and became actual by playing on the keyboard of that special part of the brain with which it was concerned."

What this means, I suppose, is that the memories (which are, of course, a knowledge of external reality), have somehow got 'into' the unconscious mind, but how we do not know, since they only appear one by one to play the brain's piano, and the brain is nothing but a selector. This means, in the Hulme terminology, that the brain separates them out of the intuitive unconscious mass and of course they must lose 'vitality' and 'reality' in the process. One must conclude that as an instrument of apperception the brain is always by-passed, except for its purely intellectual or analytic function. And one must ask where exactly Hulme himself did his thinking when, at least in intention, it was not as here, 'empirical', but 'intuitive' D. H. Lawrence's solar plexus or the apperceptive heart or liver of a pre-cerebral and pre-cortical physiology would seem to be demanded. Hulme's account of the relation between the mental and the cerebral does in

* *Horizon.* Vol. 113.

fact beg the question of that relation between the inner or mental life and external reality, which was intended to provide his whole anti-intellectualist philosophy with an empirical status and begs it quite as crudely as I have suggested. For what, says Hulme, "should we see if we were able to look into the brain and to see all the atoms in motion?" This is a miniature form of the question about the 'infinite intelligence' and its total prediction of the universe. It cannot be answered in a way which gives us any empirical information, because it is not possible to look into the living brain and 'see the thoughts'. I doubt whether any 'parallelist' or mechanical materialist has ever claimed or imagined that he could do so. But Bergson apparently thought he could do so, at least theoretically; and that when he actually looked he would see only those parts of a man's thinking which were concerned with preparations for action or were a distinct visual image. If we could thus look and if this is what we saw, I should still say that compared to Bergson and Hulme, many mechanical materialists would be in an advantageous position as far as collecting possible information about psychological reality was concerned. Many of them, that is, are able to accept the probability of unconscious mental processes because they have not deprived themselves of the possibility of judging these by effects and behaviour (ideas and actions).

But by his own apparently unconscious 'spatialisation' both of the 'inner' and the cerebral life, that is exactly what Hulme himself has done. "You may," he says, "persist in asking the question: Where are these past memories *stored*?" And naturally, since we have strayed into his spatial account of mental life, we do have to ask him for this extension of topography. His answer is that they are 'in' the inner or second self, which, as one remembers, is the vessel of duration or real time.

"The whole of your past life is in the present. This inner stream which composes your inner self bears in it not the whole of your past in the form of completed pictures, but bears it in the form of potentiality. In this stream the elements are, as we said, interpenetrated. All that happens in an act of recognition is that the interpenetrated parts get separated out."

Now it is here of no particular importance whether we regard the brain as matter or intellect, since both of these—and Bergson hardly seems to distinguish them—are thus chiefly characterised by their function of analysing out the impulses and events which otherwise remain wholly interpenetrated in the inner or mental, or, on the other hand, in the 'vital' life. (To get the full extension of meaning implied in 'vitality' we have to turn to the evolutionary doctrine which comes shortly.) But if this is the function of the brain and supposing, as Hulme suggests, that we could look into it and read its thoughts or images, I do not see what relation, if any, we should find between them and the stored and potential hosts of memories, nor between them and the past, which, according to Bergson and Hulme, ought to be continually implied in their present activity. On the Bergsonian definition, the brain's thoughts and images must exist only at the level of the superficial self, and must as it were be sloughed from the vital passage of the inner or fundamental self, through 'real time'. More strictly, it seems to me, the brain, like any other 'piece of matter', must produce only a negative of mental process, a jelly-mould without content, and it would appear impossible to have any objective knowledge at all. On the other hand, I do not see how an 'intuition' gets into the brain without instantly dropping dead. If the argument has now been reduced to a mere comparison of metaphors, that is no doubt due to the philosophy of Bergson himself, who recreated the entire universe after his own images, the metaphors in terms of which he thought he discerned his own mental life. In fact his philosophy is simply the old idealism writ large and somewhat blurred. On his view it is not possible to believe that there is any connection at all between cerebral and mental life. He has merely uncovered the old Cartesian problem—How do the mind and the body influence one another at all, if they are totally distinct substances?—but his solution is no more valid than the theory of animal spirits or of the Two Clocks.*

If the brain, as the first piece of matter on which the free unpredictable inner life has to operate, cannot, by definition, tell us anything about that Bergsonian intuition, how also can it tell us about a Bergsonian, or free, unpredictably evolving universe? Even Bergson's philosophy is difficult to account for at all without assuming the validity of some intellectual process, and in fact Hulme's main reason for quoting Bergson's evolutionary theory is that he thinks he can use it to provide the whole of the philosophy of intuition with an empirical basis as well as to show that external reality is not mechanical. The empirical nature of an empirical test does not depend only or mainly on isolated notes of experience, like stuffing a duck with snow, but on the observation that the tissues of all ducks, in these repeated circumstances, are preserved. This is the experience which results from the experiment and it calls in the mind's powers of analysis and generalisation, in short what we often briefly call the intellect.

The evolutionary theory of Bergson is briefly that the universe behaves 'as if' a current of vital impulse were passing through it, 'inserting' ever and ever more freedom and consciousness into matter. Bergson takes as his empirical 'proof' the development in totally different species, for example the vertebrates and the molluscs, of a similar organ, the eye. On either the mechanistic or the finalistic view of evolution, says Hulme, this similar development is very difficult to understand. If we are mechanists, he says, we believe that the eye was 'constructed' and if we are finalists that it was all part of a plan. One may ask, of course, in connection with both these concepts, who or what constructed or planned, and one also notices in passing that the Bergsonian creative evolution is not easy to distinguish from pantheism in

*The theory of the Two Clocks was invented by disciples of Descartes, to resolve the difficulty in which his theory has left the interaction of mind and matter. Mind and body, according to this theory, are separately wound up by God so as to synchronise perfectly. This makes it look as if it were my will which moves my body.

some form, and certainly seems to leave an individual Creator out of account, and that this should have presented difficulties to the orthodox Hulme.

Accepted scientific theory of evolution does not base itself on mechanism or finalism, as defined by Hulme, but on selection and adaptation. The eye's seeing is conceived as having differentiated itself out from a general sensitivity to light which characterises the lowest form of animal life, the amœba, and from phototropism, the tendency to turn toward the light, which characterises plants. This causes chemical change in the organism. There are, as Ida Mann says (*The Science of Seeing*), "degrees of seeing" based on the particular adaptation of the organism and its light-sensitive cells to light.

This adaptation is quite left out of account if we conceive the eye as the end-product of a wishful process. However, this wishful eye, produced because the organism wants to have vision, is Bergson's answer, as quoted by Hulme, to the mechanistic and finalistic accounts of evolution. Both mechanism and finalism, as Hulme defines them, with their 'construction' and planning, are, I suggested, forms of the usual intellectual Aunt Sally. The intellect can only analyse, therefore it can only conceive of an organism, in this case, the eye, as an individual construct, or as part of a plan, of a wider construct. On the contrary, the Bergsonian view shows us the eye as the result of a simple unanalysable desire for vision, its degree of complexity being the result of the organisation which matter has received from that development and direction of consciousness. As this desire or impulse is simple and un-analysable, the investigations of the intellect, and therefore the observations of science, are automatically ruled out—and there-fore, one would say, the empirical basis for the Bergsonian view of evolution. In fact, there is no empirical basis for Bergson's Creative Evolution. It is simply an analogy with what he imagines he discerns of free choice and consciousness, in introspection of his own mental life or fundamental self, or intensive manifold. An analogy in any case cannot be held to be evidence and, as we have seen in Hulme's account, there seems to be no kind of evidence that the fundamental self, if it exists, is free and un-predictable and no explanation of how it can be conscious.

All this however is the whole philosophical backing which Hulme provides for the essential concepts of scholastic orthodoxy —in particular for Free Will and the existence and freedom of God, implying the possibility of miraculous intervention—to which he hoped that the Bergsonian 'empirical' revelation of two kinds of knowledge would clear the way.

The chief dogmas of Catholic theology—those I have mentioned above and also, for instance, the doctrine of the Incarnation—cannot be proved empirically. Hulme, although he makes flat dogmatic statements about some of them, as we see in the first part of Read's edition of *Speculations*, particularly about Original Sin and the existence of God, is not so clear as, let us say, Mr. Eliot, on this inability, I have discussed him and his use of Bergson, for one important reason, because he illustrates a special confusion which has been and still is valuable to scholasticism. This confusion is between the fields of epistemology and of psychology. The confusion is implied already, I think, in the concepts, which theology puts all on the same dogmatic basis. For instance, Free Will, if it means human free will, is a psychological concept, whereas the existence of God is an epistemological one. The discussion about what I can know by logical implication, if anything, can never be quite on the same footing as that about what I can know, if anything, by introspection.

In the section on 'Humanism', Hulme has some interesting remarks about what he calls 'The Critique of Satisfactions'. He says, with much justification, that actual philosophy is not a pure but a mixed subject. Mixed up with the 'purely scientific and impersonal' method is something which aims to show what, according to the philosopher's conception, the world should be in reality:

". . . We should expect to find that consciously or un-consciously, the *final* picture (the philosopher) presents will to some degree or other *satisfy* him. It is these final pictures that make it true to say that there is a family resemblance between all philosophers since the Renaissance . . . the final pictures they present of man's relation to the world all conform to the same probably unconscious *standards* or *canons* of what is *satisfying*. . . . The philosophers share a view of what would be a satisfying destiny for man which they take over from the Renaissance. They are all satisfied with certain conceptions of the relations of man to the world. These *conclusions* are never questioned in this respect. Their truth may be questioned, but never their *satisfactoriness*. This ought to be questioned. This is what I mean by a *Critique of Satisfaction*."

We have sufficiently considered the epistemological, or what Hulme would himself have called the 'scientific' part of his own philosophy and we can now reasonably apply the Critique of Satisfaction to it. There are 'conclusions' at the end of *Speculations* but I think that we need not confine ourselves to these. As opposed to the post-Renaissance humanist philosophers whom he rounds up for punishment, Hulme was a quite overt apologist. He set out, not to analyse and reveal by implication, but to prove something. His 'conclusions' and therefore we must suppose his *satisfactions* are manifest from the first page. It may be true that, in so far as they do not maintain themselves as purely critical or analytical and semantic—this is certainly not Hulme's meaning, however—all philosophies are at least in part disguised psychologies.

We should ask ourselves whether or not Hulme did in fact mean *all* philosophies, including theological philosophy, or scholasticism. When we remember his division of knowledge which gives religion an absolute sphere of its own, and inorganic science another, we shall find ourselves justified in concluding that Hulme was ready to make an exception in favour of scholastic philosophy, and that his main object in trying to reduce all other philosophies to the same subjective level of psychological preference was that he wished to restore theology to its old position as 'Queen of the Sciences'. This is the Two Truths theory carried to its most extreme form. And in uncovering this wish, we also apply Hulme's Critique of Satisfaction to his own philosophy. It is not only subjectively a disguised indication of his own psychological processes—the will to power, the overestimation of order, the preference for the hierarchical. But it is primarily a claim to be an objective and final psychology, to tell us the real and absolute nature of Man, and so to nullify the painstaking, tentative and scientific effort of human generations to tell us something humbler and more reliable about human motives and behaviour. In short, his whole work is aimed at annexing the terrain of the 'muddy mixed sciences' to the 'absolute' zone of religion.

When we are making our choice nowadays between the scholastic and the scientific descriptions of the universe, which both include an account of human behaviour and its meaning, we must make ourselves clear how far the concepts of Sin, Original and otherwise, and of Free Will, which are the foundations as well as the conclusions and satisfactions of Hulme's philosophy, and of that of all the scholastics, imply a complete opposition both to common sense and observation. As conceived by them all, Sin is an absolute state and Free Will an absolute faculty. Neither is contingent upon anything at all, except divine grace, and sin has no apparent relation with my capacity to do right or wrong. The fact that I can, though improbably perhaps, and certainly laboriously, alter my character to some extent, with sufficient understanding, that is with sufficient examination of my inveterate habits, is disregarded, and therefore the ways in which I do, or may occasionally, show limited choice; are also disregarded. Yet this limited choice, this occasional capacity to see what I must do in a total given situation, is a meaning one can give to 'Free Will'. However, this possible examination of my habits and subsequent modification of my character by a more conscious 'choice' among limiting alternatives is not distinct in kind from learning to correct my mistakes in any other field, including the most practical. I learn, and I also unlearn, by changes which take place in my nervous and cortical system. To say that I am in absolute (Original) Sin or that I have the faculty of absolute Free Will is to rule out all the habits which have formed me in my existing personality, and therefore not only my capacity for education, but everyone else's. If we are absolutely sinners with absolute Free Will, then it is impossible for us to learn to drive cars or to play the piano.

CHAPTER IV

Mr. Eliot's Liberal Worms

ALTHOUGH it has been repeatedly necessary to attack the intellectual foundations of theology, it has not been my prime object to do so, but rather to make some conjecture of the kind of mental climate in which writers would have to live and write if the orthodox, by moral, social or legal pressure, could impose their orthodoxy upon our ways of thinking.

Hulme was, as I have said, an overt apologist for the theological attitude, and his expressed aim was to provide it with an objective intellectual basis. I spent so much time in examining his intellectual arguments, which are seldom more than superficially convincing and are often surprisingly naïve, largely because of this expressed aim, which is of a kind to leave a substantial residue of hope in the minds of those who want the consolations of a satisfactory intellectual conviction without undertaking the labours of establishing it.

This applies to a great number of artists, critics and writers. For them Hulme's *Speculations* may well have had the force of a manifesto. But it is interesting to ask oneself whether those of Hulme's younger contemporaries who actually read and considered his arguments, as I am sure Mr. Eliot and Mr. Herbert Read did, need have taken the trouble. For on matters of emotional importance, as we all know, people are hardly ever converted by intellectual argument. The gallant, even swashbuckling, undertakings of Hulme and the more suburban sallies of

Lewis and Sayers have had their effect on the neo-scholastic movement only in so far as nobody has seriously read them. Authority has to speak in closed books; and the authorities are quoted, not for knowing, but for appearing to know. Mr. Eliot has always had the wisdom to rest his authority on this law. Hulme is even one of the closed books to which he can refer his own more authoritarian pronouncements.

One cannot be sure whether Hulme, if he had lived longer, would have told less or more. In practice he did not get so very far with his intellectual exposition. When we look for the intellectual backing to orthodoxy in the connected part of his philosophy, we find, as I have indicated, that nothing much more than the doctrine of Free Will is covered; I suppose because it is the fundamental link between epistemology and psychology, between the description of the universe and the description of man. I myself question whether he would have gone much further in intellectual or theological disquisition; whether he would have been able to tell us, what Mr. Eliot refuses, any good reasons for believing in Original Sin or for hating Humanism. It seems to me probable that his philosophy would soon have revealed itself as just as much a negation, just as much a reaction, as any of the later forms of neo-scholasticism. By the word Reaction I mean that kind of tidal wave which mounts from the accumulation of individual frustrations and dislikes. Reactions are progressively self-suggestive and impress us with their inevitability because we are all secretly aware that emotion rather than intelligence controls us. Hulme 'foresaw' a return to religious orthodoxy and to 'classicism' *because* he hated humanism, not because he had analysed humanism and found it wanting. Humanism masquerades unquestionably in many opprobrious shapes and it is true that not all professed humanists like their fellow human beings very much better than the religiously orthodox do. But the test of the genuineness of humanism is the experimental attitude towards all human problems. This is what Hulme really hated, as his following neo-scholastics also do; but he grasped more clearly than some of them have since done that humanism was thus an intellectual method and he tried not ungallantly to counter it with another.

Mr. Eliot also knows that anti-humanism requires a method, but he has probably learnt something from Hulme's failure and knows too that direct disputation has no future.

By 1934, he had arrived in his critical work at the statement:

"Literary criticism should be completed by criticism from a definite ethical and theological standpoint. In so far as in any age there is common agreement on ethical and theological matters, so far can literary criticism be substantive. In an age like our own, in which there is no common agreement, it is the more necessary for Christian readers to scrutinise their reading, especially of works of imagination, with explicit ethical and theological standards. The 'greatness' of literature cannot be determined solely by literary standards . . ."

To know by what steps Mr. Eliot arrived at this position would be at least as illuminating to his literary admirers, among whom I count myself, at least as important a piece of documentation for our day, as St. Augustine's *Confessions* were for his. But Mr. Eliot is not going to write his Confessions. He does not instruct or inculcate, he only manifests himself with baffling discontinuity. The view just referred to, of theological scrutiny, together with the definition of orthodoxy and heresy on which he is going henceforth to take his stand, were shown in practical application in *After Strange Gods*. It is only from the time of these pronouncements onwards that his claims have been at all reasoned; and, even so, his arguments seldom refer to the metaphysics of orthodoxy, but to its practical or ethical side. In *After Strange Gods* he expressly states:

"I am not arguing or reasoning or engaging in controversy with those whose views are radically opposed to such as mine. In our time, controversy seems to me, on really fundamental matters, to be futile. It can only be usefully practised where there is common understanding. It requires common assumptions, and perhaps the assumptions that are felt are more important than those that can be formulated. We experience such profound differences with some of our contemporaries that the nearest parallel is the difference between the mentality of one epoch and another. In a society like ours, *wormeaten with Liberalism*, the only thing possible for a person with strong convictions, is to state a point of view and leave it at that."

I do not think that that is 'the only thing possible'. I think that a person with strong convictions might still examine the foundations of his convictions, even at the cost of being eaten by the worms of Liberalism. But the important thing for Mr. Eliot is *common* assumption, *common* understanding, that is, agreement is more important to him than the reasons, if any, through which that agreement is arrived at. One cannot altogether resist the suspicion that the literary Sons of the Church are sometimes almost snobbishly embarrassed by their parent, whose hold on authority is not diminished by the fact that her practical standard of morals, intelligence, sensibility and imagination is necessarily much lower than theirs. Sometimes one would dare to guess that, by the occasional tribute of a kind of petty fine upon their greater mental endowment, they purchase the privilege of its unrestricted employment during their purely professional application. Even Mr. Graham Greene, whose views must often be much more his own than they are the Pope's, has been known to bestow faint praise on a not particularly distinguished novelist, merely because she was dealing with a Catholic problem.* Mr. Eliot's very refusal to discuss with his and the Church's opponents suggests, at least to me, a similar act of devotion and intellectual sacrifice.

Yet one cannot admit that the steps by which he has arrived at his dogmatic orthodoxy are unimportant and uninteresting,

* *Evening Standard, July* 13, 1945

especially in view of the profoundly important social conclusions in which he is overtly involved by them. Nor can there be any real doubt that there was a continuous and ordered procedure, though so much of it has been subterranean. The evidence of conversion to orthodoxy which Mr. Eliot gave was indirect. Most of the people who talked and wrote about *The Waste Land* when it first came out said nothing about Eliot the Christian, because presumably they knew nothing. Even retrospectively there seems not much more reason for concluding from this poem alone that Mr. Eliot was a Christian than for concluding from Macaulay's *Lays* that he was an Ancient Roman. In his poetry, as far as the outside public could see, the conversion was a discontinuous manifestation. It happened some time between 1923 and 1930. It was a complete metamorphosis and Mr. Eliot's poetry has now no other theme than religion. In his prose the stages have been more apparent. *For Lancelot Andrewes* was the manifesto essay, published in 1926. The surface interest of this paper is secular, it is largely concerned with Andrewes's literary significance, but it is already written from the assumption of certain theological absolutes, including the continuity and importance of the English Catholic Church, and the weight and authority of her doctrines, as if no one had ever seriously called these in question. What we might call the toposcopy of this particular essay later becomes interesting. In the shuffling of subsequent collections one watches for it like the joker in a pack of cards. In *Selected Essays* (1932) it has got well away behind the Elizabethans and even Dante— many of these were of much later publication. It heads a small run of Church preoccupations, followed by a series of literary essays with theological and sociological implications (including Baudelaire, Arnold and Pater, F. H. Bradley, and The Humanism of Irving Babbitt, all of which have been or will be alluded to in this book).

In the later and most recent collection, *Essays Ancient and Modern*, published in 1936, the Andrewes paper has moved to the top. Is it fanciful to suggest that Mr. Eliot, refusing the direct or confessional, has another method of his own—the strategic?

He seems to have moved his units into position under cover of a philosophical black-out, and we awake to find ourselves occupied. The collection builds up to the last paper but one (Modern Education and the Classics), the last paragraph of which may be taken as a retrospective text for the whole work:

"If Christianity is not to survive, I shall not mind if the texts of the Latin and Greek languages become more obscure and forgotten than those of the language of the Etruscans. And the only hope that I can see for the study of Latin and Greek, in their proper place and for the right reasons, lies in the revival and expansion of the monastic teaching orders . . ."

Even the contrast between the first and last papers, between the one on Lancelot Andrewes and the one on Tennyson, is not insignificant. The paper on 'In Memoriam' is, it seems, nostalgic, and for an age in which Mr. Eliot might even have been more at home; since in the Victorian intellectual battle to be either on the side of the Angels or of the Titans was not disreputable, and a writer who lays so much stress on the intellectual basis of orthodoxy, while he never unveils it, would not have needed perhaps to be so reticent. However, by this method which, negative though it is, gives a kind of unity to *Essays Ancient and Modern*, Mr. Eliot has outflanked the agnostic hosts of the nineteenth and twentieth centuries, and brought dogmatic theology triumphantly home, so that the contemporary literary tribes take comfort without really knowing why. They are like the Ashantis with their Golden Stool. Mr. Eliot's orthodoxy is for them, if not for him, a closed symbol of power. Is it not remarkable that this considerable amateur of the Church Fathers has nothing to say about theology, except allusively in his verse, until he blossoms into full orthodoxy?* From that position, he proceeds at once to the practical application in its extreme form—for society rather than for literature.

---

*In *The Idea of a Christian Society* and in *Notes Towards the Definition of Culture*. Nothing could be more merely allusive than *After Strange Gods*, which purports to be a study of the relations of literature and theology.

The theoretical link has disappeared in the lacuna. Can we not justly call this skirting of all philosophical discussion a method— and a much more prudent one than some of his more eristic and naïve contemporaries have chosen to follow?

We saw that as far back as 1931 (essay on 'the *Pensées* of Pascal') Mr. Eliot took over Newman's 'powerful and concurrent reasons' for finding himself "inexorably committed to the dogma of the Incarnation". But he has not adduced any others for, apart from this and the statement about the very real and terrible nature of Original Sin, we know nothing positive about Mr. Eliot's theology. Apart from the allusions in the later poems to the relations of time and eternity, we know little about his metaphysics. When we would penetrate further, we are always side-tracked to the Church visible if not precisely located. It may be a good thing for his poetry that Mr. Eliot himself still remains so visibly in this world. Whatever he says about time and eternity, a significant part of the *Four Quartets* is still about the world of visual and auditory objects, even if the objects have grown less interesting, more general, less acutely observed. Yet there have been great religious poets who made a world, which seemed to them beyond time, imaginatively real to all of us. If God has been an experience for Mr. Eliot in the same sense as for Dante, Donne, Herbert and Vaughan, he does not communicate that experience. The thought and observation behind the *Four Quartets* is not mystical at all, it is in the main about human life and its in-adequacy and sin. Compared with the human life of the earlier poems, this one is over-generalised, but still we can say that where any of the Quartets is moving or exciting as poetry Mr. Eliot is living in the world of sensuous experience. I refer as particular examples to the opening paragraph of Section I and the second part of Section II ('In the uncertain hour before the morn-ing') in 'Little Gidding'. Apart from these and a few more para-graphs the language is abstract. Where it refers to felt emotion, the emotion is negative or one of general distaste, not realised in particularities.

"Only a flicker
Over the strained time-ridden faces
Distracted from distraction by distraction
Filled with fancies and empty of meaning
Tumid apathy with no concentration
Men and bits of paper, whirled by the cold wind
That blows before and after time,
Wind in and out of unwholesome lungs
Time before and time after.
Eructation of unhealthy souls
Into the faded air, the torpid
Driven on the wind that sweeps the gloomy hills of London,
Hampstead and Clerkenwell, Campden and Putney,
Highgate, Primrose and Ludgate . . ."

"The whole world is our hospital
Endowed by the ruined millionaire,
Wherein, if we do well, we shall
Die of the absolute paternal care
That will not leave us, but prevents us everywhere."

There is no reason at all why Mr. Eliot, either as a poet or a
man, should like his fellow-beings, but writers who have hated
them as a real experience have often been able to communicate
that experience so that we did not lose the sense that it was indeed
human beings who were being shown us, even fellow-humans.
Compare Shakespeare's Roman mobs, for instance, with any of
Eliot's abstract throngs on the suburban hills or in the Under-
ground. If we look at the framework of the poems attentively we
can see the cause. The religious experience itself is not intuitional,
it is 'intellectual', or perhaps I should say 'literary'. Whatever
Mr. Eliot's personal experience has been, his poetry refers only to
similar or secondhand experiences, as they have been recorded in
theological works or by mystics. This contradicts nothing that
Mr. Eliot has said himself—religion, we remember, ought to be a

matter of intellectual conviction nowadays, not of 'enthusiasm' (by which I suppose he sometimes means feeling). This is all very well, but the great believing poets were able to convey their religion to all of us as poetry. Moreover intellectual conviction ought somewhere at least to be conveyed in intellectual terms. Looking in the poems vainly for 'enthusiasm' how much more vainly we look for argument. By the time Mr. Eliot allows himself to become explicit in prose, we find that he has gone into politics. In *The Idea of a Christian Society* and in *Notes Towards the Definition of Culture* the whole question of attempting to convert has been successfully bypassed and Mr. Eliot is beginning to plan. In *After Strange Gods* he was really doing the same thing already, but at least there was that portentous statement about scrutinising our reading by precise ethical and theological standards. On scrutinising this statement in its context, with the feeling that here Mr. Eliot, however much we dislike his conclusions, is at least within his professional province and here at least we may be given some insight into the practical impingement of the chief dogmas upon literary experience, we are left still baffled and disappointed.

In *After Strange Gods*, which is about orthodoxy and heresy and about the meaning of these terms and the attitudes they cover in relation to literary criticism, but which is all the same a very short book, Mr. Eliot comes rather slowly to his only piece of practical criticism, although that is what those of us who are not orthodox, and perhaps some of those who are, are most in need of if we are to give the terms any precise evaluation. Having come thus gradually to the pronouncement that there is such a thing as 'orthodox sensibility', Mr. Eliot gives us, perhaps a little reluctantly, three contemporary illustrations—three short stories, one by Katherine Mansfield, one by D. H. Lawrence and one by James Joyce. All three turn on the theme of disillusionment and are about the relation of a husband and wife.

The first two, according to Mr. Eliot, are heretical and the third orthodox in sensibility. Admittedly when you are talking about sensibility your descriptive method may reasonably be ostensive, but somehow we do not seem to come to any very clear perception of the underlying principle which these stories either affirm or deny. Miss Mansfield's story, we are told, has, because of its slightness, practically no moral significance. Lawrence's, on the other hand, reveals "an alarming strain of cruelty and a baffling want of any moral awareness" in the characters. Joyce is the "most eminently orthodox" of modern writers. His story ('The Dead') is certainly about kindness, about a humble sense of generosity felt by a husband toward his wife's girlhood lover, now dead. But one wishes that Mr. Eliot, even in this short book, could have directed his critical apparatus instead on the vast main body of Joyce's work. Surely an orthodoxy so eminent must have revealed itself at least in a number of illuminating flashes any one of which could have been more usefully isolated for the brief quotation which Mr. Eliot's space seems to allow him. To others Joyce's 'orthodoxy' is not eminent, not even obvious, even to others whose whole literary philosophy is centred in a demand for the return to Christian cultural tradition. For example Mr. D. S. Savage in *The Withered Branch*. I quote this not because I am in general agreement with this work but because it puts this particular point bluntly:

"The most imperceptive comment ever made on Joyce was perpetrated by T. S. Eliot, when in his book on literary heresy he wrote that of the eminent writers of his time Joyce was the most orthodox. Joyce's orthodoxy was limited to the Catholic indoctrination which he suffered in his youth, and from which all his subsequent life was an effort to free himself."

I think that the reality to which Mr. Eliot is referring, whether he means to or not, is just this struggle, never successful, which Joyce continually made to get away from the effects of early Catholic indoctrination. But those in whom Catholic teaching is vestigial and unaccepted cannot by any manhandling of language be described as 'eminently orthodox'. And what is the good of all our scrutiny of our reading by Christian theological and ethical standards if at the end we not only cannot be sure what is orthodox and what heretical, but confound or invert them?

In so far as Mr. Eliot means that cruelty is immoral, and generosity and pity are moral, I am happy to sympathise with him, but even if this is all or even the main part of what he means by 'orthodoxy and heresy of sensibility' we may still deplore the terminology and its assumptions. There is indeed a preoccupation with cruelty and a revolt against tenderness to be discerned in the work of Lawrence and other contemporary writers. But does Mr. Eliot mean that authors should not describe cruelty if they observe it in the world and in human character? Or that books which describe cruelty should not be read? Or that, if read, they should be condemned as bad books? Or that authors should not appear in any way to identify themselves with the cruelty which they describe?

The first three interpretations must be excluded because a great deal of literature, including the Bible, Homer and the Greek tragedies, Shakespeare, Miss Austen, *The Waste Land*, Mr. James Joyce and Mr. Graham Greene, is partially concerned with the description of cruelty whose quality is plain, whatever its degree. If Mr. Eliot means the fourth possibility, that an author should not at all identify himself with cruel characters, I am afraid we must again dismiss almost the whole of literature, unless we are going to accept a definition of cruelty which is limited to the one type which Mr. Eliot gives, a definition too narrow for Mr. Eliot to make it clearly or even to give it much meaning.

I suggest that Mr. Eliot comes so slowly and obscurely to his main point because he is hard put to it to define, not only a sensibility which while admirable is uniquely Christian, but also a sense for cruelty which shall adequately cover all the wide varieties of this most recognisable vice. The mutual attitude of husbands and wives, offering a wide choice of cruelties, has been much studied by authors; it is therefore important, but not uniquely so. Most authors, professing Christians or not, throughout literary history, have offered us, as a consequence of their social, religious or historical status, a wider choice of varieties than this and often in unrelated fields. Their sensibility is at best partial and thus only partially 'moral' or 'charitable'. And I am not by any means referring only to their unconscious cruelty, the insensibility which may be mainly or wholly historical and for which we must not blame them. There have been authors who were at least professing Christians whose attitude, often overt, both to women and the poor, to love or money, is aggressive or un-charitable, is in fact neither Christian nor humane. It is quite difficult to think of an author, male or female, in English literature from Elizabethan times onwards who is quite free from these two vices of snobbery and uncharitableness. The poets have on the whole been freer, though sentimentality and lies about sex come under the heading of unconscious cruelty. Most of the theologic-ally orthodox novelists from Miss Burney, Miss Edgeworth and Miss Austen onwards have in these two respects been serious offenders. Miss Austen in particular often seems hard put to it to tell the difference between love and money. My point is that their orthodoxy did not help them to refrain from describing human behaviour as they saw it, and in their own circumstances, partially identified with it. So why should it help us in assessing them? The freethinker George Eliot was freer than most from these cruelties. In our day the orthodox Mr. Eliot is not free from them. His female characters are mostly neurotic, ugly or savage (it often depends whether they are rich, poor or middle-class) unless they are heavenly or mythical, or he can enchant them into statues, as with *La Figlia che piange*. His poor have 'unwhole-some lungs' and their souls are 'unhealthy' or sprout despondently at area gates.

Mr. Eliot refers specifically to the scrutiny of literature, other-wise I should suggest that what he really proposes to us, so that our criticism of contemporary cruelty should be practical and thus manifest a moral attitude, is that we all ought to do all in our power to spread the sense of charity in life and affairs, whether we call this Christian, orthodox or merely humane. This way authors, reflecting human nature, will also at last benefit. But I do not think that this is Mr. Eliot's proposal. The lack of social and moral awareness in contemporary authors and their characters is so alien to Mr. Eliot's own nature that he is "completely baffled by it", so he tells us.

But Mr. Eliot, in such eminently orthodox company as the Dean of St. Paul's, has at least as completely baffled many of us who are not orthodox, by newspaper appeals for the preparation of atomic weapons against Russia.* This demand, it should be noted, depended, not on the belief that Russia was preparing a direct attack on the democratic West, but only on the supposition that she would continue her indirect methods of infiltration. The view which Mr. Eliot supported here was in strong contrast with his lukewarm attitude to German Totalitarianism, as expressed in *The Idea of a Christian Society*. If this striking opposition between action and thought, between the demand for charity and the desire for order, is really allowed for in orthodoxy, Mr. Eliot has brought us no nearer to understanding Christian sensibility.

After Strange Gods is a book where Eliot the literary critic and Eliot the social and religious thinker meet first and perhaps last. It looks as if this experiment with the application of precise theological and ethical standards, if indeed they are precise, has dulled rather than sharpened his literary criticism, certainly if we are to judge by his selection. At the time when he was as far as we could see, preoccupied with literature (*The Sacred Wood*) his wide learning and his historical sense made it possible to choose the right problem before anyone else was keenly aware of it. This problem, of the dissociation of poetic sensibility, which he dates to the seventeenth century, he had isolated and was discussing as far back as 1921. Until the seventeenth century, 'thought' as he put it, 'could be felt', there was no necessary distinction between intellect and emotion, a great advantage to poets. "In the seventeenth century, a dissociation of sensibility set in, from which we have never recovered." On the question of poetic sensibility

*Observer, December 1947.

there is probably no one living who has more that he ought to say, and more that is worth listening to. But by the time that Mr. Eliot feels ready to give us the answer to this question—what happened to poetic sensibility in the seventeenth century and what has continued to affect it ever since?—he has become in the main a thinker on social matters with a theological bias, and the answer seems to be wrong. He begins by talking about Christian sensibility and, as we have seen, he is not very clear as to what that is. This question of poetic sensibility and its dissociation during the seventeenth century is so important and has become the central point of so much literary discussion that I shall leave it for later and fuller consideration. I shall say here only that I believe Mr. Eliot and most of those who have precipitated themselves after him into the discussion to be typically and significantly wrong in attributing the dissociation to the development of the scientific spirit in the seventeenth century.

Since the publication of *After Strange Gods* Mr. Eliot, in his prose works, has told us relatively little about sensibility, either Christian or poetic, but a great deal about how we ought to behave. This is understandable, since thought and feeling are now narrowly circumscribed for him by dogmatic standards. The dislike of the scientific, that is the critical and observational, or humanistic, spirit could be discerned in his work, even while it remained ostensibly literary, as in *Essays Ancient and Modern*, and has already been referred to (page 77).

Dislike does not improve his understanding of what scientists are doing. As we saw, sciences do *not* depend ultimately on any sort of dogma, however much the man in the street, or Mr. Eliot himself, may garble their pronouncements. Their criterion is an ultimate verifiability and their capacity to repeat their results on qualified demand. In passing, let me quote, as an illustration of what verifiability does *not* mean, the following from Mr. Eliot's essay 'The *Pensées* of Pascal', on the subject of mystical experience:

"Until science can teach us to reproduce such phenomena at will, science cannot claim to have explained them."

Similarly, of course, we might say that until science can reproduce eclipses at will, science cannot claim to have explained these also.

In the paper on John Bramhall, we may quote:

"Thomas Hobbes was one of those extraordinary little upstarts whom the chaotic motion of the Renaissance tossed into an eminence which they hardly deserved and have never lost. When I say the Renaissance I mean for this purpose, the period between the decay of scholastic philosophy and the rise of modern science. . . . The thirteenth century had the gift of philosophy or reason; the later seventeenth century had the gift of mathematics or science, but the period between had ceased to be rational without having learned to be scientific."

Here the use of the word 'rational' is scholastic, not contemporary; and behind the opposition between the words 'rational' and 'scientific' is the assumption that a deductive system of thought could increase knowledge, and that the method we choose to increase knowledge is thus a matter of arbitrary choice. Behind that, of course, is the implication that philosophies, and science itself, are all entirely relative to given periods, while theology alone is objective.

The dislike of science is carried into the field of psychology. This is worth considering here, for reasons which I have already given, in particular for the reason that the belief in Original Sin must imply the rejection of the idea of a scientific psychology, a psychology, that is, which generalises, on the basis of observation, about human mentality and behaviour. I must interpolate here that it does not much matter at present, whether we have a 'scientific psychology' or not. What is important is that we should have a psychology which is trying to become scientific, to marshal its observations in the only way which has led us to ascertainable truth in other fields. Mr. Eliot's views and the citations which I shall give are important because they do indeed clarify the fundamental opposition between the religious and the scientific ways of looking at human problems. This opposition is being more and more sharply realised, especially in certain literary periodicals, where it is now commonly implied that if religion and psychology are not at one in their general account of human nature, then psychology will have to go.* Organised religion depends on the concept of sin, and psychological theory cannot be expected to stop short of analysis of this concept, with at least the result, we must say, of very radical changes in its meaning.

Still in the essay on John Bramhall, Mr. Eliot says:

"There is a modern theory, closely akin to that of Hobbes, which would make value reside entirely in the degree of organisation of natural impulses . . . the difficulty with such theories is that they merely remove the inherently valuable a further degree."

They do not. Mr. Eliot begs the question. The quotations he gives are based on the view that the *inherently valuable* is something which cannot be meaningfully discussed. They are on the other hand an attempt to redefine 'value' as anything valued—what is in practice desired or valued. The concept of degree arises only within the practical organisation of these valued things or ends. †

This implicit question-begging is present again in the statement about Bramhall and his method of attacking Hobbes.

"He touches the point of practical importance . . . when he says simply that Hobbes makes praise and blame meaningless—'If a man be born blind or with one eye, we do not blame him for it; but if a man have lost his sight by his intemperance, we blame him justly'."

"This objection," says Eliot, "is finally unanswerable." But it is not. Hobbes's theory of morals is deterministic. We may

*Cf. also the Pope's pronouncement to neurologists and medical psychologists: reported *Times*, Sept. 17, 1952.

† Eliot, *Selected Essays*, pp. 346–7

attempt to oppose or correct his theory on philosophical grounds. But whether that theory is correct or not, a mere practical consequence of it, in this case that praise or blame becomes meaningless, cannot be used as part of the argument. This meaninglessness of praise or blame is recognised far more sharply by Bramhall and Eliot than by Hobbes, whose character however was such that he would hardly have deprived himself of an aggressive satisfaction, the right to blame, without good philosophical cause.

Neo-scholasticism however, which is essentially an objection to contemporary philosophical and scientific theories, especially when they touch 'human nature', bases itself largely on the belief that the practical consequences of a philosophical theory, as they appear in the established social and moral field, can be adduced as so many good reasons for not holding it and for rejecting its truth.

The implication that even science and all philosophies (apart from the Philosophia Perennis) have a predominant element of time and taste in them, reflects Mr. Eliot's own emotional preferences and an attitude which we have already seen in Hulme. Again and again we find allusive and summary generalisations which illustrate this bias and which remind us that the trick of hypostasis, of referring to a subjective abstraction as though it were a substantive existence, is its inevitable but misleading mode of expression. In the same essay we have "In a period of debility like our own . . ." And again "Bramhall affirmed the divine right of kings: Hobbes rejected this noble faith." It may be objected that Mr. Eliot is perfectly entitled to be traditional, conservative, a *laudator temporis acti*, even 'reactionary'. He is not bound to feel at home in our contemporary world. Moreover Charles the Martyr still has his devotees and Mr. Eliot may have his whimsies, or even, for all I know, his fun. But whether as a writer and a critic he is entitled to animate his conceptions and to marshal them as sheep and goats in separate pens, I gravely doubt. A candid examination will show that 'debility' and 'our age' are goats, while 'divine right of kings' and 'noble faith' are sheep.

These terms are all used truthfully when they are used with reference to a concept of history, implicit or explicit. When referring to time, Mr. Eliot always hankers for timelessness. 'Our age' means the age in which we ourselves, including Mr. Eliot, live, what makes us ourselves and makes Mr. Eliot himself, all of us with our emotions, our crotchets and our degrees of capacity for examining them; and also with our traditions, for in the twentieth century we receive the seventeenth filtered through the eighteenth and nineteenth. To say or to imply that this is a pity or a bad thing, is to deny both our traditions and ourselves, and to surrender the valid use of criticism. 'The divine right of kings' was an historical and political phenomenon. It was no more inherently noble than 'our age' is inherently 'debilitated'.

I have already referred to the paper on Bradley in relation to Arnold. In the present context it is again remarkable, because it reveals the same connoisseur's attitude towards philosophies, the philosophy-taster's, the deliberate innocence towards the fact that philosophies are at least an attempt towards establishing a relation to objective truth. It may be held that the assumptive and allusive attitude, marked throughout this essay, towards philosophies which Mr. Eliot dislikes is justified, because it is impossible to launch a reasoned refutation of a philosophy every time one mentions it. But one or two quotations will suggest that Mr. Eliot's ground of enmity to any philosophy is always the same. The criterion is always tradition, not descriptive truth. For example:

"This is the social basis of Bradley's distinction, and the social basis is even more his claim to our gratitude than the logical basis: he replaced a philosophy which was crude and raw and provincial by one which was, in comparison, catholic, civilised and universal. True, he was influenced by Kant and Hegel and Lotze. But Kant and Hegel and Lotze are not so despicable as some enthusiastic medievalists would have us believe, and they are, in comparison with the school of Bentham, catholic, civilised and universal. In fighting the battles that he fought in the seventies and eighties,

Bradley was fighting for a European and ripened and wise philosophy, against an insular and immature and cranky one."

Since Mr. Eliot never issued a precise intellectual manifesto, I have been trying in this chapter to extract both the method and the matter of his development into the full orthodoxy of a practical and planning Churchman. This should at least have told us something of his dislikes and of their rationale.

We know already that Mr. Eliot dislikes humanism. There are one or two paragraphs in 'The Humanism of Irving Babbitt' also in this same collection, which are worthy of comment. Eliot quotes Babbitt as saying:

"In fact, in so far as I object to the moderns at all, it is because they have not been sufficiently modern, or what amounts to the same thing, have not been sufficiently experimented."

He comments:

"We may be allowed to inquire where all this modernity and experimenting is going to lead. Is everybody to spend his time experimenting? And on what and to what end? And if the experimenting merely leads to the conclusion that self-control is good, that seems a very frosty termination. . . . What is the higher will to *will* if there is nothing either 'anterior, exterior or superior' to the individual? If this will is to have anything on which to operate, it must be in relation to external objects and to objective values."

But if the higher will is a religious will, what is *that* to will? The Will of God? But how are we to know the will of God except in relation to external objects and to objective values? And who is to decide what values, if any, are objective? Mr. Eliot would say the Church, and that is of course to beg the whole question of humanism versus religion. All values are agreed conclusions relating to experience. They are arrived at by individuals or bodies existing in space and time. Those of us who cannot help seeing that all Churches are temporary and relative will prefer to be guided, where we need guidance, as we all do, by individuals and bodies whose experience is widest, most impartial and most experimental, in short most nearly humane. I think when we consider Mr. Babbitt's use of the word 'experimental' we may pay him the respect and do him the justice of supposing that he is referring to the scientific rather than to the merely Bohemian temper. The Eliot who noticed and disliked the mere revolt and moral destructiveness, which was mixed up, in the twenties, with some genuine experimentation in new ways of living has, not for the first time, palmed another meaning of a word upon a context. This time the word is 'experimental' and the context is Mr. Babbitt's.

I must refer once more to that arch-curiosity among statements:

"Professor Babbitt knows too much . . . too many religions and philosophies, has assimilated their spirit too thoroughly . . . to be able to give himself to any. The result is humanism."

Mr. Eliot has surely made here the strangest confession of faith through ignorance. One wonders exactly *how* odious is comparison, how many religions one may safely know about, to be certain of remaining orthodox, or whether perhaps we may suspect that the logical end of orthodoxy is to know nothing but itself? The point here is that Mr. Eliot does not want religions to be scientifically studied. This gives us the clue to the meaning of his remarks on humanism and the experimental. It gives us also the essential explanation of all his other dislikes, including liberalism,* psycho-analysis, sexual relations apart from the narrow prescription of the Church, freedom of intellectual inquiry, and 'progress'. All these things when they are valuable, that is, here, when they lead to increase of happiness or contentment, do so in so far as they are the result of an observational, experimental, a scientific attitude.

*Cf. reference to Dante's childhood experience in the *Vita Nuova*: E. paper on Dante [*Selected Essays*, 1932].

Mr. Eliot and the rest of us have the choice, not least in anything which concerns the mind and heart, of being scientific or idolatrous. Moreover I believe that this is nothing new. It applies as it has always applied in religion, philosophy, art, science, politics, ethics, psychology and all our practical and spiritual activities. To take the one example of religion, there has been a continual forward movement, from Judaism to Christianity and through the different Christian reforms, away from graven images. Graven images include blood-sacrifices, dead dogma and all the stones of false abstractions offered us for the bread of meaning. Christ said with exceptional precision what he meant instead of meaning what we say. But we have continually to re-translate what he said according to our need and circumstances. The language of the contemporary experimental psychologist, for all its blemishes, is a closer translation than the dogma of the Church. It has often a noncomformist uncouthness and bareness, alternating with a kind of Lutheran garishness, but the dogmas are false abstractions, and so dead idols.

So far we have failed to discover in Mr. Eliot's prose works any theoretical illumination about the nature of orthodox thought or feeling. That such an illumination would not be unreasonably demanded from a literary man of Mr. Eliot's eminence is illustrated by the example of Arnold, already given, who was ready to write about everything that he understood of Christianity, both as emotion and as metaphysics. With Mr. Eliot, we go back as far as dogma, conventional and authoritarian pronouncements on Christian conduct and belief, and we can go no further. We have to try and find out from the implications of two works which are later than anything I have so far mentioned, and which give Mr. Eliot's constructive view of a Christian society, of orthodoxy in practice, what are his real beliefs about orthodox thought and feeling. These two books are *The Idea of a Christian Society* (1939) and *Notes Towards the Definition of Culture* (1948).

These two books may well be taken as giving us some idea of the kind of world in which Mr. Eliot thinks he would like to live; but, in a strange way, a picture of the contemporary world which Mr.

Eliot dislikes emerges much more clearly. I do not say that Mr. Eliot, or anyone, ought to like the contemporary world, but perhaps it ought to be disliked with a different sort of criticism. And what he chooses to dislike *most* is remarkable. For instance, I believe that it is fair to say, and I shall shortly illustrate this by quotation, that he really dislikes some of the things we have mentioned, such as liberalism and population control, rather more than totalitarianism, rather more than war and much more than 'the corporative state'—which, as he reminds us, was honourably mentioned by the Pope in the Encyclical *Quadragesimo Anno*.

His dislike of revivalism (Moral Rearmament) which is strong, might be accounted for by his election of dogma rather than 'enthusiasm', as characteristically Christian. However, we may legitimately remind ourselves that the previous great wave of emotional religion, the Evangelical Movement, was among other things a precursor of nineteenth-century liberalism. Psychologists observe that the repression of emotion helps to inhibit general intelligence. Moreover it does not follow that emotions released by religious enthusiasm will remain permanently attached to religious conceptions. In the case of side-tracked or inhibited intelligence, the release of any emotion may mean the release of all and even the overthrow of values which have become stereotyped. This may be a contributory reason for Mr. Eliot's dislike of 'enthusiasm'—that it is associated with the attitude which can be roughly generalised as Romanticism, and hence with the arch-enemy, liberalism.

I share Mr. Eliot's dislike of Moral Rearmament, but for the very different reason that I think it plays dangerously with the technique of psychological catharsis. But whatever one thinks of this or any particular example of religious emotion, there is very strong ground for saying that original Christianity *was* primarily concerned with the emotions and with their re-education, and with their positive realisation in personal relations. Matthew Arnold was in the right of it when he said that, at least during the lifetime of Christ, a 'right knowledge of the Godhead' was never prescribed. Christ was interested in feasts, presumably because they stimulate charity, but otherwise paid a somewhat unwilling attention to social and ritual observances. I do not see how a society which was remotely Christian could grow, unless some general attempt were made to release and re-educate our warped emotions. We are not likely to prefer to love, unless it is made worth our while in the unconscious stages of education. However unlikely it seems at present that any state—and I am afraid that it is only the state which could allow time and money enough—will let itself be persuaded by its psychological experts to undertake this vital experiment, it is still more unlikely that the hierarchical and stratified society which Mr. Eliot sketches would do anything to educate any of us into feelings and relationships which were remotely Christian. In *The Idea of a Christian Society* Mr. Eliot does, unusually, refer to charity, but with very little emphasis and only in the context of a reference to humility, and the general picture which emerges is lacking in this and in the other Christian virtues of faith and hope. That is, he does not believe that his idea will be realised and he certainly gives no indication that anybody would be happier if it were. Yet I cannot accept that happiness was a notion which was alien to Christ, for the reason that it is impossible to love without happiness. There are allusions to nature, especially to its abuse, in Mr. Eliot's book, but none to natural enjoyment. I do not think it is insignificant that the style of presentation is itself negative, always eliminative, almost a Negative Way. This we might expect from Mr. Eliot's special theological and mystical preoccupations, but it impresses itself on me at least as a technique of avoidance and its total effect is tiresome, as if one were watching someone with an obsession to avoid all the cracks in the pavement. For example:

"In using the term 'Idea' of a Christian Society I do not mean primarily a concept derived from the study of any societies which we may choose to call Christian; I mean something that can only be found in an understanding of the end to which a Christian Society, to deserve the name, must be directed. I do not limit the

application of the term to a perfected Christian Society on earth;
and I do not comprehend in it societies merely because some
profession of Christian faith, or some vestige of Christian practice,
is retained . . ."

Or again:

"I am not at this moment concerned with the means for bringing
a Christian Society into existence; I am not even primarily
concerned with making it appear desirable; but I am very much
concerned with making clear its difference from the kind of
society in which we are now living."

It is true that the elimination in these negative notions is
apparently directed towards clarifying a positive aim; and in fact,
although Mr. Eliot specifically avoids any practical discussion of
the relations of Church and State and excludes consideration of
the form of political organisation suitable to a Christian State, he
does work through to a sketch of the basic structural elements in a
Christian Society. This is however left deliberately vague. The
vagueness, considering the scope of the book, is no doubt
legitimate. The basic elements, as 'working distinctions', are then
the Christian State; the Christian Community; and the Community of Christians. The Christian State is "the Christian Society
under the aspect of legislation, public administration, legal
tradition and form". The Christian Community seems to mean
those over whom the Christian statesmen rule, considered as
a whole. The Community of Christians means those from
whom "one would expect a conscious Christian life at its highest
level".

From the point of view of the Idea of this Christian Society, the
relations among these sections are supremely important. But
though these relations, says Mr. Eliot, may be looked at in
connection with the problem of belief, the most important thing
that the rulers and the ruled have in common is that what is
expected from them is conformity of behaviour. The ruled or the

Community of Christians may realise their Christianity almost wholly in behaviour ("customary and periodic religious observances and in traditional code of behaviour towards their neighbours") because their capacity for *thinking* about the objects of faith is small. As for the 'Statesmen', whose capacity for thinking about anything may be presumed greater, it is not primarily their Christianity which matters:

"but their being confined, by the temper and traditions of the people which they rule, to a Christian framework within which to realise their ambitions and advance the prosperity and prestige of their country. They may frequently perform un-Christian acts; they must never attempt to defend their actions on un-Christian principles."

We need not at present consider the Community of Christians, the believers who have presumably both the capacity and the time to think about the objects of faith, and whose Christianity is active, whether or not their lives are completely dedicated to realising the Idea of a Christian Society. This Idea would not only be acceptable to them, but the rest of us can see why. But Mr. Eliot has given us these two other classes to consider, each of which alone must be far larger than that of the consciously devout and orthodox. There must therefore be some inducement or persuasion felt by these classes to stay in and maintain a society which they at least know to be 'Christian', some *power* which will operate the machine for which Mr. Eliot has given us a blueprint. It is difficult at first to see what this can be. I do not think that Mr. Eliot is totally Utopian, for a Utopia is abstract, it is really about ideas which are intended to give us a plan for a desirable *future*. But Mr. Eliot is not only pessimistic about the future, he is also rather more concrete than the Utopian and he is clearly referring to a state of society which he thinks *has* existed, and worked, in the past. The problem, both for Mr. Eliot and for his Christian Society, then, can be stated in another way—as How to attain the Past.

Personally I believe our present society to be developing on lines many of which are profoundly mistaken. I find an unbalanced industrialism and the wastage of human lives and natural resources as well as the immense amount of individual frustration and dissatisfaction—especially its perversion from understanding, through unconsciousness—as deeply deplorable as he does. I do not think that we ought to give either 'Science' or 'Industrialism' its head without a primary concern for human benefit. I agree that there is much to be said for some form of regionalism—which Mr. Eliot advocates in the later book, *Notes Towards the Definition of Culture* and, what would follow from this, that we ought to maintain a certain piety towards our old traditions, those that are positively beneficial such as Wednesleydale Cheese, and those that are harmless, like Bishop's gaiters. I mean by this that we should continue to live and enjoy what is living and enjoyable, not that we should necessarily insist on Morris-dancing round the village green if there is a more lively local custom arising, which brings us into more stimulating contact with all our neighbours.

But there are two practical allusions—they are hardly more—made by Mr. Eliot—which seem to me to reveal a condition which would be necessary if Mr. Eliot's Christian society were ever to be brought into being, and which perhaps he ought to state more clearly. While stating that the 'parish is certainly in decay', he gives the parish as an example of community unit, 'the traditional unit of the Christian Community in England'.

"The unitary community should be (as the parish is) religious-social, and it must be one in which all classes, if you have classes, have their centre of interest."

The other important allusion is to the education of the rulers (the Christian statesmen):

"I should not expect the rulers of a Christian State to be philosophers, or to be able to keep before their minds at every moment of decision the maxim that the life of virtue is the purpose of human society . . . but they would neither be self-educated

nor have been submitted in their youth merely to that system
of miscellaneous or specialised instruction which passes for
education: they would have received a Christian education. . . .
A Christian education would primarily train people to think in
Christian categories, though it could not compel belief and would
not impose the necessity for insincere profession of belief. What
the rulers believed, would be less important than the beliefs to
which they were obliged to conform. And a skeptical or indifferent statesman, working within a Christian frame, might be
more effective than a devout Christian statesman obliged to
conform to a secular frame."

Now what exactly can it be that *obliges* a statesman who, in
spite of a Christian education, is sceptical or indifferent to Christian
belief, to work within a Christian frame or "to design his policy for
the government of a Christian society?" And what would oblige a
Community which was unable to think about the objects of belief,
to accept his government, unless it conferred obvious and immediate material benefits which the Community would have to
be advanced enough, in an intellectual sense, to realise or 'think
about'?

What also would persuade them to revert to the life of the
parish when they are so forcibly drawn to industrial centres?—for
Mr. Eliot knows that they will also not be able to think consciously
about the advantages of that life, some of which are indubitable.
I am afraid that Mr. Eliot knows that nothing can so persuade
them but some form of force which would cover the destruction of
our present material development, and also of the ideas which
made that possible, for good as well as ill—the ideas of liberalism,
humanism and science. And who would be the instrument of this
force? The most likely answer is the Christian statesmen who
would have been 'taught to think in Christian categories'. What
exactly these categories would be Mr. Eliot does not tell us, but on
his own showing they need not be connected with charity nor with
the sense of individual and personal value, but only with the
statesmen's sense of their own power and of the prosperity and

prestige of the national unit which they were ruling. I do not know what Mr. Eliot's views on Machiavelli may be, but the quotations already given illustrate his profound contempt and dislike for Hobbes. Yet his own political views, if they could be put into practice, would surely reveal themselves as not less cynical than those of Machiavelli or even Hobbes. Since a 'Christian education', as Mr. Eliot conceives it, would be an education which left them free to think and act *primarily* in terms of their own and of national power, I do not think it would save his 'Christian statesmen' from acting as any minority class, in any community, which had been given, either by education or by the economic condition of that community, the right and the means to power, would do, in the face of a threat to that power's continuation. How much more totalitarian evidence do we want under our own eyes? However much or little education Hitler and Mussolini had in Christian categories (which their sense of power enabled them to divorce very easily from Christian feeling), it seems certain that Franco has had a great deal. As far as I remember, Stalin was brought up in a seminary and designed for the priesthood.

The Idea of a Christian Society was published in 1939, after the outbreak of the war with Hitler's Germany. Mr. Eliot no doubt did well to suggest that we ourselves might not be free from all the defects of totalitarianism. But his views on what these defects really are, and also on what they were felt to be by the majority of people who detested them, are not easy to discern and, where discerned, are difficult to accept.

"The fundamental objection to fascist doctrine, the one which we conceal from ourselves because it might condemn ourselves as well, is that it is pagan. There are other objections too, in the political and economic sphere, but they are not objections that we can make with dignity until we set our own affairs in order. There are still other objections, to oppression and violence and cruelty, but however strongly we feel, these are objections to means and not to ends."

Further, in an astonishing note:

"(By fascist doctrine) I mean only such doctrine as asserts the absolute authority of the state, or the infallibility of a ruler. 'The corporative state', recommended by *Quadragesimo Anno* is not in question. The economic organisation of totalitarian states is not in question. The ordinary person does not object to fascism because it is pagan, but because he is fearful of authority, even when it is pagan."

The order in which Mr. Eliot tabulates what he conceives to be the main objections to fascist doctrine is logical for one who holds that dogma is prior to morality. But it is significant that though he is correct in judging that the 'ordinary person's' order of objections is different from his own, he still gets that order wrong. What the 'ordinary person' primarily objects to in fascism is that it is violent and cruel. I would go further and say that where the ordinary person is 'fearful of authority' it is because authority sooner or later tends to be arbitrary and may therefore be violent and cruel. For his dogmatic purposes, Mr. Eliot has to distinguish over-sharply between ends and means. A striking fact about cruelty—this was clearly visible in the worst aspects of the Nazi regime—is that it is a means which is not sharply distinguishable from an end. To the natural morality of normal men and women it is as near to being absolutely hateful as anything can be. Moreover the objections which can be made to fascism in the political and economic sphere may still be made by the ordinary person even though he may not be interested in politics or versed in economics, and made 'with dignity' precisely because these objections too are based on his fundamental objection, his hatred of cruelty and violence. These objections in the same order apply also to the Corporative State, whether it is recommended by the Pope or not, and whether Mussolini had been taught to think in Christian categories or not. Mr. Eliot refers more than once to the *efficiency* of the totalitarian machine, for example: "I suspect that in our loathing of totalitarianism, there is infused a good deal of admiration for its *efficiency*." Efficiency for what? Not surely for the preservation of a balanced economy, for I do not believe that Mr. Eliot would so describe the short-term policy of Guns before Butter, nor even for the prosecution and winning of a world war, to which such efficiency as the Nazis had was mainly directed. There are plenty of accounts from informed sources of their wastage, circumlocution and plain stupidity in prosecuting their evil aims. Certainly they were not efficient in regard to the other political and economic aims which Mr. Eliot, often in common with the ordinary person, picks out as basic for any society which is to endure at a tolerable level of humanity, whether Christian or not. I mean that their 'efficiency' was not good enough to enable them to preserve natural resources, to give their population 'a proper and particular' cuisine (*NDC* p. 27) or, most remarkably, considering their efforts to that end, to get that population to increase. I cannot believe that Mr. Eliot is only referring to 'getting the trains to run to time' when he writes of efficiency.* Yet another quotation makes one ponder: "The fact that money is always forthcoming for the purpose of making more money, *whilst it is so difficult to obtain for purposes of exchange*, and for the needs of the most needy, is disturbing to those who are not economists." I believe that the ordinary person, who is also not an economist but does not have to think about getting to the Riviera

---

*A note made by Mr. E. on pacifism is relevant. It is because he has a moral hatred of violence and cruelty that the ordinary person hates war even if he also hates it because it is inconvenient and terrifying. Mr. E. says: "I cannot but believe that the man who maintains that war is in all circumstances wrong, is in some way repudiating an obligation towards society; and in so far as the society is a Christian society, the obligation is so much the more serious. Even if each particular war proves in turn to have been unjustified, yet the idea of a Christian society seems incompatible with the idea of absolute pacifism; for pacifism can only continue to flourish so long as the majority of persons forming a society are not pacifists; just as sectarianism can only flourish against the background of orthodoxy." This is an interesting example of the falsity which may be introduced by analogous thinking. It is fair to say that pacifists may depend for their continuance on non-pacifists. But does Mr. Eliot really mean that sectarians are more viable in such countries as Spain, which provide the most orthodox of backgrounds? Sectarians, as pacifists, flourish most where the ordinary person retains notions of liberty and is not penalised for his unorthodoxy.

this side of eternity, is also disturbed by the difficulties about money which Mr. Eliot mentions, but that once again he puts them in a different order of importance, based, once again, on a different and perhaps more natural morality. There is some evidence, as we have seen in quotations already given from his poems, that Mr. Eliot has a lack of understanding of and sympathy with ordinary persons, that he looks upon them as generally unhealthy and unhappy, whether at the dog races, the flicks, or in bed, and, as it were, worked by the roundabout of mechanised pleasure like automata. I do not think that this picture is absolutely representative. If it were so, the solution would be perhaps not to take their toys away from the people but to give them more opportunities to share our more refined enjoyments. If that were accepted by Mr. Eliot he would have to recast some of his ideas on 'education'. The dogmatic view of human nature as I have repeatedly pointed out, does not allow for the education of the emotions, the most fundamental education, because it does not permit us to discover what the emotions really are.

One may conclude that Mr. Eliot's Christian Society would not be really designed to satisfy in just proportion the needs of the ordinary person, of whom he has a poor and, I think, biassed opinion, even if conceived as part of a Christian Community. Those who would benefit most would be the class which he has described elsewhere (in *NDC*) as the Élite.

Notes Towards the Definition of Culture is a book which sticks closely to the intention indicated in its title and for that reason it is less relevant than most of Mr. Eliot's books to my main theme. One may agree that the word 'Culture', like so many other words, is abused, very often by cultivated persons, and one may also agree with many of Mr. Eliot's indications of what it ought to mean and what it may not mean: for example, on the one hand, that it is not synonymous with education, still less with 'instruction', and, on the other, that one cannot really understand it except as applied to the total way of living in which a community has grown. There are however the usual fraught statements in this book, referring to the whole background of Mr. Eliot's thought, which one would like to see amplified, and often clarified. And, as usual, particularly in the case of *The Idea of a Christian Society* we find, if we piece these and other more positive statements together, that we have quite a distinct picture of what Mr. Eliot dislikes in our present society, a much more baffling indication of what he feels he would prefer or of what he even feels may at some time have existed, but very little idea of what his answer would be to the question: 'How do you think this preferable society could be brought into being?' Without doubt, Mr. Eliot, pursuing the negative or eliminative way to which I have referred, would say that this question is 'outside the scope' of 'the present' (or any other) essay.

But if we take some of the statements, especially those to which I have referred as fraught and unamplified, we see that their scope, in necessary implication, is very large. The implication is that the ideals and the ideology which underlie our present Western society, whoever holds them or whether anyone holds them in consciousness or not, are false; and that the political, economic and educational structure which has arisen upon them is therefore wrong and unnatural. The sign which he gives is the statement that culturally our own period is one of decline. This is contrasted with a picture of the positive conditions which seem to have been necessary to maintain a flourishing culture.

The most important of these conditions are two: attachment to a religion, and a stratified society. It must be carefully noted that Mr. Eliot does not claim that the fulfilment of these two conditions will bring about a renewal of culture, only that a highly developed culture is improbable without them, and that our existing culture is certainly doomed unless the community re-attaches itself to the Christian faith. The apparent modesty of this claim may mislead some readers, especially as there is also an indication of flexibility in Mr. Eliot's view of the political and social structure which would be appropriate to his Christian and cultural community. The Élite, for instance, on whom so much depends, should continually be replenished from other classes as well as that of the rulers. There is a place for opposition as a therapeutic friction, for sects, and even for liberalism, as a necessary negative influence. That for Mr. Eliot is very liberal indeed. Nevertheless we ought not to let ourselves be deceived about the main implications of this book, which are the same as those of *The Idea of a Christian Society*. Liberalism and humanism are still the main enemies. For the ideas of liberalism and humanism (liberalism is among other things a humanistic interpretation of Christian philosophy) have, whether we like it or not, laid the foundations of our existing Western society, whether we like that or not. And the stratification of society, and the social status of the Church as well as of sects and oppositions, can only be modified by a widespread modification of the status of these ideas in men's minds. This modification can only be brought about in one of two ways, either by persuasive demonstration that they are false—that would imply, of course, as a first step making them a great deal more conscious than they are in the majority of minds—or by their repression. I do not think that the first is really possible, because the ideas have had and still have their chief value in so far as they spring from the scientific attitude. They are valuable because when they mean anything at all they are true, and because their implications are being constantly tested by the only tests we know. The second course, repression, is only possible by force or subversion. We know from experience that this is so, the repression is inevitable; it is either acute, as with fascism, or chronic as with the Roman Catholic Church.

Because we already have this experience, I doubt that Mr. Eliot, however much he may prefer an eliminative or negative way of expression, is normally entitled to maintain so academic a spirit towards the issue of power. In fact his equanimity is reserved entirely for the fate of liberal ideas. The fate of ecclesiastical Christianity, as we can see not only from the letter already referred to (see p. 117), but from the sum of implications of his social writings, does not leave him cold. And yet it has obviously been liberalism which assisted Christianity to survive, rather than the other way round. Mr. Eliot's preference as far as the organisation of society is concerned is not academic. That he ought to answer this question—How is this preferable organisation to be brought about?—is implied in his anti-liberalism and his views on the stratification of society because these opinions, in peace-time, imply a reversal of that trend in Western society which is normal and most conscious. We hear too much nowadays about the Church as the sole preserver of values, culture, knowledge and civilisation, especially throughout the Dark Ages. In fact, values cannot be preserved, only used. The foundations of what is good in our present culture were laid by the Greeks, the Romans, the Christians; and also by the Mohammedans, who made a practice of preserving the civilisation and learning of the countries they conquered and were Western Europe's first point of contact with the Greek masters, particularly with Aristotle. Because of this and also because of the attention they paid to mathematics, we might regard the Mohammedans as largely responsible for the two opposing developments of Western culture, into scholasticism on the one hand and science on the other! But perhaps their main contribution was after all something not unlike the most civilised spirit we have, that of liberalism. For they seem to have been on the whole much more tolerant of, and even interested in, alien ideas than either the Christians or the Jews, who suffered their conquest, have been when in power.

What is and was good in our society, stemming from all these sources, is and was something that expressed itself in practice as a liberal, humane sense of reality. This is how we have received the genuine meaning of Christianity, much more than through the Church in its more rigid organisations. A man at any time in the last two millennia became a Christian in practice by becoming more nearly liberal and humane. And in the latter part of those two millennia liberal humanism tended away from the rigid stratification of society. I repeat that to check or reverse this trend still needs force, as in fact we have seen recently and expensively. Liberal humanism is not merely negative, as one would gather from Mr. Eliot's allusions, not merely the destroyer of traditions, that with which society is worm-eaten, when it is most significant; nor, on the other hand, a mere party-colour or a lackadaisical habit, as Mr.

Eliot would have us believe, when he refers in intolerant tones to tolerance, that most difficult and civilised of virtues. Part of the difficulty of tolerance lies in defining its own limits, because the true as well as the lackadaisical liberal feels uneasy when he stops short of tolerating intolerance, including that of the Church, and it is indeed essential to liberalism to tolerate some degree of intolerance. 'I detest your views'—yes, I do indeed detest them. But liberalism really consists of a right and a duty—the right to think correctly, that is, in relation to reality; the duty to combat false ideas, but with truer ideas, ideas, that is, which are closer to experience.

It might be argued that the issue of force is implied here but also without being answered. Liberal humanism is primarily an attitude towards discoverable truth, but certainly today we seem called upon to defend the stocks and the channels of that truth against encroachments from all directions. Liberal humanists however do seem to have been ready to die for their belief and attitude in considerable numbers; whether soon enough or finally enough it is not my business to discuss, since neither Mr. Eliot nor myself have made any claims about the *success* of our beliefs. But the general ideal which was discoverable in the last war was that of liberal humanism rather than of orthodox Christianity, and an answer has thus been made on the issue of force. Therefore it seems to me that the onus of discussion is now with the anti-liberal side to which Mr. Eliot belongs. For the truly liberal attitude towards Mr. Eliot's beliefs implies as usual that one attributes to him both rights and duties. He has the right to ventilate his opinions. But he has also the duty of carrying them to their logical conclusions. That the cost of implementing them would be great and ugly is one of these conclusions.

CHAPTER V

Mr. Willey's Lunar Spots

ONE of the most pregnant contributions which Mr. Eliot has made to criticism is his observation on the dissociation of sensibility, the split between thought and emotion, which took place in the seventeenth century (Essay on 'The Metaphysical Poets,' 1921):

"It is something which had happened to the mind of England between the time of Donne or Lord Herbert of Cherbury and the time of Tennyson and Browning; it is the difference between the intellectual poet and the reflective poet. Tennyson and Browning are poets, and they think; but they do not feel their thought as immediately as the odour of a rose. A thought to Donne was an experience; it modified his sensibility. . . . The poets of the seventeenth century, the successors of the dramatists of the sixteenth, possessed a mechanism of sensibility which could devour any kind of experience. . . . In the seventeenth century a dissociation of sensibility set in, from which we have never recovered, and this dissociation, as is natural, was aggravated by the influence of the two most powerful poets of the century, Milton and Dryden."

While this conception, which is also related to his views on the relation of philosophy to poetry, is, I believe, central to Mr. Eliot's own thought and feeling in and about poetry, he has not been at pains to develop it. But it has been developed by other writers. It has also been contradicted by some, for example Dr.

Tillyard in his interesting and lively book on Milton. In my view, both those who agree and those who disagree with Mr. Eliot on the degree of responsibility for the 'dissociation in sensibility', have in general missed the point. Mr. Eliot it is true used the word 'aggravated', not 'caused', and it seems probable that he himself has not worked out the full implications of his statement. When we talk of dissociation of sensibility, purely poetic influence can hardly be exaggerated, but when they talk of influences, most of the writers who have discussed the idea have separated Milton's thought from his poetry. As I believe that these writers have from either side misconceived Mr. Eliot's opinion and mislaid its true and valuable implication, which is highly relevant to this book's main theme, I shall discuss the subject here.

Mr. Basil Willey's *The Seventeenth Century Background* is particularly interesting not only because it attempts to give an historical picture of the 'dissociation in sensibility' and because it at least gives the problem of the relation of poetry to truth a merited attention; but also because its theory derives from Hulme as well as from Eliot, and we may therefore look upon it as a flood-mark of the penetration of anti-humanism into literary criticism. As early as his second page, Mr. Willey makes use of Hulme's idea of the critique of satisfactions and of the subjective nature of philosophical goals, which I have already discussed.

"First it may be well to inquire," says Mr. Willey, "not with Pilate 'What is Truth?' but what was *felt to be* 'truth' and 'explanation' under seventeenth century conditions. As T. E. Hulme and others have pointed out, it is almost insuperably difficult to become critically conscious of one's own habitual assumptions; 'doctrines felt as facts' can only be seen to be doctrines, and not facts, after great efforts of thought, and usually with the aid of a first-rate metaphysician."

And further:

"The clarity of an explanation seems to depend upon the degree of satisfaction that it affords. An explanation 'explains' best when it meets some need of our nature, some deep-seated demand for assurance. 'Explanation' may perhaps be roughly defined as a restatement of something—event, theory, doctrine, etc.—in terms of the current interests and assumptions."

These early quotations seem to me to contain in germ the fundamental errors around which Mr. Willey has constructed his book. In itself the statement that it is a metaphysician, first-rate or not, whom we need to put us right and make us critically conscious of our concealed assumptions, begs the question. Mr. Willey's book is mainly about the impact of scientific discovery on seventeenth-century thought and poetic sensibility. The conclusions about the nature of the universe and of the mind which were found to be disturbing were largely those of the physicist and the astronomer, working or trying to work inductively; that is, by observation and experiment. The method and its apparent threat of unlimited applicability was what caused the disturbance; though, in general, inductive thinkers, or those who were fascinated by the method's possibilities (e.g. Bacon and Browne), refrained from applying it in the field of religion. A metaphysician, who in general feels no obligation to use this method, is hardly likely to be the one to assist us in dealing with any concealed assumptions which may lead us either to accept or deny it. The causes for our want of critical consciousness are either logical or psychological—we fail either because we do not think in applicable form or because the pressure of emotion makes our thinking subjective—and to eradicate these causes we need a logician or a psychologist.

Mr. Willey's 'metaphysician' is thus a first and early hint of his own most significant underlying assumptions—that all explanations are alike' explanation'; that they all alike relate only to subjective satisfaction; that the fact that some of them are checked and controlled by experiment or return to experience makes no important distinction among them; that there are, in short, two 'truths', one of theology and one of science, and that each has a special sphere in which its judgments alone are valid. This reminds one of Hulme's sharply demarcated spheres—with the 'muddy mixed zone' between. In Mr. Willey's case it looks as if this underlying assumption of the duality of 'truth' also covers a bias in favour of theological 'truth', because it is supposed to appeal to our 'deeper' interest—an idea which itself covers a great many assumptions of value.

A quotation from Mr. Willey's next page illustrates this underlying assumption—and bias—particularly well, and also the typical semantic shift with which it insinuates itself:

"Such a demand (i.e. for restatement or explanation) . . . does not necessarily imply the 'falsehood' of the older statement; it may merely mean that men now wish to live and to act according to a different formula. This is especially evident in our period whenever a 'scientific' explanation replaces a theological one. For example, the spots on the moon's surface might be due, theologically, to the fact that it was God's will that they should be there; scientifically they might be 'explained' as the craters of extinct volcanoes. The newer explanation may be said, not so much to contain 'more' truth than the older, as to supply the *kind* of truth which was now demanded."

I know that he might consent to expand the expression 'due theologically' into 'might be explained from a theological standpoint', but we ought not to miss the implication of value and relative degree of reality, in the positive 'due' as opposed to the word 'explained', made hypothetical by inverted commas.

The rest of the paragraph develops this imputation of subjectivity to scientific method—an imputation, we might almost say, of whim, certainly of a kind of fortuitousness, which ignores the binding and interlocking quality of historical human experience. This makes one wonder whether Mr. Willey unconsciously conceives his seventeenth century as existing in a 'metaphysical' isolation without relation to other centuries which had gone and were to follow.

No one can deny or should wish to deny that there are at all times psychological needs and drives determining the direction of our interests, either as individuals or as members of a community, determining therefore the kind of questions we are likely to ask and the kind of answers we are likely to get. But the questions, if they mean anything, will come out of a body of experience which connects us to the whole history of mankind upon the planet, while the answers, if they make sense, will appear within an existing body of knowledge, although they may extend and indeed make profound structural alterations within it. This continuity of investigation and discovery is the very foundation of knowledge and it only became possible when the experimental attitude was achieved. To ignore this historical interlocking of everything we can be said to know, to ignore the *tradition* of science whose establishment was the great achievement of Mr. Willey's Century, is simply to insinuate one of the old bad hypostatical heritages of scholasticism in a disguised form. If we were totally ignorant of the history of scientific development, within and outside the seventeenth century, Mr. Willey's 'explanation' of explanation would never give us any idea that something more than a fortuitous emotional need of a very vague entity, the human heart, had been required to set it in motion:

"A comet, for example, or an eclipse, was explained when instead of being a disastrous omen . . . it could be shown to be the 'necessary' result of a demonstrable chain of causes. No one, it need hardly be said, wishes to deny that this explanation had and still has a more 'satisfying' quality than the one it superseded. But why was it more satisfying? It was more satisfying . . . because now, instead of the kind of 'truth' which is consistent with authoritative teaching, men began to desire the kind which would enable them to measure, to weigh and to control the things around them. . . . For a scientific type of explanation to be satisfying, for it to convince us with a sense of its necessary truth, we must be in the condition of needing and desiring that type of explanation and no other. . . . Speaking generally, it may be said that the demand for explanation is due to the desire to be rid of mystery. Such a demand will be most insistent when the current mysteries have become unusually irksome, as seems to have been the case in the time of Epicurus, and again at the Renaissance. At these turning-points men wanted 'scientific' explanations because they no longer wished to feel as they had been taught to feel about the nature of things. To be rid of fear—fear of the unknown, fear of the stars or of the devil—to be released from the necessity of reverencing what was not to be understood, these were among the most urgent demands of the modern as of the ancient world; and it was because it satisfied these demands that scientific explanation was received as the revelation of truth."

If Mr. Willey means what he says by most of these remarks, it is still difficult to know what he means! Are we supposed to believe that the superstitions, fears and longings of unknown men and women, who themselves knew nothing of these individual scientists and their work, constituted any actual demand which could possibly influence the experiments, discoveries and cal-culations of Copernicus, Galileo or Newton? If we suppose that these scientists themselves felt fear or any other emotional attitude towards the phenomena which they investigated, and most prob-ably they did, can Mr. Willey say how this affected or was at all connected with the actual observations and measurements which they made? Galileo, as we all know, became conscious, after the scientific event, of reactions of fear and aggression from one organised body of unscientific human beings to that event itself, but all that made him do was to tell a simple lie which did not affect the validity of his discovery one way or the other. All that 'men's fear' here did was to cause them to repudiate science. In general one can say that the fear of science has been as strong or stronger than the fear of the gods or of natural events. Mr. Willey's evidence seems to be limited to the rather personal attitude of Lucretius. Who indeed are 'men'?—these 'men' who 'felt', 'feared' and 'demanded'? To use 'men' instead of 'Man', which must very nearly have come to Mr. Willey's pen, is a way of conferring a specious air of inductiveness. It would be amusing, if one had time, to follow out all the implied hypostases in the

statements I have quoted—these are only examples. Elsewhere
Mr. Willey says:

"All explanations of the scholastic type seemed to the new
(experimental) school to be merely statements of ignorance
masquerading in philosophic dress, equivalent, in fact, to assert-
ing that things are such-and-such because they are."

I think it will be seen that Mr. Willey's 'explanations' of
explanation are themselves of this type.

. . . "What, since the Renaissance, has been called 'science' . . .
has achieved what it has achieved precisely by abstracting from
the whole of 'reality' those aspects which are amenable to its
methods. There is no point in denying that only thus can
'scientific' discovery be made. What we need to remember,
however, is that we have to do here with a *transference of interests*
rather than with the mere 'exantlation' of new truth or the mere
rejection of error. All we can say is that at the Renaissance men
began to wish for a new life-orientation, and that this involved a
hitherto unthought-of degree of control over 'things'. Accordingly,
the sort of knowledge which dealt with the motions of bodies
came to seem the most real, the most genuine knowledge, and
scientific 'truth' the only genuine 'truth'."

Now this is not 'all we can say' although it is perfectly true that
it is 'all' that the neo-scholastics can say. It is all that Mr. Willey's
contemporary authorities, including Hulme, Maritain and
Christopher Dawson, to mention only a few, have succeeded in
saying. These are among the 'voices' which, says Mr. Willey,
have been raised in protest against the uncritical acceptance of the
'scientific' assumptions. These are the thinkers who have made it
possible for Mr. Willey and ourselves, if we will, "to consider the
two world-views with no antecedent prejudice in favour of the
modern". We should pause and consider first the semantic load
which Mr. Willey's quotation marks, as well as, for example, the

word 'modern', when he employs it, have to bear. For they both subtly beg the question: the quotation marks by implying that the comparative reality we ought to attribute to the scientific or the scholastic generalisation is a matter of unhistorical choice; the word 'modern' by suggesting that the change in the general outlook since the Renaissance is a matter of time only and its inevitable fashions. Whether consciously or not, Mr. Willey in fact considers the two world-views with an antecedent prejudice in favour of the ancient. Whether he means to or not, he has opted for the scholastics. It is not that science abstracts from 'reality' those aspects which are amenable to its methods. Science *is* a method which is imposed on us by reality or the nature of 'things' or experience, if we want to know anything about them at all. It is not true to say that any transference of interests was necessary to make men wish to have control over 'things', although it may be true that more men become aware of a wish for such power if it becomes more possible to attain it. Men have always needed and wished to have this control, from the times when they first hunted or tilled, as a condition of remaining on this planet. They consolidated their hold on their terrestrial circumstances, precisely in so far as any of their shrewder observers noted any natural recurrence, from the Nile floods to the monsoon rains, precisely in so far as their magic or religion became a form of science. We must always oppose this historical tradition of scientific observation to the mystical fortuitousness which the neo-scholastic inevitably discovers in the changed Renaissance outlook. The implication, if not the statement, that at the Renaissance men changed their ideas about the world and the nature of truth simply because they did inheres in all neo-scholastic thinking. This is 'all they can say', since, if we do not admit the hypothetico-observational method of science as the only human test of truth, we have no alternative but to adhere to the dogmatic pronouncements of the most influential authority we can find.*

*The choice between warring authorities is only a secondary difficulty, for our choices are made easily and unconsciously by our purely emotional personality, once we have cut out the difficulties of conscious cerebration.

But apart from that, if we insist that all such changes in the general outlook are thus subjective and arbitrary, it becomes much easier to claim the equal validity of our own prejudices. I quote Mr. Willey quoting his 'protesting voices'. First, from Maritain:

"In the sixteenth century, and more particularly in the age of Descartes, the interior hierarchies of the virtue of reason were shattered. Philosophy abandoned theology to assert its own claim to be considered the supreme science and, *the mathematical science of the sensible world and its phenomena taking precedence at the same time over metaphysics, the human mind began to profess independence of God and Being.* Independence of God: that is to say of the supreme Object of all Intelligence. . . . Independence of being: that is to say, of the connatural object of the mind as such, against which it ceased to measure itself humbly, until it finally undertook to deduce it entirely from the seeds of geometrical clarity which it conceived to be innate in itself."

This, says Mr. Willey, is M. Maritain's version of 'what really took place at the Renaissance'. As I have just said, it is the stock scholastic version and means that men ceased to think purely deductively because they did, that is, that the revolution was purely subjective. I do not know how the last sentence of the quotation helps Mr. Willey, mainly because I am never at all certain what the scholastics mean by Being, except that it has nothing to do with the way anything may be said to exist. But as Mr. Willey has been talking about 'scientific' assumptions and their uncritical acceptance, I suppose that he uses the quotation, as a whole, as meaning that the new contribution of 'Science' was the kind of deductive 'certainty' that geometry was accorded by Descartes and Hobbes, philosophers with no interest in the experimental method, except a somewhat hostile one. This belief about 'Science', with its implication that 'Science' is essentially a false and impious claim to mathematical certitude about everything in the universe, is, as we have seen, both untrue and irrelevant. But it is an essential part of neo-scholastic philosophy.

After this Mr. Willey quotes Christopher Dawson:

"The Western mind has turned away from the contemplation of the absolute and eternal to the knowledge of the particular and contingent. It has made man the measure of all things and has sought to emancipate human life from its dependence on the supernatural. Instead of the whole intellectual and social order being subordinated to spiritual principles . . ."

And then there is T. E. Hulme, who, says Mr. Willey, "just before the war proclaimed, in language of remarkable trenchancy, the death of the humanist and scientific traditions springing from the Renaissance, and demanded what was in effect a return to the ideology of scholasticism. 'As if,' he wrote in 1913, 'it were not the business of every honest man at the present moment to clean the world of these sloppy dregs of the Renaissance'."* Mr. Willey is not the first, and will not be the last writer to confuse such stirring sentiments as these with meaningful and critical observations. Hulme and the others are simply saying that they do not like the fundamental and inevitable development which took an irrevocable step forward about the time of the Renaissance, and would like to check and reverse it. Hulme, I think, realised the suggestive power of prophecy, and believed, not altogether mistakenly, that to proclaim that an anti-humanistic revival was gathering was the best way of inducing one. Scholasticism does still, as Bacon said of it:

"Out of no great quantity of matter and infinite agitation of wit spin out unto us laborious webs of learning. . . . For the wit and mind of man, if it work upon matter . . . worketh according to the stuff and is limited thereby; but if it work upon itself . . . then it is endless and brings forth indeed cobwebs of learning, admirable for the fineness of the thread and work, but of no substance or profit."

Thus it is typical of modern scholasticism that, not being limited, as science is, by the necessity of a return to the verifiable.

*Already referred to on p. 72.

it should organise the fears, the ignorance, the abstractions, the wishes and emotions of human beings, into a 'reality' which presumes to compete with the given and related world gradually revealed to us by scientific method. Scholasticism has seized on and misinterpreted the fact that the majority of workers in the field of physical science at present agree that there are some inherent limitations in their method of observation and inquiry, but still does not pay enough attention to the other fact that this method, depending on an ultimate return to the verifiable, is the only one that scientists recognise. When we come up against a wall, there is no excuse for saying that it is a door. If we persist in seeing doors where none exist, there is no knowing what we may see through them. Whatever it may be, its validity will be purely arbitrary.

There are two maxims which we ought continually to bear in mind—that the fact that our knowledge in any field has come to an end does not mean that we can go on to a different kind of 'knowledge' in that direction; and that authority, however deeply and widely founded upon the wishes and votes of men, is no substitute for experiment and demonstration.

This book is not Utopian. It is not offering a substitute 'religion' of Science, nor any 'belief' in Progress, itself a hypostatical notion. It tries to combat certain recent misconceptions and misstatements about the only method by which we do get public and communicable results (often negative), whose truth can be accepted by all honest people of open mind and sufficient instruction. It does not claim that all the results of such scientific inquiry in all fields are humanly encouraging or sociably desirable, and for the present leaves aside the question of what moral responsibility should be taken by governments and individual scientists for controlling these practical results.

It does, however, claim that to stifle or in any way to limit scientific inquiry as such—and this must be the practical aim of the consistent scholastic—must lead to the death of any hope of finally humanising this planet. In its special bearing it claims that poetry and literature, the arts which reveal in verbal meanings the most intimate and at the same time the commonest experiences of the most sensitive individuals, must, if they are not to wither, establish some positive relations with science, whose method alone reveals to us the structure of the known and knowable. This is particularly so because 'Man', whether we like it or not, is no longer mainly a noumenal mystery, he is a phenomenon in which the area of the arbitrary is being reduced by the same method of observation and comparison, he is becoming an object of *study* about which he himself is beginning to be able to generalise; and poetry and literature is mainly concerned with the nature of 'Man'.

I must stress as strongly as possible that I am not trying to make any pronouncements about what the abstract relations of 'Poetry' and 'Science' ought to be. No statements of this sort can be made. Poets should and generally do absorb what knowledge they need. But poets themselves often feel that they should have a definite relation to knowledge, and this implies that they have at least some assumption of what knowledge is. For example, one could develop an instructive comparison between Mr. Eliot, on the one hand, no doubt justifiably complaining of the want of learning of many young contemporaries when: "they (the older poets) are that which we know;" and on the other, Mr. Robert Graves, who believes that poets have a kind of proleptic instinct, they know by special gift where to find out what they need to know; and Théodore de Banville, who said that poets should include technical and engineering handbooks among their essential reading. The instructional point is the difference between the two underlying assumptions. For Mr. Eliot 'knowledge' is knowledge about literature (and of course theology). For Graves and Banville, knowledge for the poet is what enables him to talk about contemporary living in a way which does not conflict with the daily sense of reality; or about former living in such a way that it still continues to live in a way which we can feel sensibly. Banville and Graves are not necessarily better poets for this, they merely have a better poetic theory, which pays more attention to the fact that poets have by nature, and implication, lively minds and therefore generally are, and probably ought to be, intellectually curious.

As I have said before, it is not an abstraction called Science which is being discussed, except by scholastics, but a method of obtaining knowledge of the world we live in. For the poet this method, even in its departmental applications, may work by altering the whole structure of his experience. It is the nature of a poet to be specially sensitive to *form*, or pattern—Goethe was the supreme example of this—and I think this is what Mr. Graves's 'prolepsis' really means. A poet has an instinct for a living hypothesis, on a small scale or a large one, and in this he is not opposed to, he is parallel to, a scientist. I have said that knowledge is a method; but, more importantly here, knowledge is a *process*, essentially interlocked with living experience and practice, and somewhere along the line of this process the poet must live. Knowledge, of its nature, cannot be made static, and even Mr. Eliot, who hates progress, endangers his poetry, I believe, when he turns his back on process. My belief that to do this is the death of words is dealt with at length in the section 'Poetry and Truth', and there too I have given reasons why I think that the poet who wants an intellectual understanding of something credible about human behaviour should attend to the consortium of psychologists, which exists, though at a minimum, rather than the pronouncements of the Pope or of the whole College of Cardinals. One can say here that psychological science, for all its jargon and limitations, and in spite of its partial subjection, in common with other forms of cerebration, to some forms of philosophical nonsense, has given us new knowledge about ourselves, in the sense in which I am using the word knowledge throughout this book; and that this knowledge has had more direct bearing upon the poet's (and novelist's) world than most kinds. For poets are always feeling their way towards the awareness and the expression of dramatic relations, on the stage or in their own hearts. Denial of observational truth here is something to which not only they but their audiences are most quickly sensitive. The Church's view of sin and responsibility certainly did and does produce vivid Moralities. So of course did the Spanish conception of Honour, another powerful abstraction. But poetic drama, in its great ages, has mostly been about *crime*, which is a matter of social definition. The study of psychology has made the general sensibility towards these themes inevitably humanistic in important aspects. Poets and their audiences now live in a world where they know, however unwillingly and uneasily, that tolerance and humanity are part of the structure of virtue, because they know that criminals are also victims. Sympathy, or rather empathy, with the 'criminal' is what produces the poetical element in drama and in the novel. To try to assert theological paramountcy in the issues of human necessities and shortcomings is to remain among abstractions, an uncomfortable situation for a poet, where he may find himself stranded among verbal aridities. This appears to me to be the case with *The Cocktail Party*.

Mr. Graham Greene, who appears to work so vividly and realistically within an intellectual Catholic structure, is on the contrary successful, I believe, in so far as he remains a human realist. To be suffering and hunted, to be obstinately courageous and obstinately aware of cowardice, is a human and, historically speaking, not uncommon situation. To be mentally tortured about what seems a human necessity for deception is another such situation we can all sympathise with imaginatively. But for this we do not have to believe in the intellectual paramountcy of the ideas for which the priest in *The Power and the Glory*, or the policeman in *The Heart of the Matter*, suffer; we only have to believe that they do, and cannot help suffering. I should say that in so far as we do share Mr. Greene's intellectual convictions we miss the poetry and drama, and I have an idea that that is what he himself feels, at least to some extent. There always have to be one or more characters—for instance Father Rank in *The Heart of the Matter*—who have the function of pointing out that even the Church's dogma cannot cover all that ought to be known and said on the subject of the sense of salvation or of damnation. To my mind, many of Greene's characters, when they come to give any definition of what they mean by sin or virtue, seem alarmingly out of touch with the experiences which actually do cause human beings either the suffering of guilt or the satisfaction of genuine achievement.

Something similar may be said about Mr. Eliot, who seems now to be so Augustinian that he is positively Calvinistic. Only a firm belief in predestination, surely, could account for the extraordinary equation of values in *The Cocktail Party*, where Peter is as morally bound to make a Hollywood film about the decay of the British aristocracy as Lavinia is to stay at home and have a party, or as Celia is to go to Kinkanja and suffer a martyr's death by the startling and not insignificant means of crucifixion.

Calvinism or not, certainly no one connected with the play can be said to be particularly justified by works—not even Mr. Eliot, who has assumed too much behind the scenes and made too big a claim on at least the poetic faith of the audience.

Many poets, from Shakespeare to, let us say, Lorca, whatever lip-service they may or may not have paid to theological religion, have lived, as far as their poetic senses were concerned, naturally, in a naturalistic world, and these remarks are therefore mainly applicable when an intellectual solution of human problems seems to be demanded. But in the contemporary world, intellectual solutions are demanded commonly enough. The relation of poetry, I repeat, to intellectual truth is and ought to be an indirect one, since poetry is the product of a whole experiencing mind. Poetically a too direct relation to any theories which are not yet knowledge, which have not yet altered the structure of experience, is as bad as or worse than none at all.* This applies to scientific as well as dogmatic theories of human nature.

One of the proofs that we are building a genuinely scientific theory of human nature may turn out to be just the capacity of the theory to be absorbed and lived by the most imaginative or poetic minds. The idea of an 'absolute Science' of human nature or anything else, is meanwhile a literary abstraction and—as employed by our idealists, dualists and scholastics—a highly mechanistic one. They confuse scientific method, not only with

*D. S. Savage (*The Withered Branch*) has pointed this out in connection with Auden.

philosophical generalisations about it, but with technology. Living among and often enjoying machines, they now more than half believe that the purpose of 'Science' is solely to produce machines and eventually robots, and forget that its most important purpose is, as always, to ask and answer questions about our life on this planet.

If 'Science' is an abstraction, so, as I said earlier, is 'The Scientist'. That is the main reason, no doubt, why we find him among Mr. Willey's 'voices of protest' against mechanistic and deterministic assumptions, although the voices which Mr. Willey actually quotes are those of two philosophers, Professors Burtt and Whitehead—anyway, of two experts in other fields than those of physical science speaking as philosophers.

To give Mr. Willey every chance we can quote him some professional scientists. Sir Arthur Eddington, like Sir James Jeans, made very distinguished contributions to physical and astronomical science. But, as we have seen earlier, he also committed himself to more abstract opinions which are not essentially different from Jeans's figments, God the Mathematician, the Great Architect and so on. Though Eddington actually disclaimed the possibility of scientific support or proof for religious doctrine, he finished up, as we saw, in idealism and a mystical substantialisation of Mind which is not much less Berkeleian than Jeans's view.

Since these are hypostatical conceptions, relating to the tribal and uncritical Sir Arthur rather than to the objective and scientific Eddington, they have had more effect in confirming the popular mind in its working myths than his scientific conclusions have had in developing and changing its understanding of the universe. The quotation, however, which I have given before, is from Eddington in his professional capacity:

"Physical knowledge is based on observational procedure— more accurately, physical knowledge is hypothetico-observational. . . . This means knowledge of the result of a hypothetical observation, not hypothetical interpretation of the result of an actual observation."

A hypothesis is in fact an imaginative act. Moreover, there is nothing random about experiment. I suspect that when the average scholastic mind thinks the words 'performing an experiment' it forms an image of something like conjuring or even Black Magic. At the back is the feeling, which may even be attributed to the performer, that only God knows what the answer will be, what will pop out of the hat or out of the bowels of the earth. And indeed at the 'Stinks' age when most of the literary scholastics left off their experimental education, God alone did know what the answer would be. If we were then so helplessly driven to blow ourselves up, that may have led to our fascinated and horrified expectation that the 'Scientist' can in the end do just that and nothing else!

One of the most important characteristics of science is its continuity. A scientific worker does not 'perform an experiment', form an abstract generalisation about it and then tell the world that that is what the world is unchangeably like, but this seems to be the way the scientific Aunt Sallies of Mr. Willey and many philosophers are expected to behave. It is much more the case that the scientific worker has an idea what he is looking for, which arises more or less vaguely from the existing body of knowledge in his field, and which is confirmed or not by experimental work. It is a question of clarifying, of giving more and more meaning to experience, so that he and other men may live more and more consciously in the world given to their senses. The world was given and the world will continue to be given. Experiences become more and more related. It is philosophers divorced from the experimental attitude who are responsible for cutting short and killing this extension of consciousness which is the individual scientist's unexpressed aim.

The relation of the two complementary scientific activities has been put clearly by Bertrand Russell:

"The men who founded modern science had two merits which are not necessarily found together: immense patience in observation and great boldness in framing hypotheses. . . . Copernicus, like his great successors, possessed both . . . the test of scientific truth is patient observation of facts combined with bold guessing as to laws binding the facts together."

Furthermore, Russell, at the end of *Human Knowledge* says that adherence to the strict doctrine of empiricism is precisely what has revealed to us the inadequacy of all knowledge. But this gives us no ground whatsoever for claiming that any non-empirical theory based on what we don't know and can't know, would be more adequate.

It seems to me that Mr. Willey has the popular or even newspaper view of scientists, and does not really understand what the scientific activity is. The retorts and crucibles with which Faust ran through the whole of 'Philosophy', although he certainly did not thereby succeed in moving out of the alchemical age, still wreathe their diabolical fumes around too many contemporary minds, at least back-stage. Just about the time that Mr. Willey was probably beginning his adult reflection on the contemporary and modern, Spengler elevated 'Faust' (the Faustian) to the rank of a temporal category. Especially for the readers of Humane Letters, who are unconsciously assured of the brutality and even wickedness of scientists, it has always been confusing that science should be known in the senior university as Natural Philosophy. Whether any of this strictly applies to Mr. Willey's background or not, it is certain that he confuses the special observations of scientists with the hypotheses and generalisations of philosophers and 'thinkers' which may appear or may claim to be based on these observations.

Mr. Willey attributes the Renaissance change of outlook to a mere change in demand—men began to wish for a scientific 'explanation' and no other. This idea is also implicit, as we saw, in Hulme.

To my mind, it is an exaggerated estimate of the power of human wishing to believe that it could be decisive in bringing the scientific outlook to dominance. Nowadays when people talk, as Mr. Willey does, about 'wishes', it is natural to suspect that Freud's unfortunate expression 'wish-fulfilment' is at the tip of their tongue, for use against the opposition party. Hackneyed by everyone and understood by practically no one among the newspaper public, it has by now hardly any use save as a weapon convenient to both idealists and materialists. Freud himself clearly recognised that a wish-fulfilment was essentially an ineffectual wish, a substitute for reality, which consoled for a failure to alter the observable in a desired direction.

That was a classification intended as a basis for the further study of wishes, so that some estimate of their possibility of real fulfilment and of their general relation to observable reality could be made. Freud's own philosophical edifices are not always soundly erected, however good his observations were. There is, in fact, an enormous psychological subject-matter by now, to which philosophers might well begin to turn their training; beginning with what nature has supplied, their own minds. Yet at present hardly anyone, even as part of a philosophical education, certainly not as part of a general education, receives any training in understanding that wishes are a proper and indeed necessary subject for observation in themselves and that, though they are in a different category of experience from that which understands and observes, they are not in a different category from the rest of what is observable and observed in the world. Mr. Willey attributes seventeenth-century science to a change in general wishing. But of course the only wish which ever issues in science is the wish to find out. Mr. Willey's study has taken a wrong turning. It would have been useful indeed if he had examined the characteristic 'wishes' of the seventeenth century and had shown how these issued, not in 'Science', but in substitute philosophies which had no relation to the experimental method, and were unconsciously based on fear and hatred of the wish to find out.

CHAPTER VI

Old Puritan Writ Large

IT is unlikely that Mr. Eliot's reference to the 'dissociation of sensibility', the split between emotion and intellect which characterised poetry between the seventeenth and twentieth century, was, in his own mind, intended to develop into a direct attack on the method and outlook of science, whose advancement has been parallel. In general, Mr. Eliot's direct references to science are slighting but slight. The allusion to the influence of Milton and Dryden which ends the quotation I gave at the beginning of the last chapter suggests that he might have carried on, if at all, with a more literary emphasis. This might have been fruitful. Mr. Willey and others, assuming that the dissociation was genuinely schizophrenic, that is, that it was necessarily pathological, have not been content merely to describe the change in relation which took place among poetry, science and religion in the seventeenth century but have looked round for a toxic agent. This they have found in 'Science'. This in any case assumed, I think, that poetry is primarily, and was primitively, a religious activity. Certainly it was early associated with religion. But primitive religious activity covered a great many functions and forms of apperception which time has separated more or less completely. The imaginative organisation of sensibility was one of them, the kind of inquiry and practice which later developed into science was another. Poets, at all times living primarily in the world of immediate sense, have an underlying interest in both these functions. What discourages them from this sensuous

159

immediacy, this preference for seeing the general only through the concrete and particular, may disqualify them as much for scientific as for poetic perception. It may not be irrelevant or insignificant that Mr. Willey can be found saying:

"What the cold philosophy did destroy was the union of head and heart, the synthesis of thought and feeling, out of which major poetry seems to be born."

The point is that Mr. Willey's cold philosophers, though for him they are destructive of poetry because they base themselves on 'Science', harmed poetry in so far as they, just like any other sort of ideological middlemen, traded in generalisations and abstractions. It is just as harmful for poets to read about 'Science' without due awareness of the kind of abstraction inherent in such literature as to have a staple diet of theology. Both are potted, or lack verbal roughage. Certainly a poet who swallowed Descartes or Hobbes whole and uncritically would do himself no good. But I doubt if anyone ever did. I shall suggest that the issue is one of verbal influences, and that this has been misunderstood by Mr. Willey and others whose interests, whether consciously or not, are vested in the traditional, the theological or the scholastic.

It is particularly to the mechanistic views of Descartes and Hobbes that Mr. Willey attributes the change in the status and value of poetry which took place in the seventeenth century. Though both these philosophers pay lip-service to Christianity, we can agree with Mr. Willey that the absolute dualism of Descartes, the really unbridgeable gap between mind and matter, or thought and 'extension', did probably reinforce

"the growing disposition to accept the scientific world-picture as the only true one"; while "the criterion of truth which it set up, according to which the only real properties of objects were the mathematical properties, implied a depreciation of all kinds of knowing other than that of the 'philosopher'."

The æsthetic psychology of Hobbes may also be described as poetically discouraging. His distinction between Fancy, which finds 'unexpected similitude' in 'things otherwise much unlike', and Judgment, which 'discerns dissimilitude in things that otherwise appear the same', is not only too limited to illuminate us strongly on the whole poetic activity, it is also typical of the one-sided intellectual who feels that he ought to include art in a coherent philosophical system, while he still feels ham-handed in its presence; typical, too, of all those who, whatever their æsthetic sensibility, still have an intellectual axe to grind. Mr. Eliot, for instance, advocating the closed theological system, tells us that poetry is only a 'superior amusement', a view which would not be alien to the eighteenth century, with its generalised, abstract and mechanical conception of poetic language. It may be well that the Hobbesian attitude that "Fancy without help of judgment is not commended as a virtue" whereas judgment was commended for its own sake, has, as Willey says, encouraged the degeneration of poetry.

We may agree anyway that a degeneration followed, while still being unable to go the whole way with another critic, Mr. Cleanth Brooks, who says that it lasted essentially unchecked until the twentieth century, when what he calls the Third Poetic Revolution took place. Throughout the whole of the eighteenth and nineteenth centuries, he says, no successful attempt had been made to heal the split in sensibility. Poets had either accepted an inferior status in relation to truth or science which had forced them to limit their apperception of real objects and accept a specialised range of 'poetic' subjects, those that were suitable for 'fanciful' or generalised treatment, or they had indeed revolted and had attempted to free the imagination from the limiting categories of Fancy and Judgment or generalised 'good sense', but had done so by opposing only another range of subjects, vaguely indicated as 'poetical'. This is how Mr. Brooks sees the Romantics; the Platonic categories of apperception which poets such as Keats and Shelley, and Wordsworth, when he is being professionally high-minded, seem to impose on themselves give him some support. These poets failed, he thinks, in so far as they accepted a specialised status and did not boldly claim the whole of reality for poetic apperception. In effect, he thinks, they were still suffering from Hobbes and his kind, whose influence on poetry Brooks finds as sinister as Mr. Willey does.

"We have abundant evidence of the esteem in which such poets as Cowley, Davenant and Dryden held . . . Hobbes, and as Ransom . . . put it, 'what Bacon with his disparagement of poetry had begun in the cause of science and protestantism, Hobbes completed'. . . . The name (of Hobbes) stood for common sense and naturalism and the monopoly of the scientific spirit over the mind. . . . The weakening of metaphor, the development of a specifically 'poetic' subject matter and diction, the emphasis on simplicity and clarity, the simplification of the poet's attitude, the segregation of the witty and the ironical from the serious . . . all these items testify to the monopoly of the scientific spirit."

We ought to note the expression 'the scientific spirit', which is itself, as we might expect in this connection, a type of hypostasis. Actually it implies that science is identical with its analytical and classificatory aspects. If this were all that could be said about scientific method there might at least appear to be more sense in equating the abstractions and generalisations of a philosopher with science. It would also be possible to agree that such a verbal dilution might well wash the very stuff of poetry, that special concrete grit, out of circulation. But this is not exactly what happens. Not all, nor even perhaps most, poets read *about* science; while, on the other hand, poetic apperception, the apprehension of the universal in the concrete, is something very like the basic scientific intuition.

Mr. Brooks thinks that the Romantics failed to accomplish the needed poetic revolution because they were not witty, they did not succeed in fusing the discrepancies and oppositions of experience, as the Metaphysical poets had done; and that this again was due to the fact that they accepted the separation of truth and poetry, of prose and fancy. I should say, on the contrary, that they succeeded, as they often did when they simply went back to what had always been the poetic muttons, when, for a beginning, they went back to living in their senses and put down what, as poets, they actually saw, heard and smelt; and, not less importantly, when they allowed themselves to become aware of the operations of their own internal world, each poet's mind, with its hinterland of archaic and universal symbolism. This seems to me the specific excellence of the 'Romantics', their inexhaustible contribution to poetic reality. For though with Wordsworth, Coleridge, Shelley and Blake this quality appears in a revolutionary form, so that the Passions need not any longer be confused with the Vapours, but could be written with a small p, described and delivered it appears as a basic quality in many later and modern poets. Verhaeren is a good example. Much critical attention has been given to Mr. Eliot's dictum that "Poetry is not a turning loose of emotion, but the escape from emotion". (In the context, Mr. Eliot makes it clear that he finds it necessarily unpleasant to have emotions.) Now this opposition does not circumscribe the poetic situation. But if we take it in conjunction with Mr. Eliot's other much-quoted generalisation—that the task of the poet is to find the 'objective correlative', in words, of his emotion, we can see what it ought to mean: that the words of a poem contain the particular, concrete and individual shape in which alone we are to experience the poet's 'universal', the imaginative hypothesis which he has formed relating to some aspect of the world. But if he is to recognise this universal and to deliver it in particular shape, it is his business not to escape from his emotions, but to be aware of them with peculiar exactness and intensity. To know what one's emotions are, one must make an act of detachment from them, but detachment is by no means the same as escape. To escape, or rather to try to escape, from one's emotions implies that one ceases in the end to know what they mean oneself, they become irrecoverably private. To detach oneself from them, on the other hand, is a first step towards discovering what in them is representatively human. The end of such detachment is to bring a relatively formless intuition on to the plane of the observable. The poet's detachment results in bringing his emotion on to the level of sensuous apperception, making it move among rhythms and images where other people can see what he is expressing. This effort of conjunction of an inner with an outer world is the greater category and subsumes Mr. Brooks's lesser one, of metaphysical-type wit. The conception does of course imply what he claims—that there are no specifically poetic subjects—but for a quite different reason, that there is no opposition between truth, either of feeling or of sense, and poetry. The idea that there is such an opposition would probably never have been suggested except by philosophers of various schools who always live *ex officio* one storey above the apperceptive and intuitional level of both science and poetry.

There are, it seems, other factors which we must observe if we wish to account fully for the decline in poetic language during the eighteenth century, and these have been consistently under-estimated by Willey and Brooks, and all those who are suspicious of the increase of knowledge.

During the seventeenth century the poet was certainly told, both sharply and frequently, that truth was what was wanted, and that he was a producer of fictions. This was not new, however. The view dates from Plato, and it had provided a flourishing controversy in the previous century. It would be interesting to speculate how far this attitude towards poetry goes with a particular kind of mind, the authoritarian and institutional. Certainly we can say that the authoritarian and institutional kind of mind inclines to think of Truth in the abstract, as hypo-statical and deductive. It is likely, that is, to split our way of knowing sharply into generalisation on the one hand, and observation on the other, and to confer too high a status of reality on generalisation, the 'Universal'. It will be unwilling to return constantly to experience. Hobbes, in fact, who had a poor opinion of the 'Gentlemen of Gresham College' with their 'mean, common' (and probably smelly) experiments, is the type of such a mind. To either the imaginative or the inquiring intellect the word experience means something living and new, one's own experience first of all. To the authoritarian it means essentially someone else's experience, something which has already been accumulated, is traditional, formalised and dead. This kind of mind is the enemy of both poetry and science.

That is certainly true of Hobbes, who comes in for most of the blame for poetry's down-grading during the seventeenth century; and although we find it natural to ascribe 'enmity' to the passionate Hobbes rather than to the mild-mannered Locke, it is in fact true of Locke also. Neither Hobbes nor Locke apparently understood what men of science were up to. Nor did they understand that the concept of knowledge had radically changed. So if we blame them for not liking poetry, let us not blame them under the title of 'scientists'. They were probably still determined, as are many contemporary philosophers, let alone theologians, that philosophy, in virtue of its very abstraction, must maintain the status of a superior *kind* of knowledge.

Locke is described as empirical, but he had as little real interest in genuine experimental method as Hobbes himself, whose philosophy is the final expression of a fear-driven and violently selective dream of 'geometric' certitude. Locke's psychology, no doubt, could not be empirical in the sense we accept today, when we no longer have to rely on individual introspection or the limited objectivity which literature or conversational discussion can give us. We have better techniques of introspection and unlimited comparative data, and we know enough to be able to say that Locke's *tabula rasa* is wrong as a description of human mind, whether we get all our 'ideas' from externality or not. There is no point of experience at which we can say that a mind is blank. This is a mechanistic conception. Locke's psychological animal was just as much an abstraction as Hobbes's 'political animal' and the selection involved was not less personal because it was less passionate.

Both men were enemies of science as well as poetry because they misunderstood or denied the mind's imaginative synthetic activity, which may reveal itself either in poetry or science.

I am convinced that both Mr. Willey and Mr. Brooks are subconsciously aware that what is bad for poetry is the confusion of abstract and deductive systematisation with reality. Surely nothing can be much more abstract and deductive than theology? It is interesting to note that the two deductive systems which are strong enough today to have a bad effect on poetry, those of Catholic theology and Soviet Marxism, also have a bad effect on experimental science.

We can agree with Mr. Brooks when he says that we have had the Third Poetic Revolution, whose:

"importance . . . lies in the fact that it attempts a complete liberation of the imagination. The successful use of prosaic or unpleasant materials and the union of the intellectual with the emotional are symptoms of imaginative power—not, as F. L. Lucas would interpret them, symptoms of the death of poetry."

The poets of the twentieth century, in short, were able spontaneously to heal the 'split in sensibility'. According to Mr. Brooks, this showed that they had ceased to be cowed by the scientific conception of truth which had dominated the late seventeenth and eighteenth centuries and which, he suggests, had been merely by-passed by the Romanticism generally identified with poetry throughout the nineteenth century.

Now how are we to suppose that the poets achieved this victory, this reassertion of poetic values *against* scientific, if that indeed is what they were doing? Certain of them, for instance Tate and Ransom, whom Mr. Brooks quotes, had beliefs and attitudes about the nature of science and its impact on imaginative life, and Tate wrote poems about not being scientific in a way which reminds one of Wordsworth writing poems about writing poetry.

But the best of the new poetry, including Mr. Eliot's, did not come out of this attitude to science or out of any systematised attitude to truth or the nature of reality. It is obvious that systematised attitudes one way or the other do not produce poetry, they can at most produce attitudes towards poetry, and restrictive attitudes at that. An anti-scientific attitude produces beliefs about poetry, among other phenomena, which are not only restrictive, but restrictive in just the same way as a philosophy based on misguided and uncomprehending pro-scientific enthusiasm is said to have been by Mr. Willey. So to the anti-humanist Hulme the important element in poetry is *Fancy*, a dry quality opposed to the more emotional imagination, while to the far from pro-scientific Mr. Eliot poetry is a 'superior amusement'. The word 'superior' even has an Augustan ring.

Thus I do not deny that a restrictive philosophical practice, from whichever wing it comes, is harmful to poets and poetry in so far as it really affects them. The reason is the same in either case. Abstractions are harmful when they get loose among a poet's words. But it is generalisations about scientific activity which are abstract, not scientific investigation and work, in so far as they are allowed to act on and change reality. What happens to language is the point where anything happens at all. In trying to assess any poetic revolution or reaction one ought never to underestimate purely poetic influences, as they are likely to be the most important of all, at least the *sine qua non*. It is therefore strange that Mr. Willey, who gives considerable space to Milton, should treat him as an effect rather than a cause. He studies the Milton who has been affected by 'experimentalism' (to Mr. Willey for this purpose the essence of Milton's Protestantism is 'experimentalism') rather than the Milton who did extraordinary and powerful things to the English language and so acted directly on the cortex and nervous system of *other poets*. Poets in fact are governed primarily by their senses and by what other poets are or have been doing—the second is more often of prior importance. Shelley said that "Most wretched men Are cradled into poesy by wrong, They learn in suffering what they teach in song." It was typical of Shelley's own sidetracking by philosophical abstraction (of whatever sort) that he should make this false generalisation. Far more often, quite buoyant men are cradled into poetry by a fascination felt at what has been done with language in poetry, and by a desire to do as well or better. Hypostatising the common unpleasant experiences of growth into general concepts of 'Wrong' on the one hand or 'Sin' on the other will only delay the process of artistic maturation or of converting these realised experiences into poetic meaning where it is all in the words. This primacy of language is the main reason, one certainly not ignored by himself, why the fortunate and, one may believe, lasting influence on English poetry has been that of Eliot the poet rather than of Eliot the scholastic theologian. For what inaugurated the Third Poetic Revolution, to adopt Mr. Brooks's classification, were facts such as Eliot's vivid concrete and accurate poetic apperception as well as such a markedly technical movement as Imagism.

The poets returned to business. I do not say that they had been unaffected by misconceptions of science. The first business of a poet is rhythmical, auditory and visual receptiveness. He ought not to allow any purveyors of abstract generalisations to harm that receptivity by predigesting his material for him. In the days of Dante the theology of the Church provided a highly visual and, one may say, rhythmical material, created a universe of high imaginative order in a space not previously occupied by the probabilities of physics and astronomy. The material could be realised with sensuous immediacy; it was not predigested. Nowadays theology cannot provide this imaginative material; like other abstractions it has a devitalising effect on poetic language, as it has done with Mr. Eliot's, and takes the grit out of it.

On the other hand, doctrinaire and systematising mechanists, such as Hobbes, while they are just as bad for poets, are often a godsend to the scholastic-minded, since by abstracting from the working generalisations of scientists, they appear to be more 'scientific' than other hypostatisers. 'Matter' in such usage is just as much a hypostasis as 'Spirit'. We have already seen that Hobbes was not a scientist nor particularly interested in scientific method, and though he may for instance have been interested in Galileo's work, there is no sign that he grasped its real importance as an illustration of a new way of looking at things. We know from Aubrey that Hobbes was a favourite companion of the peripatetic Bacon and took down the Master's thoughts. But it is quite clear that the great inductive method made no impression on Hobbes at all. Hobbes may have suffered from Renaissance pride, but he took in little Renaissance science. The 'great patience' in gathering facts which Russell coupled with 'great boldness in framing hypotheses' as characterising scientists was surely lacking. Particularly in the fields of political science and of psychology, one may regard Hobbes's collection of facts as unusually and significantly partial. In the first field, the selective agent was dissatisfaction with his own social and material position, and in the second, satisfaction with his own impulses. He wished for a policy which would make Hobbes secure and for a psychology which established his own aggressive nature as humanly representative.

We must return to our position that poets not only ought to be, but are, influenced more by poets than by any other users of language. What went wrong in the seventeenth century is for the purposes of this discussion a matter of language. It is therefore reasonable, if we want to find a major factor to account for the prolonged dullness, artificiality and poeticism which blighted much of eighteenth-century poetry, to look for some historical accident of language itself. I do not agree with Mr. Willey that the phenomenal Milton is to be understood either as an effect of 'experimentalism' or as a successful evader of a harmful dissociation between 'truth' and feeling, which had already taken place. I think on the contrary that Milton the poet was the portentous and comet-like cause which accounted for much of the devastation in poetic language. One can and does admire his music, rhythmical genius, sense of form, intellectual ease and power, and even his 'gigantic loftiness', while still believing that it would have been better if no one had tried to imitate him or even perhaps to learn from him in the sense that most great poets can be learned from; and that his influence alone was enough to inflict a hampering sense of inferiority on a whole poetic generation even if there had been no false æsthetic from philosophers to spread the damage.

This is not to disparage Milton, merely to say that he was not the sort of poet who starts a successful school. It may be that we can say this of any artist whose individual achievement was both highly specialised and near perfection in its specialisation. There is nothing more to be done in that particular direction. In diction there are thus two orders of poet. The other order, the one to which Milton did not belong, is of those whose use of language starts a new mode of apperception of the ordinary living universe, and includes some major poets—for instance Dante—and many minors. We can only quote Shakespeare and Milton. But we can inherit the language of Dante and also of poets who, compared to him, were minors, even though its radio-activity diminishes from generation to generation. Blake and Tennyson were among such minors who alter both poetic and common experience more than the rarer monumental and finished masters. From their originality or uniqueness, from their own special qualities both of vision and diction, not in any case readily separable, much could be learned. More indeed could always be learned and bequeathed by contemporaries, and would be perhaps, if they thought less about grading so-and-so as a major or a minor, and more about illustrating the fact that the poet was valuable. A minor poet may dwell more fully in the universe of general experience than a major poet with a more comprehensive vision, even if the frame through which he looks at the world is esoteric or unusually personal or abstract. From a major such as Dante on the other hand there may be so much left over that other poets who do not share his vision, can still learn to see a different view with the same eyes. Of Milton one can almost say that the substance of his great poem exhausted the language available for it.

Mr. Willey is more interested in the fact that Milton achieved a great poem which was recognisably religious, at a time when the critical spirit was unfavourable to religion, than in the poetic means by which the poet projected his vision. So we do not hear very much from him about what poets thought of the poet Milton —just as we do not hear what scientists thought about poetry, or science. We hear in general only what philosophers thought about the imagination. He quotes at length the unduly complacent remarks of Thomas Sprat (1635-1713), in his *History of the Royal Society*, on the advancement of modern learning, which among other triumphs has 'removed the rubbish of ages' and 'freed our understandings from the charms of vain apparitions'. Disliking fairies, animism and primitive beliefs in general, Sprat also disapproved of the figures and tropes to which these had given substance. These he regarded as the chief characteristic of poetry. He recommends to his readers a clear and workmanlike prose as the highest means of modern communication. But, says Mr. Willey:

"He would have been staggered to know that one hundred and fifty years after him, men not out of their senses (though poets) would be lamenting that glory and loveliness had passed away; that later on, the recovery of every fragment of information about primitive beliefs would be the life's work of a distinguished succession of scientists; and that an outstanding mind of the third century after his would be passionately striving to bring back the pre-scientific consciousness, and reanimate the world which science had 'killed'."

In another context these words would mean that, ignoring the rationalisations of philosophers, scientific method in our century advanced normally into the psychological and anthropological fields which previously could not be investigated, but I do not think that that is what Mr. Willey intended by them. I am not sure whether the allusion is to Frazer or Jung. If to Jung, it probably occurred to Mr. Willey because Jung's implied attacks on causality have made him hopeful of finding support for the Two Truths theory, rather than because he has been willing to estimate Jung's contribution on the archaic contents of dreams in its context with the rest of experimental investigation in this particular branch of psychology.

If the allusion is to Frazer, the same essential estimate applies. Both were "striving to bring back" material for study which had been lost or disregarded, or to reveal new material. At least that is the actual value of their contributions. They had no reason to suggest, and Frazer certainly did not suggest, that contemporary human beings ought to return to a pre-scientific mode of consciousness. To study the thought-processes of savages it often helps us if we think ourselves imaginatively into their skins, and neither scientists nor poets should rob themselves of this enriching empathy. But we should not put on their skins. Such extreme identification is indeed characteristic of the totemic stage in human development and we might come too late to find that meanwhile the clothing of our right minds had been stolen. At best we should be beachcombers and at worst rabbits.

Willey has confused the subjective with the objective, one of the commonest of current philosophical mistakes. He has confused a belief or an attitude or a mode of consciousness with the study of that belief or attitude or mode of consciousness. What is implied is that he cannot grasp that psychology or anthropology are 'scientific', and indeed in his use of the word they are not. For behind his assumptions, exactly as in the case of Mr. Norman Nicholson, quoted on page 59 lies the old test-tube-and-caliper myth. This has no more bearing on the method by which we live truly in a given world than Sprat's panegyric had.

Thus for the study of poetry and indeed of the 'dissociation in poetic sensibility', Mr. Willey's remarks on Sprat and his like, which precede a consideration of *Paradise Lost*, do not tell us anything very illuminating. "This great religious poem" appeared in the middle of the seventeenth century when "all these forces scientific and philosophic, working together for 'Truth' " were "tending more and more to show up the traditional imagery of poetry and religion as obsolete, phantasmal or fictitious", and Mr. Willey feels that he has to account for what must have been either an astonishing integration or an equally astonishing disregard for the need of integration of poetry and 'truth'.

"It is true," says Mr. Willey, "that Milton's outlook seems never to have been influenced by the post-Restoration and Royal Society atmosphere; he had nothing about him of the 'experimental philosopher' . . . but Milton was 'protestant' to the core, and this meant that in the moral sphere he *was* an 'experimenter,' and had the same disdain for all that was not 'truth' as the natural philosopher had in his. . . . Intolerance of all except what seemed to him *most real* was, then, a characteristic of Milton which linked him with his age and vitally affected his choice of poetic subject. . . . There still remained one source and one only from which the seventeenth-century protestant poet could draw images and fables which were not only 'poetic' but also 'true': the Bible."

We may agree with Mr. Willey that Milton, as far as his poetical work was concerned, did not pay much attention to scientific discovery, or rather—for this is what Mr. Willey is talking about in practice, as we have seen—to the philosophical and speculative conclusions which had been rightly or wrongly drawn from it, although from his prose writings we can find that he was aware of what was going on in the sciences and interested in it. We may further accept that to draw his fable from the Bible gave him a sense of unchallengeable veracity, because so far no serious challenge in this field had been issued by scientific investigation.

Concern for truth and even more importantly for every human being's right to know available truth, and even to discover it for himself according to his abilities, was in the air and had been for a very long time. We will, if so inclined, regard the Reformation as the injected poison of the Renaissance, if not exactly part of its 'sloppy dregs'. However inherited, or acquired, concern for truth and for liberty of thought and expression were in Milton's blood and bone and the speculative results in *Paradise Lost* are no doubt individualistic and unorthodox even from the Protestant angle. We must note however that Raphael answers Adam's inquiry about the relative merits of the systems of Ptolemy and Galileo only doubtfully, concluding with an exhortation to intellectual humility which should satisfy the most authoritarian. But it is, I suppose, this idea of Protestant individualistic inquiry which regarded itself as limited only by the authority of the Bible, to which Mr. Willey is referring when he calls Milton an 'experimentalist', while describing his great religious poem as an 'isolated volcano' or a lucky accident of time, which no one could have expected in the seventeenth century, when intellect and emotion, truth and imagination, were at the point of dissociation. Milton, as it were, only just got it in, before the vandals of reason and empiricism fell on the cosmogony and history of the Bible and reduced them to literalities, subject to the need of verification.

I think that Milton *was* in the line of 'experimentalism' and it must be clear that I also think that it was natural, inevitable and right that he should be so. Once he had appeared, all those striking characteristics which made Milton might have been seen as historically conditioned and therefore inevitable. This does not mean that they all sprang from a single root or that they were all directly connected with each other. Something, we agree, debilitated poetry. I think that a vital part of that something was Milton's successful exploitation of language, not the 'experimental' in Milton's thought and view of life.

It is common, especially with anti-humanists, to lump experimentalism, individualism, rationalism, liberalism, protestantism and even capitalism together in this fashion. But an individual may be connoted by any of these attitudes and activities without necessarily sharing in all or any of the others. If Milton, as poet, felt comfortable in relation to the 'truth' (as Mr. Willey prints it) of his subject-matter, we cannot take that as meaning that those who employ scientific method in any field, including that of biblical criticism, ought to drop it in case they make poets feel uncomfortable, or even that the use of any scientific method whatsoever is wicked. Accepting that Milton was both a poet and, in morals and psychology, something of an 'experimentalist', we might take that, instead as evidence that great poets are great poets, for one important reason, because they characteristically try to integrate their poetry with truth; that is, they try first to integrate themselves with their experience, emotional and intellectual. If they fail, they may conceivably also feel that their poetry has failed, not that they have been misinformed about the nature of existence.

We cannot know that Milton, if he had lived in one of the difficult centuries which have followed the seventeenth, would not have been able to find the imaginative equivalent for the contemporary conditions of life, would not have been able to make a new and different effort of integration. It seems to me highly likely that he would have been able to make this effort successfully.

He was in one important respect at least more typical of his immediate age, less of an 'isolated volcano', than Mr. Willey indicates. What Milton thought about 'Science' might or might not have been similar to, or influenced by, what Hobbes and other philosophers thought about the subject. What Milton did have in common with them was something which I refer to for convenience as Puritanism, although I mean by the term something at once more special in origin and more general in psychological application than is usually meant. Critics of all kinds who have observed the severe and 'lofty' quality of Milton's powerful uniqueness, have used his 'Puritanism', in the more commonplace sense of the word, as an explanation, and have either ignored or been made merely uneasy by reminders of his Renaissance sensuality. I think that the Puritanism is, indeed, for this discussion, the important quality, but that the essential in Puritanism can be described as a preference for the Old Testament over the New.

The dominant view of *Paradise Lost*, especially among those critics who have no great interest in grinding a theological axe, is that the Christianity expressed in it is far from strict orthodoxy. This is true, not only of Blake and others who have commented on Milton's at least covert weakness for Satan, but of Saurat and Tillyard, who have compared the theological implication of Milton's poem with his professed theological beliefs and also with the theology generally accepted as orthodox. Mr. C. S. Lewis, who has a theological axe to grind, tells us that *Paradise Lost* is an overwhelmingly Christian poem and largely dismisses the imputation of unorthodoxy.

I think that, when we consider the *poem* and what has got into it, what Milton *thought* or anywhere stated that he thought is secondary. The *feeling* of the poem is not essentially Christian, if by Christian we mean related to what Christ is reported as saying in the New Testament, and we must not let Mr. Lewis and his like obscure the issue with a false emphasis on intellectual orthodoxy. Milton like other Puritans took his stand on the Bible, which means on the Bible as a whole—Mr. Willey will perhaps grant that a belief in the 'veracity' of the Bible implies also a belief in the Bible's unity. It is observable that in the psychological attitude which this generates, the Old Testament becomes dominant as an emotional factor. We observe this clearly when Puritanical reformers thump the Bible and do not merely take their stand upon it.

It is not only orthodox Christians or Biblical scholars who can observe that the Bible is in fact not a unity; that there is a radical change in psychological and social meaning between the Old Testament and the New while, more importantly, as a child can often see, they are in their most fundamental conclusions even contradictory. The Christianity of Christ was a totally new pronouncement about punishment and sacrifice.

Whether Milton was a Satanist, "of the Devil's Party without knowing", whether he was theologically an Arian, believing that the Son was inferior to the Father, and other similar questions are interesting according to one's speciality. But unless we see them in relation to a more fundamental attitude in Milton we shall miss both the literary and the psychological significance of the poem. We shall also miss the significance of some contemporary re-actions to it, Mr. Lewis's for example, with everything that those imply about the nature of 'orthodoxy'.

What the poem is about is *punishment*. That is also in fact what the contemporary 'orthodox' and neo-scholastics, with their emphasis on the Fall and on Original Sin, are talking about. The awareness of 'Sin', or of Original Sin or personal Sin, is the expectation of punishment, a main preoccupation of Hebrew theology; and the attempt to justify the ways of God to men always means the punishing ways of God to Man, because it is not necessary to 'justify' the love of God. This justification is also a Hebraic compulsion.

It may not appear very striking to say that *Paradise Lost* is about punishment. But it is a striking fact, and it is worth our while to remember that punishment, in the old tributary and retributive sense, is not only *not* an integral part of Christianity as stated by Christ, but that his main purpose was to supersede it. Two thousand years of 'Christian' history have consisted largely of intellectual and practical manifestations that human beings in general cannot without great difficulty understand this simple and profound revolution. The many gentle and mystical interpretations of the ideas of sacrifice and atonement must not mislead us. When we start to formulate our ideas about human nature and about man's place in the universe, we are predominantly liable to talk in fact about our own most primitive fears and passions, the shadows of which we dimly perceive and try to objectify. As a result, our theology, by whatever name we call it, reveals itself as still tied to the God of Wrath; patriarchal, aggressive, tense, aware of danger within and without, particularly aware of the danger of love, and deeply preoccupied with payment of a more or less material kind, which ranges from out-and-out simony to merely telling one's beads, or to the various neurotic compulsions.

Preoccupation with sin, one's own or other people's, also has the mechanical quality which subsumes it under payment in kind. For the belief in Original Sin is psychologically a *tribute*, a mechanical confession that we are incurable, and that therefore we must pay endlessly in order to be allowed to live.

One may readily understand how St. Paul and the early theologians of the Church became dominated by the death of Christ and saw it out of due proportion to his life; but one should not fail to note how this negative interpretation, with its emphasis on Sin, hatred of sexual life (which means in practice Hate) and punishment, has foisted itself on the whole of explicit theology since. When we build intellectual structures, we all drive more and more towards the crudely mechanical and away from the life of imagination and experience. The scientist, the poet *and* the ordinary person who is making any conscious effort to find out about human life by living it are all concerned in checking this drive. For many purposes of communication we have to abstract from experience and imagination, but we must always be aware that we are doing so, and we should try not to kill our symbols. When we try to turn them into Absolutes, we do kill them, for an Absolute is just that which is never experienced either in our imagination, our inward awareness of emotional existence, or in our observation of the world around us; and the average human mind can do nothing with it except substitute some crudity of sense-perception whose grossness is in proportion to the degree of abstraction.

The symbol of Christ's redeeming Blood illustrates both this general human attitude towards all symbolism and the unconscious retrogression of theological orthodoxy, since Christ, to a psychology more compatible with the Old Testament than with the New. Because that is what we can see, we think much more readily of blood as something which is shed than as the circulating medium of life. It has been comparatively easy for the orthodox to associate it for us with violence and death. We may say that it is thicker than water, but when we use it of kinship it is one of our worn and automatic words. We have to imagine it flowing in battle or in crime, if we are going to make a song about it or even to reach the creative level of the detective story. The redemption by blood too easily becomes a very mechanical and economic notion, not morally superior to the cruder Old Testament beliefs about sacrifice and atonement, which were essentially payment. Those who infect Christian feeling and psychological truth with the notion of an absolute Original Sin, whatever they may tell us about Matter and Spirit, are trying to import a Thing into the Mind. Such a very material stain needs a material agent to cleanse it.

Christ's reference to his own blood occurred at the supper which celebrated the Passover, normally a feast of thanksgiving for deliverance. For two centuries after his death, the Eucharist was celebrated as an Agape, or Love-Feast. However much Christ's view of the Last Supper was dominated by his premonition of his own death, we may reasonably conclude that the more positive and living symbolism of the Bread and Wine, the idea of sharing one's substance with the brothers and the beloved, was not obliterated from his mind any more than from those of his disciples. Such a poetic awareness of life continuing and circulating is more in consonance with the gospel of love than later interpretations have been, however orthodox.

The efforts of Reformers in religion have usually been directed towards recovering the truth of Christianity, the actual meaning of Christ's words behind the current theological misinterpretations. But they have repeatedly failed and have stopped short at some new justification of the hatred of opponents, in their more abstract theory, and some rationalisation of their own guilt, as far as their practical precepts are concerned.

The most unarguable meaning that Christ's words have is the biological observation that 'We must love one another or die', but this is seldom marked in any new outbreak of orthodoxy. As I continue to point out, our most recent orthodox are far more concerned with establishing codes of behaviour and belief than with helping any of us to live in the actual world around us. It may be that they know, as we all do, that to love one another at present, as heretofore, appears impossible. But it may still be necessary for survival that we should learn to do so and it serves nothing to offer people instead mere talismans of salvation.

Puritanism got no nearer to the psychological truth of Christianity than any other reforming movement, to the idea that the fundamental sacrifice human beings must make, if they would be rewarded by learning to love, is of their *self*-hatred, their compulsion to *self*-punishment; but it may have stabilised the human burden by giving a new range of objects on to which hatred could be spread.

Milton's puritanism then cannot be understood in its perennial significance for poetry and for human life, if it is treated as an historical accident, merely as an effect of a contemporary outlook, which has been accorded a capital P, although this is the way in which it is generally treated by literary critics. Puritanical austerity has many embodiments and it has often accompanied periods of 'greatness' (of rising or successful aggressiveness) in a nation's history. Towards Christianity, as towards everything else, it is a Spartan attitude. It does not always, by any means, deny itself splendour. But it does always tend to repudiate anything which may be called 'effeminacy', and this too often has included the more passive and sensuous kinds of awareness which are necessary to poetry and art. Hence the occasional view that poetry and music are mere accomplishments, the perquisites of the young ladies in the drawing-room and directed towards their temporarily relaxed admirers. This view when it arose did debar these arts, because of the accompanying situation of young ladies, from making any authoritative pronouncements about life as a whole. That is an extreme situation, but whether the view expresses itself in the form that poetry is a 'superior amusement' and whether it is promulgated by Plato, by Mr. T. S. Eliot or by a Victorian novelist, we can reasonably suspect that, in spite of the wide differences of philosophical and æsthetic outlook, the old Spartan and puritanical spirit is at work. Secretly this spirit is always over-concerned with 'greatness', a concern which masks an excessive self-assertion. This, if it becomes obsessive, is bad for poetry and many other things. It makes one progressively blind to *goodness*, which, as Aristotle remained aware, is always of its kind. One cannot *aim* at sublimity without missing one's way or falling into bathos. It is a by-product of looking where one is going in the circumstances of a splendid imagination. Milton's 'gigantic loftiness' was the effect of a powerful intellect and an exquisite sensibility in a unique combination, and therefore, though it awed his successors, it was the one quality they certainly could not imitate.

This Spartan or puritanical attitude, with its accompanying loftiness and contempt, is really what is dominant psychologically in many of the writers and thinkers whom Mr. Willey blames for being at least fellow-travellers with 'experimentalism', in Hobbes particularly as well as Milton. It is in fact opposed to the experimental, which is a humbler and more passive attitude, and it therefore works against both science and poetry. According to

Mr. Willey, Hobbes, for one, disliked the fictional in poetry because he liked 'scientific truth'. It would be much more accurate to say that Hobbes plainly disliked poetry (as so many people do) and was interested in preventing it altogether. A similar effect of Puritanism in Milton merely made his attitude to the elements of poetry dangerously selective, at least by the time he was ready to write *Paradise Lost*.

It is not at all surprising that something which also expresses itself in a contemporary dislike of graven images and of stained-glass windows should be paralleled in a poet's apperception by an avoidance of the more spontaneous and idiosyncratic kinds of imagery, since these often originate internally and unconsciously. From present-day psychological investigation we learn that repression works against the merely non-rational nearly as much as against what appears to be obscene. It is obvious that without the Reformation we should not have had Puritanism in the formulation of a sect: and because Puritanism is also an attempt to escape from dogmatism by exercising the right of private judgment in relation to available sources, those with a bias in favour of authority have found it easy to connect it with the humanistic and experimental outlook. A logical result of dogmatism, of Hulme's Two Truths system, or of any attempt to oppose an Absolute to the scientific field of free experimental inquiry, is that we are left with 'stills' of human mental history, selected and static aspects. These leave out of account the way that all manifestations of formal belief, including Catholic Action and Communism alike, apart from the merely reactive element inevitably present in everyone's formal beliefs, are part of a shuttle movement. It is interesting to speculate how far one can carry one's disapproval of history. Why stop at the Renaissance? The doctrine of the Fall must contain the implicit delusion that human history somehow, somewhere, *ought* to have been different, and the feeling, probably unconscious, is discernible, for example, in Mr. Eliot's *Ideas* and *Notes* about Christian Society and culture.

But it does not much matter where we stay our regressive wishes as far as human history is concerned. If we deplore a total way of looking at the world which has grown up historically as a reaction to that given and unavoidable world, there is only one meaning which can be attached to this emotion—that we wish we could extirpate a section of human experience, or of reality. In our public thought, as in our private emotions, this is a dangerous delusion. The Two-Truths system has been taken over as a description of *reality* by Mr. Willey and others, who ignore the fact that it is a denial of past reality, since it implicitly denies the way in which we have come to know anything *about* the past. The failures and evils of history since the Renaissance are all traced to the experimental spirit which, working in historians, has given us the facts we distort, and an experimental spirit in any subsequent manifestations is then used as an excuse for their wholesale identification.

I said that the Puritan tends to repress his childish imagination just because it is childish, if for no other reason, for childishness may be felt to be disabling in a competitive world. We may justifiably look on the present competitive world as evil but we should recognise that its evil is the result of many strains, not all of them in themselves evil, and many of them necessary. We should try to save ourselves from identifying any one of them we happen to dislike with all the evil which we discern. It is by now almost a commonplace of writers on social history to identify Puritanism with Protestantism, Protestantism with individualism, indivi- dualism with the experimental spirit, and the whole lot with aggressive competition in economic life. But this is to telescope history and all the natural stages of inheritance. Mr. Willey has achieved just this sort of identification—of the experimental spirit with all our present psychological evils.

The result is that he sees most of the poets of the seventeenth century as sired by experimentalism out of inferiority, but Milton as if, with the same sire, he had had a different dam, the absolute truth of the Bible, that saved him from the verbal penury his poetic half-brothers fell into.

My family tree reads rather differently. I find it more illuminating to see in Milton a fortuitous marriage between an experimental spirit which is natural to a poet, and the repressive psychology of the Puritan (how his puritanism had lived through a rich and strange past with classical learning, we can leave out of the story). This marriage begot the uniqueness of Milton's language, and the third generation was the repressed and distorted eighteenth-century poets who could only compensate for their feeling of inferiority by a pretended identification with their dominating sire.

It would be a juster view than Mr. Willey's to say that the practical results of science have restored to the modern poet much of the material, if he cares to use it, which the Puritan in Milton, and in others, rejected—an extended, a magnified world of fascinating objects either grim or beautiful. A poet ought not perhaps to be primarily so 'gigantically lofty', so purely Attic. Much of Milton's poetry springs from this aspect of Puritanism, and his great technical achievements ought not to blind us to the rejection involved. While we admire the resources and devices with which poetic efficiency, making something positive out of its very limitations, has achieved just this particular triumph of negation, we ought to wish that these limitations should not be compulsively adopted.

The mental archetype is still present with the neo-classicists, however different the verbal results may appear. No one could say that Mr. Eliot, for instance, has learnt obviously from the Milton he used to deplore, but certainly he might have learnt much about the poetry of austerity, of sensuous rejection, while his underlying mental approach may not be so very dissimilar.

It is difficult to draw a comparison which is based on a common negation, but a study of the imagery and dictions of Milton and Mr. Eliot does suggest that the poetic apperception, in either case, is related to a similar form of intellectual selectiveness; it derives, as I say, with Milton, from his Puritanism, and with Mr. Eliot from the sense of personal and also of Original Sin covering the general human situation, which has received a structure from his theology.

The qualities which result were always characteristic of Milton. With Mr. Eliot they have become more marked as his scholastic and theological persuasion has become dominant, overgrowing the sharp and concrete apperceptions of his earlier poetry. They are a preference for the abstract and general term, coupled with an avoidance of the particular and concrete, a reluctance towards fused metaphor, and another characteristic which, when it becomes a disease, as it does, we can call audilism. This is referred to later.

Milton's language, as we all know, was heavily Latinised. This was probably not due to the mere habit of classical scholarship. It seems certain that he had the poet's sense of the history of words and that when he used such expressions, as the 'palpable obscure' or the 'vast abrupt' or the 'torrid clime', his mind's eye was well aware of thick darkness that might be felt and that *shielded* all objects from sight, or of something steep and broken away, or of parched sand. I do not say that Milton would have written better or as good poetry if he had kept mainly to words of Anglo-Saxon origin or even if he had not laboured rather to exclude them. We cannot say that a thatch would look well on a classical temple. Milton's Latinised usage was architectural and the neatly jointed Latin constructions are as essential to his poetic technique as the meanings and sounds of the words. But the Anglo-Saxon words are the natural language of an immediate and concrete apperception which lives willingly in the present of time and the presence of fellow-humanity. There is no good poetic reason why a poet should not prefer or think he would prefer the past nor why he should like his fellow-beings—there is every reason, on the contrary, why his awareness of all aspects of the present should be exceptionally critical. But it is poetically dangerous if he does not like using his senses to obtain the most precise awareness of what that present is. Milton's Latinism put a verbal veil between himself and contemporary, that was, living, reality. The result is literally monumental, static, relating more to the acoustical medium of stone than to the word becoming flesh, and to the past and dead rather than to the continuing present and future.

The characteristics of diction and imagery which I have mentioned spring directly from this attitude of abstraction and sensuous withdrawal—withdrawal, that is, from the concrete and in particular from the sharply visualised:

> "First in his east the glorious lamp was seen,
>   regent of day, and all the horizon round
>   invested with bright rays, jocund to run
>   his longitude through heaven's high road."

Or

> "Meanwhile the tepid caves and fens and shores
>   their brood as numerous hatch from the egg, that soon,
>   bursting with kindly rupture, forth discloses
>   their callow young."

There are one or two quotations which are worth while giving here, under the general heading of abstract language, from Adam's instructional conversations with the Archangel Raphael, because of the comparison they invite with Mr. Eliot and also because of a possible contrast with Dante, whose philosophical or theological passages seem similar, but serve, I believe, a quite different intellectual structure and a form of apperception which remains consistently poetic. For example:

> "The swiftness of these Circles attribute
>   though numberless to His omnipotence
>   that to corporeal substances could add
>   speed almost spiritual."

Or

> "He ceased. I lowly answered:—'To attain
>   the highth and depth of thy eternal ways
>   all human thoughts come short, Supreme of Things.
>   Thou in thyself art perfect, and in thee
>   is no deficience found. Not so in Man,

> but in degree—the cause of his desire
> by conversation with his like to help
> or solace his defects. No need that thou
> shoulds't propagate, already infinite,
> and through all numbers absolute, though One';"

Such passages, which attempt, often with borrowed means, to round a poetic vision intellectually, can fairly be paralleled with Mr. Eliot's

> "Time present and time past
> are both perhaps present in time future,
> and time future contained in time past.
> If all time is eternally present
> all time is unredeemable".

Or

> "In order to arrive there,
> To arrive where you are, to get from where you are not,
> You must go by a way wherein there is no ecstasy.
> In order to arrive at what you do not know
> You must go by a way which is the way of ignorance.
> In order to possess what you do not possess
> You must go by the way of dispossession."

Or

> "It seems as one becomes older
> That the past has another pattern, and ceases to be a
> mere sequence—
> Or even development: the latter a partial fallacy
> Encouraged by superficial notions of evolution,
> Which becomes, in the popular mind, a means of disowning
> the past."

Both these sets of quotations seem to me to be apart from the author's purely poetic vision, although they may well be part of his general philosophical or intellectual vision; hence their coldness and prosaic quality. Mr. Eliot has given much consideration to the problem of the philosophical poem and, according to the Italian critic Luciano Anceschi, has shown signs himself of wishing to write the poetic equivalent of the *Summa* of our time. Whether any poet from Lucretius onwards has ever really solved the problem of writing a *whole* philosophical poem, rather than one of whose philosophy is the string on which the poetic beads are strung, is doubtful. Dante seems to me to be the only poet who is not much in doubt. Théodore de Banville, one of the extreme advocates of the 'poetic moment', went so far as to say that the chief way in which the poet shows his real poetic artistry is in his production of the *chevilles*, his filling of the interstices between these moments of 'pure' poetry. Milton, according to this test, succeeds more obviously than Mr. Eliot. He has succeeded, as usual, in making a self-pastiche—of his own rhythmical and verbal music. Mr. Eliot, on the other hand, may have got a theological tune on the brain, but he hears it only himself. It is not unusual for him thus to hear inwardly an incantatory music from rather abstract words.

The importance and the similarity of the quoted paragraphs lie not so much in their substance as in their kind. They both show that any didactic or intellectual statement must at least be beyond argument, it must not be in such a form as to tempt prompt intellectual dissection, if it is to be poetically effective. Browning's dialectic trick—of providing his own questions and answers—had something to be said for it, but it can hardly be repeated, since it provided him with the major individual quality of his style. As Mr. Eliot himself has said, an intellectual structure must become a *vision* to be valid as poetry—it has to be *seen*, not reported. Poetry is the felt truth of experience, where the reference can be immediate, and very great poetry is the macrocosmic vision which has also this immediate validity. For an intellectual poet this means absolute conviction, which again implies an absolute intellectual authority. Since history catches up on philosophies so much more quickly than on poetry, this vast equilibrium is very improbable. Nothing was much more unlikely than the intellectual conjunction of Aquinas and Dante. But Dante's intellectual vision was in fact a whole with his poetic, and his use of language, in particular of imagery, is the sure indication of this. (Shakespeare I believe had at least an equal wholeness though his vision was humanistic and, as far as one can see, materialistic.) Though there are long passages of didacticism in Dante, with Beatrice as celestial school-marm, we are never far removed from the concrete and vivid image which makes these poetically real and which shows that for Dante the mythos was all part of a living truth which to the poet was only an extension of the living world around him.

Both Milton and Eliot are characterised by the absence or the avoidance of the fused metaphor. The earlier Eliot of course did occasionally use such metaphors often forcibly (cf. the yellow fog in 'Prufrock'). Now he substitutes the particularities of prose ('Dry Salvages') or the associative symbol. Descriptive particularity, I know, has always been a characteristic of Mr. Eliot's style. It is common also to good prose and, allied to dryness and wit, it is natural and legitimate in a poet who is trying to show that poetry needs a clean surface sometimes more than it needs 'depths' and always more than it needs decoration. Precision is, after all, the goal; and where the unlimited has become the meaningless, then the localised and time-pointed actuality, which is the particularity of prose rather than of poetry, may be the best kind of precision. But not all depths and distances are false. It is unnatural that a poet should never feel the need of that special kind of precision which is the most central rendering of many dimensions of apperception, that 'real presence' which is given by the fused metaphor. That it is one of the most natural poetic activities is shown by the fact that it is the chief poetic contribution to ordinary speech.

The associative symbol which abounds in the later Eliot—'the rose of memory', 'rose of forgetfulness', 'the bowl of rose-leaves', 'the blue of larkspur, blue of Mary's colour', has certainly nothing to do with *precision*—it is also not an attempt to make the experience of the world, or even of the community which is held together by the particular language, present and real. And though, with Mr. Eliot, it refers to a society in time, that does not necessarily make it universal. It may well have no more than archaic force, and be as specialised as the emblems of freemasonry.

The fused metaphor on the other hand always appeals to living sense; and some dislike of living sense, with considerable implications about a too partial view of the world's intellectual structure, is what we may suspect when it is conspicuously absent, as it is with Milton and with Eliot. In Milton the predominant image is the classical simile, which selects, intellectually, a common quality out of a host of dissimilarities. This is at best a purely denotative decoration, a kind of abstract illustration, with the maximum suppression or avoidance of associative overtones. We can say that it is centrifugal from precision, and just because of this want of fusion of the many dimensions of qualities. Even if the effect is pleasing—generally only with a certain flat quaintness —the reader's mind shoots off at an unlimited tangent and has to be brought back on a string to the main poetic intention. For instance, Milton's well-known description of the Fiend's shield and spear:

> "The broad circumference
> hung on his shoulders like the moon, whose orb
> through optic glass the Tuscan artist views
> at evening, from the top of Fiesole,
> or in Valdarno, to descry new lands,
> rivers or mountains, in her spotty globe.
> His spear—to equal which the tallest pine
> hewn on Norwegian hills, to be the mast
> of some great admiral, were but a wand——"

which not only takes us on a tour of Italy and Norway but gives us a rapid view of the recent Galilean advances in astronomy, with a glance at the condition of the British Fleet, before coming back, rather disconcertingly, to the main picture of the geology of

Hell, which had quite ceased to affect our associations. Milton's poem can support this immense diffusion; but the instinct of a poet writing anything less spacious, is, I am sure, against the blind and tentacular wavings of such similes. Matthew Arnold in his shorter efforts does not do them well. The point, however, for us is what they represent, how the underlying attitude to experience affects the choice and type of imagery. Eliot, as I say, now avoids imagery, and he does not of course substitute any such form of mere decoration. But his earlier apparent similes are worth looking at, as they serve to illustrate the change which has taken place in his later work. I call them 'apparent' because the 'like' or 'as' is merely syntactical, they are actually metaphors fused with the whole real and living scene which is present to the poet's eye:

> "Like a patient etherised upon a table."

> "Streets that follow like a tedious argument
>   Of insidious intent
>   To lead you to an overwhelming question."

> "And you see the corner of her eye
>   Twists like a crooked pin."

In all of these the compared characteristic is provided directly by the visual and temporal setting which has given the poet his immediate inspiration. Or, to put it another way, the imagery is revealed still in the matrix of experience, not detached from it. Dante's images which use the syntactical simile form are also often really fused metaphors. This is the more remarkable since, as I have said, they often had to deliver a purely intellectual content and might well have remained merely illustrative and also, like Milton's, something of a poetic archaism. I have indicated above why I think it was uniquely possible for Dante to achieve this. Here I shall merely give examples of the way in which I think it was achieved:

"quando incontrammo d'anime una schiera
   che venian lungo l'argine e ciascuna
   ci riguardava come suol da sera
   guardare uno altro sotto nuova luna;
   e si ver noi aguzzavan le ciglia
   come'l vecchio sartor fa nella cruna."

(When we encountered a troop of spirits, coming towards us along the verge, and they all of them peered at us as if it were by the faint light of a new moon; puckering their brows at us as an old tailor does at the eye of his needle.)

At first sight, one might say that the old tailor squinting into his needle's eye is as remote from the theme as the Tuscan artist from the burning sands or marl of hell. But this is not really so. All the emphasis remains on the act of peering, and this old professional concentration is all within the total dramatisation of the urgent need to 'make out'. It clinches and at the same time universalises the actuality.

And then from Canto V, the famous double image of Paolo and Francesca:

"E come li stornei ne portan l'ali
   nel freddo tempo a schiera larga e piena,
   cosi quel fiato li spiriti mali . . .
   E come i gru van cantando lor lai
   faccendo in aere di se lunga riga,
   cosi vidi venir, traendo guai,
   ombre portate della detta briga——"

(And as the starlings in the cold season are borne away by their wings in a broad close flock, so these lost spirits were borne upon the blast. . . . And as the cranes depart with their mournful chant, making a long streak in the air, so I saw them come wailing, the shades tossed on this turmoil.)

This is by no means a mere point-to-point comparison of kinds of physical flight. It has many dimensions of similitude—helplessness, the pathos of being a creature, waning light, all used to extract and concentrate the maximum emotional meaning from the vision of this flight of dead lovers, and to evoke for us at once its automatism and its naturalness.

Finally there is the particular and significant use which Dante makes of his imagery, to make an immaterial conception part of a vision which, though ecstatic, is still earthly:

> "Cosi parlòmmi, e poi cominciò 'Ave
> Maria' cantando, e cantando vaniò
> come per acqua cupa cosa grave."

(Thus he spoke to me and then began to sing 'Ave Maria', and still singing vanished like a weighty thing through deep water.)

Or

> "La mia letizia mi tien celato
> che mi raggia dintorno e mi nasconde
> quasi animal di sua seta fasciato."

(My bliss holds me hidden in its radiation as a silkworm is hidden in its silk.)

Of course, images of light and translucent media are dominant in the 'Paradiso'. I doubt if this is purely emotional and associative. It was an attempt at exact description. Abstract vision in poetry needs to be implemented by as much sensuous experience as possible. But there are limits to the possibilities of finding earthly 'objective correlatives' with which to fuse the ecstatic. Dante does wonders within the limits of his cosmogonical information. *His* sensibility was not dissociated—even his traditional and orthodox symbols and his mystical mathematics were feelings to him. That does not mean that he can always convey the feelings to other sensibilities which through lapse of time have become alienated from what was knowledge to him. But the starry dance of the twenty-four Fathers of the

Church (in 'Par.' Canto XIII) at least reminds us of something more wooing than the odour of sanctity, while Dante himself, becoming roselike at one point:

> "E io a lui 'L'affetto che dimostri
>   meco parlando, e la buona sembianza
>   ch'io veggio e noto in tutti li ardor vostri
>   cosi m'ha dilatata mia fidanza
>   come'l sol fa la rosa, quando aperta
>   tanto divien quant'ell' ha di possanza'."

(And I said to him "The affection you show me when you speak to me and the warm intention which your glowing conveys to me dilate me and encourage me as the sun does the rose when she opens to her fullest extent.")

is moving because he does so in the natural atmosphere of emanation and sunlight and response to warmth. Moreover the symbol is defined anew by the sensuous materiality of the whole poem, in which the vision is always that of a living eye. It is in no sense archaic and shows no signs of wearing down to cliché as even the classical and verbalist roses of the Pléiade did. Finally there is the great vision of the vast white rose of the empyrean in Cantos XXX and XXXII. At the point at which we feel the full poetic force of the whole great Vision of Dante, we are all inside this Celestial Rose and the bees are a simile for ourselves.

But still the similes are limited—mostly roses and bees, and light and water. Hell and Purgatory are more like home; and the chief benefit of this familiarity for poetry is that it supplies the imagination with inexhaustible and detailed sensuous nourishment. In poetry, distance may lend a kind of disenchantment.

CHAPTER VII

Poetry and Truth

IN treating Donne and the Metaphysicals, Mr. Eliot picked the
right problem, but whether he has stated it accurately or not I
doubt. Mr. Eliot refers to the disintegrative effect of the new
learning upon Donne.

We can certainly recognise the effects of the collision in 'this
sensitive mind' between the old tradition and the new learning,
but may question whether or not 'disintegrating' is the right
adjective when we are referring to the poetry. We ought to
consider the earlier Donne apart from 'The Metaphysicals', none
of whom, to judge from their poetry—the only valuable way to
judge them in this connection, passed through anything like his
curious rich vivid and analytic naturalism with its extraordinary
range and subtlety of experience. Then we shall realise that in this
earlier work, Donne did indeed represent a tradition which was
later broken and one which the twentieth century, in so far as it
has done anything good at all, has been trying to restore.

For these poems are in the true tradition because they are
'Renaissance'. What neo-scholastic critics dislike in the 'Renaissance' spirit, which gave us humanism and science, is precisely
that which gives us the most complete poetry. That is, fidelity
to experience, which makes either pure Ugliness or pure Beauty
irrelevant categories. The most important experience for a poet is
full experience of his own human nature. This does not mean that
the good poet is in the mothlike condition of the girl in the song
who went up to London 'just to see the bright lights gleaming,

'Eeding not temptation'. It is not important that experience should be sought, only that it should not be denied. In between Donne and our older contemporaries the split in sensibility has been real enough. The older psychological tradition, based on orthodox theology, with its abstract conception of sin and its over-emphasis on suffering, frustration and emotional defeat, could not in fact come to terms with the new learning. Since that was primarily a method of inquiry, it had no inherent limitation and must eventually be applied to 'human nature' itself.

The result was that the old tradition tried to defeat the new learning, and largely succeeded. But poets, in so far as they *are* poets, are always the last victims of this defeat, not the first. Anything that we can subsequently recognise as a 'Renaissance', however minor, of poetry, always turns out to be a resuscitation of the 'Renaissance spirit', of the wish to find out and learn, to receive experience, and to enjoy the experiences one has received. Fundamentally, the poetic impulse is an openness to perceptive living in the human world, which is enjoyable to the poet because it is willing. It is a law of human psychology that the full realisation even of conflict or opposition in oneself, or in the external world, brings a peculiar satisfaction, if what is realised is some form of the truly inevitable, if it is a vision of law or pattern. This must have been included under Aquinas's '*Quod visum placet*'; and Shelley, in the *Defence of Poetry*, implied the same thing:

"For from an inexplicable defect of harmony in the constitution of human nature, the pain of the inferior is frequently connected with the pleasure of the superior portions of our being."

This potentiality of enjoyable realisation of their own duality, of the opposition and alternatives which are inherent in their own impulses, is the basis of men's capacity to adapt themselves to the laws of the physical universe and of their own natures. This capacity remains perhaps in most men only potential; it is readily misinterpreted and perverted, and its development in any considerably depends on the spread of genuine knowledge among all. But a developing capacity for realisation of law and inevitable pattern leaves less and less room for Sin. Again I am not talking about Crime, which, I have already stated, is a matter of social definition.

Sin is a subjective state, interpreted in some variety by those who experience it. But in practice it is the sense that man is a doom-laden freak on his own planet, who can never know what he is or where he stands. Sin may be described theologically as the condition of being cut off from God, but its realisation requires belief in the Devil, in essential Evil, very much more. In essence, the neo-scholastics, with their belief in Original Sin and their Aunt Sally attacks on the *possibility* of moral progress, are trying to deny that men have this inherent potentiality for adapting themselves to the laws of nature and the laws of the mind, that men can by any means acquire the freedom to recognise their own necessities. I am not a Christian Scientist; and I do not deny that, up to date, pain, cruelty and ugliness are more typical of our human planetary performance than are their contraries. But the cure lies, not in the conviction of Sin, not in the war of body and spirit and the crucifixion of the flesh, but in the enjoyable admission of our own dialectic. The essential of a poet is that he should be someone who in some degree does realise and enjoy this representatively human dialectic. If that is not his essential nature there is no way of accounting for our love of tragedy. If it is, one must ask what on earth Mr. Eliot means by the 'escape from emotion', as a definition of poetic activity.

We can say that poetry which we can reasonably recognise as such is always an attempt, however limited, to prevent or to heal the split in sensibility which our unwillingness to be conscious forces upon us. The victory is generally only partial or occasional. The bulk of the work of most poets is a record of failures, though the failures of a poet are generally interesting and instructive enough to other poets. Only the rarest poets have been able to live continually in a positive relation to the available knowledge of their time. In the battle to force words to express the experience of natural law, a vision which is at once whole and concrete—and this is what every poem from the smallest lyric to a full-scale drama is really trying to do—abstraction wins again and again. The mind of the poet, which should engage gear between the inner and the outer rhythm, slips its clutch. Even the innovating poet too often devises some mechanism of language, some technique of welding rhythm and imagery with emotional certainty, only to lose the hang of it, though someone else may make it serviceable again. Words become ghosts, and poets parody their earlier full-blooded selves when they cease to be able to look directly at their emotional experience—and this may happen at any time in a process which is essentially dialectic. It did happen with the elderly solemn Wordsworth, with the Coleridge, who let himself be seduced by Germanic idealism, as well as with Swinburne whose words, as Mr. Eliot has said, developed a 'life of their own'—and a strange ectoplasmic kind of life indeed. Yet this is not peculiarly a disease of those poets who may be lumped together as Romantics. The Romantics—Shelley, the early Wordsworth, Beddoes, Blake, Keats—had in fact only this in common, that, far from soaring into the empyrean and beating their poetic wings in a void, they were all trying, unconsciously, to unify sensibility again, to see with the true poetic vision, which is tragic, naturalistic and myth-making. Whatever any of them may or may not have said or thought on the subject of 'Science', each of them in his most successful work was trying imaginatively to be faithful to his experience and to work inductively. They did not fail more frequently than other poets. When they did fail, they failed as other poets have done—the range of merit may run from Crashaw to Mr. Alfred Noyes—through confusing abstraction with experiences.

What Mr. Eliot means by 'dissociation of sensibility' is further illuminated by his references to philosophical poetry. There are some in his essays on Dante, on Shakespeare and Seneca, and on Blake. In all of these there is the implication, if not the statement, that the poet need not, in fact had better not, do any thinking for himself, as it is on the whole bad for his poetry. A philosophical poetry is certainly permissible, we are to understand, but, as Lucretius and Dante illustrate, the poet is safer, as poet, if he borrows his philosophy. Now there is a curious but not untypical æstheticism in this view which results, I think, from Mr. Eliot's fixated conception of the split in sensibility. He is determined to see it and to maintain it as a 'split' rather than to see it and to accept it as a natural dialectic conflict in the development of poetry and of human mind, the resolution of which might be fruitful and renewing.

He says in the Shakespeare-Seneca essay: "You can hardly say that Dante believed, or did not believe, the Thomist philosophy," a statement which does not tally with the quotation he himself has given from Dante's *Convivio* (in the essay on Dante in *The Sacred Wood*)—"the principal design is to lead men to knowledge and virtue, as will be seen in the progress of the truth of them."

Again, in one of those fraught references which one would like to see analysed, Mr. Eliot says: "It happened that at Dante's time, thought was orderly and strong and beautiful." There is really nothing fortuitous about thought, whose 'strength' depends on its truth, its tie with given reality, while its order and beauty are qualities dependent upon this tie.

Referring to Blake, Mr. Eliot says his "occasional marriages of poetry and philosophy are not so felicitous" as either his "naked vision" or "naked observation". Mr. Eliot quotes: "He who would do good must do it in Minute Particulars," etc., and goes on "One feels that the form is not well chosen. The borrowed philosophy of Dante and Lucretius is perhaps not so interesting but it injures their form less."

This is highly arguable. The Blake quotation has at least an excellent gnomic quality; it is one of those statements which are always being proved valid in the course of individual experience, and this gives it the same kind of poetic merit as we find in much of 'Proverbs' and 'Ecclesiastes' where ancient traditional wisdom may for any one of us at any time be transmuted into the warmth and felicity of personal rediscovery. Parts of Dante, on the other hand, which paraphrase the borrowed philosophy extremely concisely, and often with the greatest skill, are surely often very crabbed as poetry. This is not to deny that the borrowing philosophical Dante can be translucent and felicitous, or that the private philosophical Blake can be boring, bewildering and vaporous. But it may be that when either is good or bad, in the sense of poetically acceptable or inacceptable, the underlying cause is the same for both poets. Credibility may after all have something to do with it.

What seems to follow from all Mr. Eliot's references to the relation of thought and emotion, and of philosophy and poetry, is the implication that when a 'split' or an opposition occurs, when, for instance, an objective situation which demands critical application of the intelligence, from those who can think without undue inhibition, arises in history, as one did in the seventeenth century, the poet's duty as poet is to retire from the battle upon the charity of some system which will give him intellectual food and shelter for the rest of his days. Only one system can really afford this vast intellectual philanthropy, although within the Soviet frontiers a rival philosophical system is claiming a similar abstract inclusiveness with equally bad results for poetry and art. Many poets do avail themselves of their institutional privileges in their old age. However, it is then revealed that there is no pure charity about it. The benefits of the system are really only for those who have contributed most of their poetic working life. They will not become believers in time to receive their orthodox poetic dole, unless they have been preparing to believe for a lifetime. Belief, to produce poetry at any level, must be emotional assent as well as intellectual assent. One way of unifying sensibility, of 'healing' the split between thought and emotion, is to give up thinking for oneself. But this necessarily impoverishes *sensibility*. The tragedy about giving up curiosity and speculation is that one will never know precisely what one has given up. For the ability to think freely is a necessary condition of feeling freely and fully also. This does not mean that what is popularly called 'Free Thought' is necessarily free. It may be a safeguard against sensibility and tied to moralistic internal prohibitions. Thought that appears to be liberal and in favour of 'Humanity' may well be an attempt to impose a new abstract orthodoxy. For 'negative capability', as Keats called it, the capacity to be sensible of reality freely, that is, passively, without trying to interfere with it, flickers and often goes out, even with poets; how much more so with the majority of human beings for whom, by training and habit, mere 'activity', mental or physical, is felt to be much more valuable, indeed more virtuous than thinking and feeling.

All this leads to the question whether or not any general statements can be made about a characteristic relation of poets to their subject-matter. There has always been a wide range of opposing opinions as to what constitutes the basic material of poetry, what poetry is 'about', if it is about anything. Behind this there is the further question: what is the relation of poetry, through its subject-matter, to objective knowledge or truth? These questions should be kept distinct, but it is clear that they are closely related. When a critic has strong and positive beliefs about objective knowledge, about the nature of reality or truth, he usually has little doubt that poetry should be in a positive relation to this universal frame, and he is inclined to estimate 'greatness' or poetic merit always with this extra-poetical standard in mind. Plato, for instance, thought that poets had inevitably a wrong relation to their subject-matter; that they were liars, because they treated the absolute and divine, too often, in terms of the temporal and fleshly. This is an attitude which continually recurs, in whatever disguises. At the other extreme, I. A. Richards makes a sharp opposition between the scientific and the emotive uses of language which implies that whatever any poet is trying to tell us, it is not in any meaningful sense true or false; its value to us is not the value of a piece of information which might enable us to correct either our actions or our direction. Then there are all the rather more negative definitions: Sidney's, that poets are not liars because they 'nothing affirm', or Coleridge's 'willing suspension of *disbelief* for the moment which constitutes poetic faith', or Dr. Leavis's 'pseudo-statements' which seem to lie somewhere in between active deceit and suspension of disbelief. But on the whole the consensus of critical opinion has been against the idea of Art for Art's sake and in favour of the belief that some highly important relation always exists between poetry and 'truth' however difficult it may be to define.

With Mr. Eliot one can detect a curious divergence between the critic of poetry and the critic of society. As the first he inclines towards Valéry's extremely æsthetic view—poems are, after all, written with *words*. If this means that every successful poem is a piece of verbal one-way traffic, that the words never get out again quite the same, I suppose one can accept it, because that is only an intensification of what is always happening to language. But I think this view shares a defect with all those to which I have referred above, except Plato's, which is in a quite different category: that is, it does not take into account what the words do to our emotions, in poems their most considerable function. By this I mean that poetry is a language of extreme precision; and that implies that it has a frame of reference and therefore a standard of truth. But its frame of reference, as has often been observed, is not the 'dry biscuits' or 'tulip-streaks' of particular facts, but general or symbolic situations. They are not general or symbolic because they are hypostatical, but because they are existent and common. They exist, for a large part of all our lives and for all or some of our lives, below the verbal level. Poetry brings them into verbal life and does so more accurately than any other use of words can do. Our test of poetic truth comes after the poetic event. We cannot judge a poem *a priori* because we become aware of the frame of reference, one of our own basic emotional situations, only after reading the poem; but the frame of reference is there.

The second Mr. Eliot, the critic of society, nowadays with Plato applauding somewhat hollowly from Limbo, departs from his æstheticism and looks at poetry and literature partly as a social phenomenon, from the angle of what he himself believes to be true. In a statement which I have already quoted, Mr. Eliot tells us that literary criticism must now be completed from a definite ethical and theological standpoint, and concludes that "the 'greatness' of literature cannot be determined solely by literary standards; though we must remember that whether it is literature or not can be determined only by literary standards."

To his own and to his readers' advantage, Mr. Eliot might elucidate this last sentence, written with his common evasive prudence which is so often nearly prudish. He should begin by trying to define what he means by 'greatness'. As it stands, the sentence seems to suggest the 'dissociation of sensibility'. At what point does the literary evaluation merge into the theological? Either 'greatness' is a point on a continuous scale of values and we had better try to find some more central standard which is not purely literary, or else literary evaluation and theological evaluation should each stick to its own business.

My own view is that poetry cannot be evaluated from a purely semantic angle, nor on the other hand from the angle of any particular subject-matter, claiming objective 'truth', in its own terms. But I claim that there is a relation, and an intimate one, although indirect, between the objective and categorical use which he makes of his ordinary and public understanding and the poetry which a poet produces. The more generalising capacity he has (the more he is an 'intellectual'), the more obvious this will be. Poets are not and on the whole never have been naïfs. Moreover they always in some important sense belong to their age, even if they claim to detest it. Hence it is probable that the analytical and comparative faculties will be much more highly developed among our contemporary poets than among their forebears of only a hundred years ago. I do not mean that contemporary poets have better brains or even more learning than earlier poets. It is obvious too that Coleridge, for example, had powers of abstraction and critical comparison which were above the average of any time. I only say that a higher capacity for abstraction and critical comparison is now necessary for a useful and general education. The 'meaning' and applicability of the abstractions of scientists and mathematicians cannot now be left out of account by the poet. I do not believe that he can retain the romantic alternative of just disliking them. For outside his ken and control they really decide, in a very important degree, what sort of person he is. They decide among other things the fact and the length of his life, and much of the quality and content of the emotion with which he lives it.

Words are symbols, and therefore as a means of communicating our experience they are inherently imperfect. They always exist at some degree of abstraction. But since this is their natural defect, the best effort of the poet and the scientist alike, as well as of the ordinary man when he is trying to be exact, is directed towards continual awareness of the fact that, as the late Alfred Korzybski said: "Words are not things."

This is not so obvious nor so simple as it sounds. If we think of the Nominalist-Realist controversy and of the problem of the reality of universals, we see that a large, perhaps a major, part of philosophical discussion has centred round the opposition of words and sensuous experience. The controversy is by no means ended. A scientific inquirer seeking exact communication tends more and more to leave words behind and to take to mathematics. This is true even in the social sciences. Unfortunately it means in our day that he leaves more and more of the possible audience behind. The result has been that, left to themselves, they generally begin to gossip, anyway to talk about something else, unaware and unwilling to become aware that they are doing so. More unfortunately still, the ordinary man, especially when he has become the advanced political animal, can live on an inflationary circulation of mere language for too long, quite unaware that he has been off gold for years.

If we believe that poetry has still some important human function, that it cannot be described, with such lamentable want of definition, as 'a superior amusement', we must also believe that a poet cannot neglect 'meaning', the way in which words are tied to experience. We must even believe that he has a more serious duty, not a lesser one, in this direction, than the ordinary person, comparable in its own way to that of the scientist. Loss of the continual awareness that 'words are not things' may account for a great many immoralities, from bad style (including the style of the 'split sensibility' from which, we all agree, we have suffered since the seventeenth century) to false philosophies with their pernicious effects on social life.

That the poet's relation to meaning is, of all, the most difficult to determine, does not mean that it does not exist.

The contemporary philosophical interest in semantics has developed side by side with and at about the same pace as the movement to revive scholastic thinking. They may be called the poles of contemporary awareness of our intellectual predicament. Both have a long historical development behind them. In fact their opposition expresses the basic conflict of western philosophy. I stress the fact that it is contemporary, because Valéry's view that poetry is made with *words* predominates among modern poets and because some reaction to the statement that 'words are not things' is implicit in this view. Scholastic thinking implies that Words are some sort of Things.

The semantically trained inquirer has ceased to ask questions, anyway while he is functioning as a philosopher, to which experience shows that he can expect no answer, and lives in the world of statements. He considers the relation of these statements to each other and to sensory experience, which may be direct or which may depend on further statements made by other people. The acceptability of these further statements will in their turn depend on their relations to each other. That is, they are acceptable while other questions do not arise which cannot be resolved by further resolutions into 'meaning', by finer analysis of the relations of the statements concerned to someone's sensory perception. The semantic inquirer lives in a human and historically determined world of maximum probability. 'Meaning' is in fact just this 'World', the relations between the tacit or explicit statements made by visible human beings—whose behaviour implies a social and biological past, itself capable of further and further analysis and realisation—about the perceptions which they believe themselves to have or their forebears to have had. They constantly test their beliefs by their very statements and by their discussion of these statements. It must be remembered that the semantic standard of verification is not perfectionist. There is inherent, on the other hand, in scholastic thinking a demand for such an absolute—at least from the opposing school. The scholastic-minded are known, for example, to adduce that history is unverifiable. In other words, historians expect to work by collection and comparison of data, by analysis and elimination, and also by their contemporary understanding of human motive and conduct, all normal inductive and deductive methods. They do not work by necromancy, summoning their subjects back to write their books for them. Scholastic thinkers forget, as good historians and the semantically trained do not, that history is about the *past*. The past, like the future and also the present, is part of the world of maximum probability. Here pride and perfectionism, it seems to me, are on the part of the absolutists. Behind them is the old fantasmal hankering for a universal knowledge.

In the semantic world of probability there is plenty of room for error and correction. But many statements, according to the semantic view, will not be part of this world, this web of human and historic corroboration. They are 'noise', something like the radio operator's 'static', they come out of the ether and return to it, they affect our nerves but not the network of our communication. This is the semantic classification of most of the terms which scholasticism (and idealist philosophy) use; for example, God, Being, Eternity, Sin and Mind (as opposed to Body).

However, just because he recognises another *use* of words (which he opposes to direct meaningfulness), the semasiologist may be tempted to regard poetry as a dumping ground for these otherwise unemployable 'noises'. I have never found I. A. Richards's distinction between the communicative and the emotive uses of language wholly satisfactory. It apparently gives the poet latitude to use any words he likes (including those mentioned above) and not only to give them some sort of meaning but to re-define them within his own poetic context. At the same time it seems to reveal a curiously absolutist view of language. Words, after all, are all the time, both in poetry and prose, becoming subject to redefinition, for this is the organic behaviour of language. Also implicitly, in the very vagueness of this view about the 'emotive', Richards gives up the attempt to classify poetry, at a much earlier stage than usual or necessary.

I suggest, on the contrary, that while the relations which he makes between his words and statements may be special, unusual, and also circumscribed or even isolated by the poem, the poet is even more concerned than any other user of words with 'meaning' —in the semasiologist's sense of something which is verifiable. Certainly it is the experienced fact that the poet works through emotion. Perhaps we could have even greater certainty on this point if we were clearer as to what emotion is. But it seems to be some physiological disturbance accompanying experience, visual or auditory, or a combination of these and of other forms of perception, which has *not* yet been analysed out into conscious and intellectual statements. Theoretically it would be possible, I believe, to take any poem, from the intensest lyric to the most unified drama, and analyse it into a number of statements, no doubt approaching infinity, which would cover its total meaning. Of course I have no wish at all to deny that the poem would vanish in the process. But that is the point. The poem achieves its poetic effect by choosing its moment of concentration, of 'representation' of meanings, which are, as it were, visible to the poet at that point, that moment.

How can we say that the poem's meaning is in any sense verifiable, especially when we can thus see that by continuing the analysis too far into verifiable statements we lose the poem itself?

I think that the poet's relation to the verifiable is certainly never one of making atomic statements. He is rather like a fisherman who has caught in his net—the poem—a shoal of statements which were swimming towards a verifiable meaning. (This, let me add, has nothing to do with F. R. Leavis's 'pseudo-statements'.) Moreover, to go back to the metaphor, the shoal was naturally spawned and was proceeding to its natural biological work of growth, reproduction and participation in biological process. In other words, something with all the complexity of the organic was 'given' in experience and the poet caught it in words. I do not think that the point of attachment to an external verifiable is unimportant or that the poem is merely a matter of self-coherence. That is what Dr. Leavis's 'pseudo-statements' suggest. I think that a poem always 'means' something, that it is always trying to communicate some form of experience, even though in the end, because the words and the feeling are inseparable, the communicated experience may be different from the one which caused the first stimulation.

In an enormous number of cases, perhaps with the majority of not overlong poems which have lingered in the world's memory, it would not occur to us to undertake any verification of the reality of the poet's emotions, of the accuracy of his references or of the truth of the general statements which may appear in the structure of the poem. Doubt does not enter in any more than it does when a normal acquaintance tells us that he has lost his mother, or fallen in love, or has just recovered from an operation. I have deliberately chosen examples which would cause some slight, at least social, difficulty in verification, so as to make a rough analogy with the mood in which we 'believe' a poem. We react in each case with immediate sympathy. There is no visible reason for believing what is said, there is just no reason for doubting it.

But on the other hand a great many poems, and perhaps the majority of long poems, include in their structure references to the 'world' of general statement, from opinion to some form of philosophy, and here there is always the probability, indeed we may say the inevitability, of contradiction.

I say inevitability of contradiction since it is just because 'truth', the only truth that we have, is a method of discovery, that it cannot be completely divorced from historical circumstances. A long period of intellectual stability giving a static appearance to 'truth' will have clear advantages for some poets and may indeed provide a comfortable framework in which great poetry may be written. Another kind of poet of an inquiring (and answering) turn of mind may work out such a system for himself, though it will tend to be less stable and will probably be useless to other poets. Dante is an example of the first type, and Wordsworth of the second.

This may seem to suggest the opposite of what I intend: that truth is so entirely relative to epochs that it does not matter what beliefs a poet adopts or, much more serious, that he should work only within a framework of beliefs which has been laid down by an external authority. If one really believes that there can be an external 'authority' for truth in the sense, in which the word is used by the neo-scholastics, it is indeed logical to try to restore the framework of beliefs as it was at the time when, for the poet's use, it worked best. Unfortunately we have had in our time plenty of evidence of the working of authoritarian systems. Authority as used by the neo-scholastics does not mean merely moral authority, it means authority with the power of sanctions. Mr. Eliot, in his various attempts at definition of a 'better' society, always, to my mind, dodges this issue. It should be clear, however, from quotations which I have already given that he must favour some form of 'censorship'. I use this word in a dual sense which increases rather than splits its significance. The first is practical and political. A Church cannot work as an intellectual author-ity without limiting the freedom of intellectual inquiry, either actively, by some form of 'index', or passively, by a *distractive* education. The second meaning is psychological, even Freudian. By their emphasis on Original Sin, the Fall and other concepts which are repressive of emotional truth, Mr. Eliot and others are helping to restore a moral atmosphere which hinders the growth of sanity and indeed of charity. And, as far as we can see from contemporary authoritarianism, of poetry also.

The point is not 'authority' but belief. Intellectual authorities are only valid, and indeed healthy, for poets and everyone else, when they do not seriously defy belief. The 'authority' of science is based on probability, not on 'certitude'. For this reason, the fact that truth is relative makes it more and not less important what beliefs a poet adopts. Certainly in a philosophical poem of any scope, the development of objective truth, which is a method of discovery and therefore historic and progressive, may break down much that previously seemed acceptable as its poetry.

Mr. Eliot has referred to the *Divine Comedy* as the finest *structure* of emotions that we have ever known. This statement should be taken in conjunction with the other one made by Mr. Eliot, that we cannot say definitely that Dante did or did not believe the Thomist theology and cosmogony.

If we regard the poem as primarily a 'comedy', a single dramatic presentation of the resolution of the soul's despair and conflict in a happy vision of order, peace and significance, then we may say that it is a fine structure of emotion, if not indeed the finest. But Mr. Eliot says 'emotions'. It is certainly true that in the 'Inferno' and the 'Purgatorio' there is recorded the widest variety of human feelings and passions. These become resolved into the single predominant emotion, beatitude, of the 'Paradiso'. The dramatic presentation is *not* carried over from the 'Inferno' and the 'Paradiso,' we do not see the resolution of the despair and conflict of Paolo and Francesca nor even of Belacqua and the other Purgatorial characters who, though they are certain of eventual redemption, are too slothful to wait for it in perfect hope:

> "Ed elli 'O frate, l'andar su che porta?
> che non mi lascerebbe ire a'martiri
> l'angel di Dio che siede in su la porta.' "

(And he said, 'Brother, what is the use of going up? For the Angel of the Lord who sits at the gate would not let me proceed to penance'.)

It is true that the poet Statius, an interesting and moving character, is described as purified and ready to rise up to Paradise, and he actually accompanies Dante and Virgil on the last Purgatorical stages, and is invited by Beatrice to join Dante in the final ascent. But after his original introduction he seems to be intended mainly as a sample of salvation. Apart from Beatrice's arraignment of Dante for his earthly disloyalty, and Dante's confession and repentance, the human interest in the last cantos fades into beautiful and discarnate abstractions of theology, which are in continuity with the 'Paradiso'.

The resolution consists entirely in Dante's vision of an underlying universal truth or meaning. This resolution is not achieved by dramatic means internal to character. It is achieved by purely intellectual means. The 'Paradiso' taken alone is didactic. It is emotionally satisfying to its readers—and I claim must also have been so to Dante himself—in so far as it is intellectually satisfying, in so far as it answers the questions posed or implied in the 'Inferno' and the 'Purgatorio'.

I do not see how we can deny that it mattered to Dante whether he believed or did not believe the philosophy on which his poem is based. And it matters to us whether we believe or do not believe. All of us, whether, like Mr. Willey, we believe that truth is an answer to a demand for emotional satisfaction; or whether, like Mr. Gladstone, we regard a preference for the 'Paradiso' over the 'Inferno' and the 'Purgatorio' as a test of poetic taste; or whether unlike these two, we believe that the approach to truth is unified and scientific and that there is not a special order of theological truth, have still something in common. We are all in fact made uncomfortable by poetry whose statements challenge verification, much more when we can discern flat opposition to the truth.

We have reason to suppose that Mr. Gladstone* ("Ah, there's my test!") was much more sensitive to the emotive than to the scientific use of words, and because of his theological bias it was comparatively easy for him to confuse poetry with mystical vision.

Mr. Willey has a more difficult task. The reader will remember the quotation I have already given:

"The spots on the moon's surface," Mr. Willey wrote, "might be due, theologically, to the fact that it was God's will that they should be there; scientifically they might be 'explained' as the craters of extinct volcanoes."

*Quoted in Morley's 'Life'.

The spots which vex Mr. Willey's vision are the same as those which Dante, in Canto II of the 'Paradiso', asked Beatrice to explain. It is legitimate to assume that in order to maintain the feeling of the poem's unity with truth, Mr. Willey would be willing to revert to Dante's cosmogony—and indeed to something even vaguer and less scientific. Neither Dante nor Beatrice are satisfied with the 'explanation' that it is God's will the spots should be on the moon. Both give a 'rational' explanation according to the lights of Dante's time. But they go a good deal further, for Beatrice in the process of refuting Dante's explanation that the spots are caused by relative density or rarity of the moon's substance, so that the reflected light of the sun has a lesser or greater distance to travel, suggests that he should undertake an experiment with mirrors, to settle the point. For, as she justly observes: "Experiment is the fountain-head from which flow all your arts." This recognition even if incongruous with the rest of the *Commedia's* philosophy, is sufficiently remarkable. Mr. Willey and others of our generation are less open-minded than Beatrice. C. S. Lewis has provided us with a notable illustration of a present tendency among theologically-minded men of letters to keep the door open on an older cosmology which agrees with the claims of theology rather than with those of experiment and observation. In his *Preface to Paradise Lost* he refers to the medieval account of armed men fighting in the sky. "I myself have not seen them," he admits, but implies quite clearly that that is merely his bad luck.

The significance of these examples, in particular the one quoted from Mr. Willey, is that they show that even those who claim one sort of truth for theology and another for experimental science are in fact troubled by this disunity of truth to which they have committed themselves. They are also aware that poetry cannot safely detach itself from verifiable meanings. They wish, after all, that there should be one truth and that it should be theological.

The rest of us, who suffer the same discomfort in the presence of a philosophical poem whose philosophy we can no longer accept as true but whose structure *is* that philosophy, must say that the

'Paradiso' is not, after all, 'pure poetry'. Parts of it which express
a concrete vision are unsurpassed. Parts of it are versification of
outmoded ideas and beliefs, intellectually ingenious but poetically
dull, other parts are simply antiquarian. The purely human
passions and emotions, or rather the emotions which can only be
understood as referring to human experience, are at a much lower
level of intensity than those drawn in the 'Inferno' and the 'Purgatorio'. Sometimes, when taken in relation to the intellectual
structure, they are unpleasing or even ridiculous. Beatrice
continually and meanly scores off Dante, rebuking instead of
enlightening his ignorance. Since she is wrong quite as often as
not, her assumption of absolute authority becomes insufferable.

We come back at present to Coleridge's view that a poem of
any length cannot be 'all poetry', at least we do so if we cannot
find a better or more useful term for whatever it is which gives its
unity to a poem of great scope than 'structure of emotions'.

Am I claiming that, because the system of thought behind the
Divine Comedy is only archæologically 'true', the poetry itself,
in so far as it is a structure of thought, becomes disintegrated
with the passage of time? In so far as the poem has a philosophical
or didactic intention, I think this claim must be made. We see it at
once in poetry where the philosophy is of private or idiosyncratic
invention and therefore of less durability, for instance, in Blake's
or Wordsworth's long poems. The philosophy behind the *Divine
Comedy* has been much more ably, carefully and determinedly
preserved and has therefore lasted much better. It is clear however
that Dante has been quite as often read with devotional as with
æsthetic excitement. Many people beside Mr. Gladstone have
preferred the 'Paradiso' to the 'Inferno', as poetry, on these unanalysed grounds, and the renewed public interest in Dante, for
which to more than anyone we must be sincerely grateful to Mr.
Eliot, is surely rather more because of his 'orthodoxy' than because
of the unique intensity of his poetic vision?

This lability is the occupational risk which the philosophical
poet must run, and there is no poem 'of any length' which may not
have to be read at some later date, even by its most ardent and

specialised students, with more historical than immediate interest. This is even so with poems whose structure, chosen by the poet with perhaps greater instinctive wisdom, is dramatic or epic. It may also be so with quite short poems of lyric intention whose reference is to a system of thought or to a social code (also inevitably a system of thought) which is arguable and therefore no longer intellectually *acceptable* by anybody. This applies, I should say, to all the poetry of 'courtly' love. By using this term I do not confine myself to poems written by the Troubadours or by Dante and his contemporaries. I mean love poetry written at any period which conflicts with the naturalistic unconventionalised experience by one sex of the other. We might compare Alice Meynell's 'She walks, the lady of my delight' with Wyatt's 'They flee from me that sometime did me seek', or with 'The expense of spirit in a waste of shame'.

My point is still that there is no way by which a poet can absolutely ignore his relations with objective truth; but that there are ways by which he can smooth them, by which he can heal 'the split in sensibility'. At moments of the 'purest' poetic excitement this is what he does quite naturally. But the relation of a poem to the various references which constitute its meaning, and therefore to what is verifiable, and furthermore to any form of philosophy or belief, is, in so far as it is a poem, never one of direct transcription. To see what this relation really is, we must obviously consider the agreed moments of the 'purest' poetry. We do this without prejudice to the 'long' or 'structural' poem simply in order to see whether those various arrangements of words which cause the greatest admitted pure excitement have also in common any residuum of typical meaning.

> "It was no dream for I lay broad awaking,
>   but all is turned now through my gentleness
>   into a bitter fashion of forsaking."

> "Mad in pursuit and in possession so,
>   had, having and in quest to have, extreme.

> A bliss in proof, and proved a very woe,
> before a joy proposed: behind a dream."

"Since there's no help, come let us kiss and part."

> "Beauty, truth and rarity,
> Grace in all simplicity,
> here enclosed in cinders lie . . .
> To this urn let those repair
> that are either true or fair,
> for these dead birds sigh a prayer

> "But hark! my pulse, like a soft drum,
> beats my approach, tells thee I come;
> and slow howe'er my marches be,
> I shall at last sit down by thee."

Or

> "Helen, thy beauty is to me
> like those Nicean barks of yore
> that gently o'er a perfumed sea,
> the weary wayworn wanderer bore
> to his own native shore."

or Gascoigne's 'Lullaby of a Lover' or the ballad of Clerk Saunders: or Wordsworth's 'A slumber did my spirit seal', or Yeats 'Sailing to Byzantium'.

All these seem to me to have in common an awareness of the living, intense moment in the waste of time, dead or gone. This awareness of intense individual vitality in the midst of or against an awareness of natural inevitable change, or even destruction, enters the reader's mind directly as a simple unanalysed excitement. I do not say that this acute awareness of standing on the shore of time is the only poetic theme, anyway the only conscious poetic theme. I do say that this awareness is the sine qua non of poetic experience in general. It *is* the poetic emotion. This view has something in common with Housman's idea about the 'physiological' basis of poetry to which he refers when he is trying to analyse the effect of such a poem as 'Nymphs and shepherds dance no more'. It has nothing in common with the idea of the preference for 'infinity' which was a defect of some Romantics, as pointed out by Hulme. Time is the point, not eternity.

These extracts however much they differ in period and expression, have another quality in common which is a matter of the use which they all make of language, and which in the view I am indicating here, is a quality distinguishing poetry from all other kinds of speech. This is a form of concentration which I call representation. I mean this word in the electoral sense. In all of these quotations and in all poetry as such, whether we are using that word in the meaning of one of the high moments or whether we are referring to a poem's unity of structure on any scale, the words mean what they say and they also stand for a number of other meanings more or less directly implied. This is to be found sometimes by actual research and interpretation but more often perhaps as possibilities of meanings, as hints and half-hints which we could follow up, elucidate and exhaust if we cared to, but which we may well prefer to keep in this prime state of exciting poise, as an initial disturbance of many strata of meaning. This preference in itself illustrates poetry's essential hovering between the impulse to creation and the impulse to destruction which I have referred to above as the poet's instinct for a naturalistic or biological choice of theme. The completely destructive or analytic process, the complete elucidation and exhaustion into single meaning, of course, yields prose. And poetry struggles to maintain itself in the teeth of prose, as life does against death. Elucidation, it may be suggested, is always weakening to poetry. Moreover, if we look historically at poetic imagery, we can, I think, see how poetry is a resistance movement against the normal development of language from the synthetic to the analytic. Poetry moves away from simile (which is diffuse and elucidatory) towards metaphor, essentially an aid to fusion of meaning and to the kind of concentration I have mentioned.

But of course metaphors are always getting rubbed away and in time obliterated. It is as if they lose their organic vitality, which depends less even on the multiple meaning which we can see in them as soon as we grasp that they are metaphors than on their unanalysed power to suggest further ranges of meaning. We do not of course absolutely destroy this power, in the case of any given metaphor, by its analysis, but the risk of an irreversible disintegration into prose meaning is always there. That some images retain their power after indefinite intellectual analysis is due, I think, to the fact that the metaphor always establishes a relation of some sort between conscious mental process and unconscious association at different depths, some of these very hardly won into conscious understanding and easily vanishing from it.

By metaphor I do not mean only the kind of image in which one idea or sense-impression is expressed in terms of another—'When to the sessions of sweet silent thought', or 'When that fell arrest, Without all bail, shall carry me away'—I mean all kinds of imagery, and of the verbal economy which is one example of what I have called 'representation', where fusion, in any degree, has taken place between the terms, so that they affect the mind with something like equivalence in meaning.

Shakespeare is full of such highly fused imagery—one can almost pick examples at random:

> "You sulphurous and thought-executing fires,
>   Vaunt—couriers to oak-cleaving thunderbolts,
>   Singe my white head!"

> "That memory, the warder of the brain,
>   shall be a fume, and the receipt of reason
>   a limbec only: when in swinish sleep
>   their drenched natures lie as in a death,
>   what cannot you and I perform upon
>   the unguarded Duncan? what not put upon
>   his spongy officers? . . ."

"Farewell, thou art too dear for my possessing
and like enough thou knowest thine estimate.
The charter of thy worth gives thee releasing,
my bonds in thee are all determinate . . ."

Or Donne:

"I wonder by my troth what thou and I
did till we loved? Were we not weaned till then?
But sucked on country pleasures childishly.
Or snorted we in the Seven Sleepers' Den?
T'was so; but this, all pleasures fancies be.
If ever any beauty I did see
which I desired and got, t'was but a dream of thee.
And now good morrow to our waking souls . . ."

where the whole of the first part at least of the poem, while being
one extended image, even perhaps a form of 'conceit', yet evokes
another and unlimited world which while, expressing, even
illustrating, the 'idea', is equipollent with it.

Or we have Dylan Thomas:

"Never until the mankind making
bird beast and flower
fathering and all humbling darkness
tells with silence the last light breaking
and the still hour
is come of the sea tumbling in harness,"

"And I must enter again the round
Zion of the water bead
and the synagogue of the ear of corn?
Shall I let pray the shadow of a sound,
or sow my salt seed
in the least valley of sackcloth to mourn
the majesty and burning of the child's death?"

Or Mr. Eliot, the superb poet, himself in such a passage as:

"In the uncertain hour before the morning
Near the ending of the interminable night
At the recurrent end of the unending
After the dark dove with the flickering tongue
Had passed below the horizon of his homeing
While the dead leaves still rattled on like tin
Over the asphalt where no other sound was
Between three districts whence the smoke arose
I met one walking loitering and unhurried
As if blown towards me like the metal leaves
Before the urban dawn-wind unresisting.
And as I fixed upon the down-turned face
That pointed scrutiny with which we challenge
The first-met stranger in the waning dusk . . ."

This is almost beyond imagery, the fusion of all the sensuous elements which compose the total poetic meaning is almost complete, the purity at which I am sure Mr. Eliot aims, and which is perhaps always the aim of the poet in his manage of his images, is nearly attained. And of course at the moment of this intense synthesis, language is ripe to fall back again into prose. It seems to me that, in our generation, Kafka at his best has, with his allegories whose surface meaning is so well digested, attained this point of synthesis more perfectly than any verse-poet.

What decides the degree of fusion in imagery is not grammatical structure. I have chosen examples which do not employ the word 'like' in the images giving the particular effect to the lines, because 'like' is the grammatical sign of the simile. Some similes however, in this grammatical shape, are also highly fused imagery, metaphor in the sense I am trying to indicate here. We can quote Mr. Eliot again in the well-known lines:

"Where the evening is spread out against the sky
Like a patient etherised upon a table."

This, although its sensuous quality is far-fetched, is an orthodox simile, that, is it is a kind of analogue in the natural historian's sense, where a single functional characteristic is selected from two natures or organisms essentially different. But I think that this is all the same, in my sense, more of a metaphor, an example of fused or focused meanings. The likeness is not a mere bridge between an abstract and a concrete meaning; the impressions exist upon the same plane of apperception and the meanings have the reflexive quality of highly-fused metaphor, presenting us, even as the Donne quotation does, with a whole evoked *world*, in this case the roofs and the high buildings, which may be public ones, including hospitals where life and death go on although the offices are shut.

Mr. Eliot's tendency, with a few startling exceptions such as I have quoted, has been to avoid metaphor. Now, in the later poetry which includes *Ash Wednesday* and the *Four Quartets*, he goes in much more for stock images, turning more than ever away from individual imagery based on unconscious primitive association. But this is not really a new thing. In spite of many forms of verbal incantation, the repetitions, the half-punning and almost obsessive internal rhymes and assonances, Mr. Eliot's poetic method is still what it always has been—very near to prose, his most striking qualities as a writer being particularisation, selection, wit, avoidance of metaphor. All these qualities of good prose in verse were most obvious in the poems from 'Prufrock' to 'The Waste Land'. We certainly needed him at that time as a corrective. Such verse plus such good prose were perhaps the best combination against bad verse and *ce qui n'est pas prose*, the post-Swinburnian hangover, the various forms of automatic writing, although of course there were a number of other people doing their best to keep the language awake and sharp and bright, both before and after the published Hopkins. And not only Yeats, but Wilfred Owen, Harold Munro and de la Mare, being perhaps less afflicted than Mr. Eliot with a sense of sin, did not so much fear the inevitable fall of their poetic nature into imagery.

Not all of these poets have Mr. Eliot's importance. Especially when the literary histories are being written in a hundred years' time and assessments are being made, some of them may be classified as minors, while Mr. Eliot will probably have the minimal chapter due to a great innovator—whether anyone then reads him or not.

But if we analyse the distinction between Mr. Eliot's characteristic diction and imagery and theirs, we may come to think that in 'purifying the language of the tribe', Mr. Eliot has become something of a martyr for poetry's sake. He has sacrificed, or is trying to sacrifice, too many of the naturalistic advantages of poetry. For choice of imagery indicates a whole intellectual and emotional outlook or use of the poet's total capacity of attention, and highly metaphoric language of an individual or original kind indicates the process of freeing emotion from its imprisonment in the unconscious. In Mr. Eliot's case we can speak rather of avoidance of imagery, and this again is not fortuitous.

T. E. Hulme's anti-Renaissance manifesto was a demand for the return to the ideology of scholasticism and to something which Hulme called Classicism. Mr. Eliot's *For Lancelot Andrewes*, which followed this, was another anti-Renaissance manifesto, anti-humanistic and implicitly anti-scientific, and in favour of 'Royalism, Anglo-Catholicism and Classicism'. To many people the Christian conversion of the author of *The Waste Land* was the most striking feature of his career, especially as testified by the poem-sequence *Ash Wednesday*. But Mr. Eliot's conception of classicism bears even more directly on the development of poetry, his own and other people's, and more perniciously than Hulme's, which was positive, though limited. For Hulme had not developed as Mr. Eliot has done a merely guarded and indeed puritanical attitude towards imagery. For practical poetic purposes, Hulme meant by classicism merely dryness, wit, and fidelity to perception, and this demands the help of new and precise imagery. In romanticism Hulme disliked the vagueness, abstraction and woolliness which characterise any bad poetry; and there is no necessary connection between his views on poetry, which were shared by the Imagists, and the body of his philosophy. Mr. Eliot's classicism, as we have seen, contains the same core as his theology and is inseparable from his political and social philosophy.

With his followers, classicism has become a posthumous title conferred on the products of a bygone age which is seen—for various reasons, including romantic nostalgia—as more unified, peaceful and orderly than our own. But unity so often results merely from the selective view of the observer. And there is no special merit in being past and dead. By implication, Mr. Eliot often suggests that there is such merit. Rebuking the opinion that there is any advance, even in knowledge, hé says that the past and dead poets are 'that which we know' ('Tradition and the Individual Talent'). This ignores the fact that good contemporary scholars do actually know more about the times and conditions in which the dead poets worked than the poets did themselves. A poet often speaks more forcibly and originally, says Mr. Eliot, when the voice of his dead poetic ancestors speaks through him. I will not stress the opinion, which may be merely personal, that when we decipher, as we so often do, another piece of Mr. Eliot's deliberate mosaic of quotation, we experience some, no doubt irrational, disappointment, because after all we were unconsciously looking for Eliot. But I do say that what we want from these poets is their reincarnation. What remains interesting in them is precisely that which is still living, not that which was capable of death. This living quality, whatever else it may be, relates directly to the awareness of natural law, and not to the awareness of the laws of any society, past or present, of God or Man. And it is common with the quality which the best Romantic poetry was trying to reinstate. What this is I shall try to show.

Coming down against the 'Modern Side' in public-school education, Mr. Eliot stated, as I have already mentioned:

"If Christianity is not to survive, I shall not mind if the texts of the Latin and Greek languages become more obscure and forgotten than the language of the Etruscans."

One of the best ways, surely, of 'healing the split', as far as education affects it, would be to increase the higher criticism of the classics. Never let the young, from the very begininng of literacy in Greek and Latin, be allowed to conceive them un-historically; that is, without regard to at least the rudiments of economics, politics and even anthropology. The effort to link classicism with Christianity is over-strained. The Church helped to re-discover and preserve the classics. It did not invent them. What the Renaissance discoverers found in them was the human, men like themselves. If we are to achieve in education any of the aims which Mr. Eliot sees as desirable, in particular if we are to preserve the tradition, that is, the continuous life of poetry, we must behave more and not less like the discoverers of the Renais-sance. We must, for one thing, teach the young, not that the classics are models to emulate, but living poetry written by people like ourselves. The classics are alive because we are alive, not the other way round.

The older way of teaching classical literature, after which Mr. Eliot seems to hanker, taught Greek or Roman history as a mere parallel without causative influence. Men have only lately begun to think historically, and therefore this chance of bridging the gap between scientific method and imaginative sensibility could not have been earlier seized. But we can see that the upholders of 'Classicism', including Mr. Eliot, do not wish it to be seized. In particular, they do not wish the adjective 'classical' to be limited to a historical meaning denoting at best a special kind of virtue in composition or outlook, because that would imply something temporary and conditioned. They wish, as usual, to hypostatise the classics, to give them an absolute status and value. Hence their attempts to link classical teaching indissolubly with Christianity.

In fact, 'Classicism' manifests itself in relation to recognisable historical epochs, often short. In the case of European poetry, the genuinely 'classic', in a sense which would be accepted, I suppose, by Mr. Eliot as well as by myself, has been a few drops in the ocean of time. With Western music, the only one which is on a sufficiently macroscopic scale for verifiable generalisations to be made about it, the classical was surely a peak, almost a moment, which emerged only to disintegrate.

In all arts, change seems to be of the essence, because, apart from anything else, the avoidance of imitation and a contribution of novelty are, for the creator, also of the essence, whatever his unconscious relation to sources and influences, and whatever Mr. Eliot, who has sought to cover this point in *After Strange Gods*, has against originality. Artists seldom know they are being classical, when they are. 'Classicism' is generally an epiphenomenal concept for the use of critics.

What then are the neo-classicists trying to pin and restore? In this case I think restoration as such is also of the essence, and in hypostatising the 'classics' they are really trying to restore certain conventions and a certain agreement about values on which they believe a secure and ordered society (secure for whom?) has been based and could be based again. Underneath everything, what the neo-classicist wishes to restore is authority, as opposed to free discussion and opinion. Hence the attempt to by-pass or at least to undermine the whole of the modern development of philosophy and retire on the old base of scholasticism. No such absolutism is really possible, as I have already said, without, for one thing, a censorship which would be as unmanageable as it would be monstrous. In using the word 'unmanageable' I do not mean that it could not be imposed, for, alas, we see that it can. I mean that it would never achieve what I must believe would be the sole deliberate aim of those despots—who, like Mr. Eliot, would remain in a conscious sense benevolent—the mere selection and preservation of the agreed best human values. For freedom—and the preference for it, both for ourselves and other people—is also of the essence. Without it, *all* genuine mental creation fails even in those aspects which manifest the real classical or Christian contribution; let us say, proportion or charity. By freedom I do not mean license or anarchy; I mean that the creator in any sphere, artistic or social, must not be at all coerced and should not be interfered with in the process of finding his necessary elbow-room within the limits of his proper material. Since we are all, in proportion to our enlightenment, responsible for the education of our fellows, the propagation of irrelevant dogma by those who are able to know better counts as interference. Humanly speaking, it may be said that the most blowsy mistakes of the liberal-minded have done less harm, since they do not inherently propagate hatred, than the thin-lipped disciplinary solemnities of the formalist who mistakes his repressions for classicism.

In fact, by classicism the neo-scholastics mean an arbitrary and fixated definition of poetry and spiritual and mental creation, and by this selection imply that the great main stream of art has followed a largely mistaken course through history. It is just because the periods of recognisable order and authority have been in the minority that we can state with some confidence the contrary although at present less reputable, view that poetry, and artistic creation in general, have on the whole expressed an impulse which can be loosely but more readily classified as 'romantic', at least humanistic. When T. E. Hulme, we may note, expressed dislike of the 'Renaissance' spirit he is referring to qualities and views which reached a peak of expression in the Romantic movement.

What we call classical art—and we call it so, as I have said, after the event—may be said to depend on agreed and therefore largely conscious conventions about values and also about the rules of artistic production. I do not imply any kind of contractual state. Rather I mean that what we now call the Unconscious played relatively little part. It is also true that the rules have often been extracted from practice by later thinkers, for example Aristotle and Boileau, but that fact merely gives point to the generalisation that classical art has been the product of small societies (small either as cities or in caste) where the rules of behaviour, both social and artistic, were immediately visible and did not have to be made explicit. This single fact of the inevitable association of classicism with the small community (in one of the senses mentioned above) is of prime importance if we wish to understand whether we can or ought to restore a new classicism.

Mr. Eliot has a good deal to say on this subject of regionalism in *Notes Towards the Definition of Culture*. There is much to be said for a sane regionalism, and Sir George Stapledon* has said it well enough in practical terms which have nothing to do with our sin but only with our idiocy. A 'sane' regionalism, as I mean it here, would be one which grasped, through the concrete idiosyncrasies and environmental activities of men, that sense of universal man which we have in fact *gained*, through many conditioning forces, including what we call the Romantic impulse, in its essential humanism.

We must, however, never forget that regionalism, with the movements allied to it, including craft and brotherhood movements, is not necessarily sane or does not necessary remain so. It readily loses the real advantage of the universal and become exclusive and what we may call Luddite towards those forms of universal communication, spiritual and technical, which, as one must maintain, do confer a real benefit on the human race. The Pope at least knows that you must use the radio to combat those uses of radio which you deem undesirable. Similarly, regional cultivation requires a central production of tractors. If we do not tolerate what I have called the blowsy mistakes of liberalism, if we deny real value to the increase of general knowledge, mistaking its at present inadequate and partial character for a kind of inherent evil or impossibility, we, or those who may come to power as the representatives of this illusion, will do as the Nazis and as the Russian Communists have done; simply impose a limitation on human development which has the rudeness without the naturalness of savagery. Truth, because it lives and grows, dies of any arbitrary amputation. The 'limits', the nothing-too-much, which neo-classicism wishes to impose, if we are to take the imposition as more than a technical corrective, imply this real danger. After all, it is very important that the 'limitation' of the Greek City State was not merely a product of the regionalism which was inevitable at the time, but also, and more significantly, a product of caste and therefore of oppression, social and sexual. I do not wish to believe that the neo-scholastic opponents of 'progress' would reject the real advantages which we have gained

*In *The Land*.

from the spread of knowledge and techniques. By this I mean that they should be glad, not only that they can catch an aeroplane when they are in haste to get to some desirable and moral goal of their personal choice, but also that the same aeroplane *can be used* to be more humane and more intelligent about human relations in general. The aeroplane will, in fact, as we all know, be monstrously abused in too many instances. But it is the opponents of 'progress', at least in recent times, who have erected that idea into a dogma and at the same time identified it with The Machine. Christopher Dawson, for example, writes as if a hope for some kind of 'progress' were always the same as a belief in its inevitability. D. H. Lawrence, with a distaste for the automobile, implied a similar hypostatical view of the idea of progress when he described the horse as the optimum human means of absorbing a change of scenery. Lawrence had a peculiar mystique of flesh. If the problem were only one of relative speed, one sees no valid objection to the bicycle.

The fact is that 'The Machine', whatever that may be, is not to be identified with progress. On the other hand, machines have been necessary for any advances, including moral ones, which human beings have made. A machine, in the technical sense, is something calculable and exactly reproducible. But all the ways, since the beginning of human history, in which we have organised and passed on our handling of any part of nature are essentially machines. A church is a machine for worship. The Church is a machine for the unification of human living. Like other machines, it was a good machine while it worked. And, like other machines, it worked while it conformed to the laws of its material. But 'human nature' is never a raw material in the same way as electricity or steel. The conception is always partly a convention, an artifice. Not to recognise this is the first step towards becoming a mechanist. The doctrine of Original Sin based on a fixed conception of human nature is certainly at least as mechanical as many of the more liberal attempts to organise human relations. Churchmen can point to the period of cultural and psychological unification when the Church produced a common language of conceptions, as Greece and Rome had done, so that the great dramatic case-book, represented by such extremes as the *Divine Comedy* and the Elizabethan drama, still only proved the rules. No one can fairly deny the immense value which this unification once had, nor that humanity paid a high price for it, as we pay for all the steps of our devious human progress—today we may say for the advances of technology. But that must be looked at also as a step in our history, that is, as a conditioned choice among our human evils.

At the back of all was this agreement about Sin and therefore about the nature and definition of Man. The concept worked because it was agreed, because it was a convention, not because it was Original, not because it was an absolute description of human nature. In seeking 'classicism' the neo-scholastics are seeking the convention, without regard to the fact that the classicism of Greek and Rome were based on quite different conventions about sin. What the neo-scholastics will not accept is that we cannot really know about Man until we know about men and women. Art has to maintain a balance between the abstract and the concrete, the universal and the particular. In one sense poetry is just this balance, or rather this fusion. What we vaguely indicate as classicism, in either its pagan or its Christian form— and this is something real in so far as the movement is spontaneous and not artificial—is valuable as a corrective to romanticism run wild, the romanticism which makes a virtue of formlessness. This wild romanticism may be either an insane realism or an un-controlled fantasy, these terms covering exaggerated stream-of-consciousness literature, unlimited surrealism, utterly free verse and Udolfan thrillers. But the classical corrective has been and should be of relatively brief application in human history, and it has been applied best when it has been applied casually, in-dividually and not too consciously; above all, wittily and humorously. Jane Austen was a classical corrective, in this light and casual sense, to the Udolfan and other mysteries in which fiction had entangled itself, but we do not have to limit the novel to her neat framework. Jane Austen's method was by no means satirical—chiefly it was limited, by the natural limits of its chosen material, and it was 'dry'; but the possibility that the true classical *genre* is Satire is perhaps worth considering.

In fact what we call classicism has been a benefit of limitation based not merely on men's unconscious acceptance of a set of conventionalised beliefs about the behaviour of mankind and its significance, but on men's real ignorance of their actual fellows. The great dramas of the past have blazed against a brutish, somnolent and superstitious background. They were a type of education without general literacy. That I believe we ought not again to demand the privilege of the 'classical' at the social price of obscurantism does not mean that I claim any great virtue for literacy as such. It is too easy for Mr. Eliot in *Notes Towards the Definition of Culture*, to ask an implicit question—'That education makes people happier'—pointing out an Idol of the County Council Chamber, and making an Aunt Sally of it. That our education today is still largely wrong means in practice that we still want more of a different kind. Roughly, we need to educate people to know about people. We must begin to do this, not only in the nursery, but at the breast—and before that.

If we had education in this true and fundamental form, an education of the emotions, we should not need to worry much about the advantages or disadvantages of literacy, still less about the classics, and not at all about the evils of state interference. By this I mean that if a few basic biological and psychological *laws* of an intellectually rather simple character were to be accepted by the practical authorities, even as far as they accept the rulings of scientific workers in the fields of the inanimate, the state could automatically limit its interference to removing barriers.

Those who dislike and habitually misconceive the nature of all sciences are also those who often tell us that psychology is not yet a science. For this belief they commonly give two main reasons: that psychologists cannot reduce the description of a human being to exact mathematical formulæ, and that medical psychologists do not succeed in curing neurotic illness as often as patient, doctor or general public could wish. The basis of scientific method however is the observation and verification of laws. In this sense psychology as well as sociology in all its branches are sciences like any other. The insistence on the quantitative or mathematical is an example of a valuable technique of attack on the views of our adversaries. The shocked disapproval of anti-Marxists for any deviation from Stalinism is another: the attempt to counter Church theology with the actual statements of Christ is one more.

The real reason for neo-scholastic attacks on contemporary psychology is a wish to preserve the theological view of human nature, in particular the doctrine of Original Sin, with its implication that the one thing which human beings inherently cannot learn is the one thing they most need to learn: the truth about other human beings and therefore about themselves. I see no reason for supposing that human beings are radically unteachable in this respect. Mankind as a whole seems to have an unlimited capacity for learning. As far as medical psychology is concerned we have no right to draw absolute conclusions of disappointment from the rate of 'cure' any more than the majority of us do from the present results of cancer research.

In psychology there is even now an agreement over simple and yet revolutionary fundamentals which is quite sufficient to provide us with a working conception of the child who is father to the man, a conception moreover which flatly gives the lie to the scholastic conception of the original sinner.

In a way which should indeed gratify our neo-scholastic battlers for the idea of a continuous 'Christian' heritage, the beliefs of our public and social authorities, whether Protestant or agnostic, are still unconsciously dominated by a conception of the child as a pocket adult, a forlorn being who is born wearing his father's psychological trousers already cut down. This conception, by whomsoever it is held, denies in effect the existence and role of unconscious mind. But all learning, by which I mean all change of character and capacities, takes place in the unconscious mind and the unconscious nervous processes. And unless unconscious process is affected, learning, however useful and desirable, even from the individual's point of view, does not take place.

Different schools of psychological thought do differ profoundly about the contents at any given moment of unconscious mind, about their ætiology also, and about their ultimate social orientation. But they agree that these unconscious processes are our instrument of education, the means by which we absorb and also make available for change, our learning of all kinds. It is not surprising that the Catholic priesthood is faced by a mass of recalcitrants and recidivists. An absolute dogmatic morality taught as a science of human nature is totally indigestible by our real mental organs.

This role of the unconscious is precisely one, and the most important, of these fundamental points of agreement among all psychological observers who have not themselves been too deeply touched by the dogma of Original Sin which in some form infects us all, and who therefore can think of unconscious mentation as something other than a static sump of wickedness. But the temptation to think of the infantile mind as not merely aggressive but knowingly sadistic, and of the child merely as a *bad* adult, who wants at best licking, at worst bludgeoning, into shape, is still strong with all of us. Those who have been driven out of their childhood by a rain of either intellectual or physical blows will not willingly return to it in imagination. They will naturally prefer the view that the way they now are obliged to deal with their 'adult' fellows is and always has been the best. From this static view of human beings we learn only one method of dealing with them, to counter their aggression with aggression. It implicitly denies the observable fact that a human being develops from a more primitive condition and, having clearly some original principle of growth in him, is also clearly educable. The dogma of a static 'Nature'—which is also the basis of the dogma of Original Sin—is an intellectual resting-place and a big comfort, like all absolutes. It is, however, observably wrong, therefore socially immensely dangerous and, like many ecclesiastical dogmas, singularly opposed to the meaning of Christ.

To deny the dogma of Original Sin does not mean that one has fallen into the Pelagian fallacy. I use this term to indicate a distinction from the Pelagian heresy, which has a definite meaning in theological history. The Pelagian fallacy is the form of a charge levelled by neo-scholastics against romanticism —that all romantics believe with Rousseau that 'man is born good'—and in this form it is important for the slight survey I am trying to make of some of the unconscious assumptions behind the neo-scholastic criticism of poetry and art. Rousseau certainly said that man was born good, but romanticism is not precisely described, nor is the nature of the romantic impulse exhausted, by lumping them altogether with the ideas of Rousseau, nor indeed by making them out to be a mere contrary to 'orthodoxy' or classicism.

The essential feature of the romantic impulse is its humanism, and humanism is essentially the belief that men and women have the right and the duty to ask what questions they please, to question the state of society and the state of their own emotions, the starry heavens and anything that appears to be a moral law within them. But such an exploratory attitude is not usually so unnaturally and obligingly simple as to be a mere contradiction of any 'orthodoxy'. Several of the most discussed poets of the Romantic Movement were recognisable Pelagians, for instance Keats with his belief in the holiness of the heart's affections and probably Wordsworth with his belief in the unwillingness of Nature to betray the heart that trusts her. But Coleridge was not a Pelagian. The Ancient Mariner's sense of guilt attached to a wickedness which was not absolutely redeemable in any human terms. Baudelaire, a poet with many romantic affinities, was certainly no Pelagian. On the contrary he shared, and is applauded by Eliot for so doing, our neo-scholastics' unctuousness about Sin. In passing it is worth our while to note the ripe moral flavour on their tongues every time they open their mouths to pronounce the words 'good' and 'bad' or conceptions associated with these. Whatever the orthodox view may be, there is no doubt that, for example, Eliot and C. S. Lewis weight their conception of Sin with a curious sexual obsession. Lewis, oddly troubled about male domination, knows, like Paul in this respect, much better than his Master. Eliot, as I have already pointed out, is concerned lest lack of a sufficiently puritanical morality should cause poets to die of sexual boredom.

But poets and artists if we take the sum of them through history, have not been dominated by the obsession of this puritanical moral flavour and, whatever they became in the course of their lives, they were certainly not, as a majority, cradled into poetry by the notions of sin or of other-worldly redemption. Most of them, especially dramatic poets—and all poets have the dramatic instinct—have been more interested in showing a pattern of behaviour, which is sometimes biological or even social error, than in Sin. Christian poetry is certainly often cautionary, and so is some 'classical' drama, Corneille's, for instance, and the Spanish 'honour' drama. Certain defined rules have been broken and the defined penalties must be paid. But this very definition is a ruling of a society, whether of men or of the Church. The biological penalties, on the other hand, are for the *undefined error*, the error which is one fruit of trial or discovery. It is this process of discovery, of living by trial and error, that most poetry has been written about. There have been many Christian poets, and the Christian, mystical and theological pattern of Sin, Atonement and Redemption (or Damnation) has penetrated into many literary fields, including that of the popular novel. But not by any means all, even of those poets and writers who regarded themselves as belonging to a Christian society and philosophy, have been predominantly preoccupied with this pattern. Far more have been naturalistically concerned, let us say, with the brevity of life and love, of happiness and worldly blessedness, with the conditions of mortality as such. This seems to have been quite as true of the bulk of the Greek and Latin poets who were rediscovered at the time of the Renaissance as of the eager Renaissance poets who studied them. In particular the tragic flaw in the Greek dramatists is much more comprehensible if we think of it as biological error, or even social error, than if we try to equate it with Sin.

CHAPTER VIII

Poetry and Truth (continued)

II. Romanticism and Classicism

IF those among the Renaissance poets who were Christians, for example the Pléiade, had been better theologians, they might have been troubled by the pagan flavour of their more naturalistic passages. I have never been able to understand how the neo-scholastics, particularly Hulme and Eliot, have been able to feel satisfied with the kind of identification they have made for themselves between classicism and Christianity. Christian monasticism certainly had a practical hand in helping to produce the materials for classical study, but what the poets did with this material can only be understood in terms of poetry, of what poets are usually doing with their material. Ronsard and the Pléiade were notably humanistic and man-centred, even mortality-centred. If we merely studied the works of these poets, who helped so indispensably to bring 'classicism' to Europe, I doubt if we should ever discover any indissoluble connection with Christianity in the theological sense of that term. They were, however, passionately interested in trying to reform their own poetic language and so of course they produced books of rules whose significance and value could as usual be misunderstood by later, more pedestrian minds. It seems to me possible that when our neo-scholastics think of 'classicism' they think first and foremost of 'rules' and oppose these to the supposed 'licence' of romanticism.

This was done before by Boileau, who ignored the genuine Renaissance humanists and also misinterpreted what Aristotle was trying to do, in his *Poetics*—that was, of course, to understand, not to legislate.

It seems to me inescapable that both Hulme and Eliot, whatever other theories they may hold, and whatever they may say which appears to be inconsistent with this view, really believe that 'rules' are a good thing in themselves, because rules are like dogma and because they give us the feeling of an absolute authority, stern but reassuring.

I believe that both Classicism and Romanticism, as applied by the neo-scholastics to poetry, are false and arbitrary abstractions. There is a health of poetic language which flourished in the times of the great Greek and Latin poets and which flourished when Christian cosmogony was dominant in Europe and may equally well flourish when a more scientific view prevails. And there is a disease of poetic language which might have appeared, and sometimes did appear, at any of these periods.

What looks like highly individualised mannerisms among contemporary poets may sometimes be merely a symptom of this absolutely stock failing, which is a form of hypostasis.

Sir George Rostrevor Hamilton wrote an acute essay on the high incidence of the definite article in Auden and other contemporary poets, pointing out that Eliot is by no means free from the disease. For example, 'The infirm glory of the positive hour'.

The 'the' in this line and many others confers a pseudo-concreteness on an abstract and even artificial conception; it is in fact a piece of hypostasis. A symptom of the same disease in Mr. Eliot's later work is that he builds his more emotional passages so often out of auditory imagery, and that the visual images are much nearer to stock, apart from being redolent of Time Past. The roses are fallen or about to fall, a dust of memory to be swept up; they are quite different from the roses of the Renaissance which poets so often wished they had gathered.

"My words echo
Thus in your mind.
But to what purpose
Disturbing the dust on a bowl of rose-leaves
I do not know."

Then there was the passage in *Ash Wednesday*:

"If the lost word is lost, if the spent word is spent;
If the unheard, unspoken
Word is unspoken, unheard;
Still is the unspoken word, the Word unheard,
The Word without a word, the Word within
The world and for the world;"

Even the theology and philosophy (not his own indeed but part
of his piety) do not in general read boldly out from the page.
When they are not like a piece on a parchment lampshade which
we have to twist ourselves to read, he has turned them again into
a sort of tune in his head.

"I shall say it again.
Shall I say it again? In order to arrive there,
To arrive where you are, to get from where you are not,
You must go by a way wherein there is no ecstasy.
In order to arrive at what you do not know
You must go by a way which is the way of
ignorance . . .

And what you own is what you do not own
And where you are is where you are not."

Let us remember that this insistence on the auditory is often a
disease which implies a dislike of *meanings*, of which, after all, our
world is made up, and which are in inception, concrete and *given*.
For underneath all the qualities I have mentioned as characteristic
of poetry there is the natural and passive use of sensibility, which
Keats called 'negative capability'. The Romantics, like others,

often failed to be poets. Ideas, as such, in poetry, are always seen sooner or later to be partially false, for one thing because, like anxiety, they are so often an illusion of activity, a feeling that we can do something direct about the given material of our sensibility and experience. Ideas in their general form are always somebody else's, and the poet cannot seize the general except through the particular, through the idiosyncrasy of his own physical and nervous nature.

Shelley suffered, in a way which, far from classifying him with the Romantics, sharply distinguishes him from them at their best, from this afflation of ideas. He found it very difficult to keep his eye on the object, not to lose the skylark in the diffusion of light. Much of his work suffered from the disease of hypostasis which has so infected the philosophy of our neo-scholastics, the disease of multiplying entities, of mistaking words for things. Shelley probably suffered from an ill-conceived Platonic education. The Church in our day, through Aquinas, refers to Aristotle as an original secular authority, so that no one quite knows why he does not accept an honorary canonisation, but not even the Church through Aristotle or any of its present theologians could have taught Shelley to solve the problem of universals. Yet this problem, if it exists, can be solved by poets. They solve it continually. When we discuss whiteness or blackness, or snow or pitch, we are always losing either the abstract or the concrete. But a prime characteristic of the poet is that he can make us experience whiteness or blackness.

Our view of the problem of universals decides where we belong philosophically. When we have decided that our poetic taste can be labelled Romantic or Classical, the fault which we impute to the opposite party's language is always that it is a form of false abstraction—that it is emptily generalised, or that it is freakishly individualised.

For myself, I find that those poets who are generally called 'The Romantics' were, when they were being poets, as pure and precise, as faithful to the object, internal or external, as any the world has seen.

In their general opinions, moreover, systematic or scattered, they produced many of the essentials of a 'scientific' æsthetic, because they observed the facts of mental life and of poetic behaviour with unusual fidelity. The test is that their comments on each other were so often on the mark. However Germanic Coleridge might be in his metaphysics, however Platonic Keats became when he talked about Beauty, the opinions of the one on Wordsworth, and of the other on Shakespeare or Shelley, were based on the given poetic material.

If we look at the work of the poets who preceded them, Collins and Gray, for example, since, at least in the school-books, these two are held to be 'Romantic' precursors, the quality of vivid precision which characterises the Romantics strikes us with the most forcible contrast.

How many, in these two poets I have just mentioned, are the 'rosy-bosomed hours', the 'gilded swarms', the 'purple light(s) of Love', the 'incense-breathing morns', 'the pensive pleasures' and the 'wanton gales', compared to the few, the very few, lines such as 'Her conscious tail her joy declared', 'Cold is her breast like flowers that drink the dew', or 'the weak-eyed bat With short shrill shriek flits by on leathern wing'—in which it looks as if the poet were paying the slightest attention to *what* he was talking about.

If we compare some of the poems of Blake, who certainly had a more intellectual conception of experience, as well as a commoner gnomic habit, than the other 'Romantics', we can see the point of the Imagist classification of poetic accuracy into fidelity either to an external or to an internal object.

Compare for instance Blake's poem *The Prince of Love* with Gray's 'In vain to me the smiling mornings shine'. The difference lies, I think, in this. We can say not only that Blake's experience strikes us as real whereas Gray's does not, but, much more importantly, that Blake has told us all we need to know about his experience. That is remarkable enough, since nobody really knows quite certainly and distinctly what Blake's objective experience was, whereas we can presumably check the dates of

Richard West's death, which Gray mourns. In Blake's poem the words *are* the experience. He has found a form of words which, as nearly as it is possible to guess, recreate in our minds the experience in his. The only test we have of this is of course the fact that it is not possible to think of other or further words which would give us a better or more precise experience within the limits of thought imposed by the kind of words. The Gray poem on the other hand is at best notes for a poem, if that, and the last two lines might come out of a rather stilted letter to a friend. But with its clichés, its blurred and swollen imagery, its purely verbal abstractions, it can only lead us to inquire, if our curiosity is not totally enervated by it, *what* on earth, if there, it is talking *about*. The experience, if any, remains incommunicado, and the words are *nothing*.

Am I saying then that poetry is just this vividness of precision? If I were I should not be saying very much more or other than T. E. Hulme with his 'accurate curve' which the artist is trying to express. At least I am saying that this quality is always present in true poetry if we include fidelity to an internal as well as an external object. At the moment, however, what I chiefly wish to point out is, first, that this quality is present even more obviously in those poets who have been described as 'The Romantics' than in the rather more vaguely indicated 'Classicals'; and, second, that it is much more characteristic of them, it defines them much more recognisably than the qualities for which they are generally and loosely labelled 'Romantic'; for instance, as being Pelagian, rationalistic, liberalistic, humanistic, emotionally 'wet' rather than 'dry', loose in conception or in living, imaginative rather than fanciful, subjective, wild, and preferring their architecture ruined. Further I want to point out that this is in no way accidental. The quality of poetic precision is related to these other vague qualities which, in friendship or hostility, we discern in them and, for good or bad, although probably for bad, lump together as 'Romantic'. It is true of course that if Virgil or Pindar can at all meaningfully be described as 'Classical' poets, then there is not much sense in describing Gray as such. His use of the language, the verbal tricks rather, which he picked up from his Greek and Latin education is largely negative. It does not indicate a positive Classical point of view—which is, as I have said, an epiphenomenon —but is a way of avoiding direct experience and therefore meanings which were dangerous, indecorous and certainly not acceptable by his contemporaries, anxious for stability. I do not see any reason to suppose that Gray could not have communicated these experiences and meanings if he had been able to allow himself to have them. What is worthy of note is that his world of classical verbiage is highly subjective. His diction is really in the main a trick of quotation not so very different from Mr. Eliot's although rather more generalised. But the aim in each case is the same, the evocation of authority and the exclusion of the world of direct sense. That it is possible to retain some of both the virtues and vices of the Latin and Greek poets—and even to retain a Latinised diction—while still writing good verse, even recognisable poetry, and without excluding the external world, is shown of course, not only by Milton, but also by Pope and Thomson. But what makes these poets great or good poets is what makes 'The Romantics' also great or good poets—and what makes Mr. Eliot often a good poet: to have one's eye on the object, to labour continually to release the exact, the true word, which is knocking about all the time in the poet's unconscious. To have this unconscious verbal *preparation for experience is* to be a poet.

Now I have used the word 'release' and earlier I referred to 'freedom' as a poetic essential. These words here relate to a mental process, but I must note that it is just this accent on freedom (in all its manifestations) for which the Romantics are accorded, by the neo-scholastics, various adjectives of pejorative intent. The Romantic resistance to mere convention is only the negative side of a continual effort to formulate experiences and to know in so doing what these are. Again I refer to Keats's 'negative capability'. But I must add that, though a certain passivity towards the given is a mark of the poet, his is not a mere formless passivity. He waits, but he waits with a kind of words, and of rhythms conditioning and conditioned by these words, which he has inherited and accumulated. These words *are* the way in which he receives his experience. A transmutation happens in his mind—Mr. Eliot has described this process very well—and later the poem is born. It is a reproductive process, and one thing that cannot be reproduced by such a process is any book of rules.

The rules which Boileau or Pope or Dr. Johnson have implied or explicitly stated, and which are as good a handbook of classical composition as any with meaning for modern writers, cannot possibly teach anyone how to produce a poem (unless it were entirely a patchwork of quotations from a poet's 'dead ancestors', and that would be indeed a very 'superior' example of Mr. Eliot's 'superior amusement'). In other words, a definite and recognisable psychological process, what formerly with necessary vagueness was called 'inspiration', has always been at work whenever a poem is produced. One quite valid definition of the poem, which is not more vague than any other attempt at definition, is just the account, as precise as possible, of this psychological process in the given case.

Naturally the mere transcription of psychological states is not poetry. States are not the process; and the free associations of an analysand upon his couch can hardly be confused with poetic creation, although many modern poets write as if they were not clear about the distinction. A poem always exhibits the signs of some sort of unified vision and some sort of control, but, on the other hand, we can still say that there is a kind of psychological intuition, an experience of the mind on the hop between its unconscious and its conscious conditions, which is exciting in a way we can hardly distinguish, if at all, from the purest 'poetic' excitement.

I mean that the 'poetic moment', the isolable line or lines which make us catch our breath and say "That's it", are a final statement of a psychological truth, as it is being perceived. We feel that it is being said to us by a living person in a state of unusual wholeness, that is, of awareness of himself and of the universe, about what he himself sees and feels at that moment, however often the moment may be repeated. This psychological peculiarity is what is responsible for the dual character of poetry, as at once universal, and concrete and particular.

Many of Shakespeare's characters speak to us in this bare, true, universal but concrete and living form—'Pray you, undo this button', 'Look, look, her lips'. 'She should have died hereafter, there would have been a time for such a word'. Even 'Never, never, never, never, never'.

It is significant that these lines are directed towards, even if they do not absolutely require, dramatic performance. The 'representation' is a visible and audible organisation of human relations. It is essentially economic, a marshalling of experience for the maximum avoidance of the explicit, as though the very aim of poetry were to supersede speech.

These lines are nodal unifications of the formless data of psychological behaviour. What causes the excitement is the feeling of our own minds leaping with the poet's from an instantaneous visual survey of the whole factual truth of the emotional situation into a form of conscious speech which is its plenipotentiary representative. It gives us at one and the same time the feeling that it is so accurate that we could pass back again into the elaborated total emotional situation, and the feeling that we do not need to try. This looks as if poets might still be only the most convincing liars. But in fact they have to stand up to unending generations of the feelings they have grown and altered in ourselves. It is the lies which die in poetry, and its truth is discovery, within the limitations of those emotional acceptances which are biologically possible.

A bridgehead from the remote unknown part of the mind into the conscious, the available, the free and powerful, has been secured, a victory of experience won. But though we can, at least in theory, find out what a poem 'means', we can analyse the poem out into discursive prose, the poem disappears in the process.

A good poem exactly opposes itself to the discursive in so far as it is a unified poem and not a collection of poetic 'moments'. I have laid emphasis on the poetic process, on the shift of experience between the poet's unconscious and conscious, his sleeping and

waking mind, because I believe not only that this shift of experience is the way in which poetry is written, but also that there is
no other way in which poetry can be written. In other words, I
would go as far as to say that if the human mind were other than
it is, if the human brain and nervous system had developed in
such a way that we did not function dynamically between conscious and unconscious processes, we should not write poetry at
all. Because a race of beings, if that were conceivable, which
functioned always on a flat level of consciousness could not
write poetry, we may say that the purely discursive is always bad
for poetry, or anyway strictly useless. 'Ideas' as such, it has often
been noted, are bad for poetry, and this is the reason. While they
are still recognisable as 'ideas' which can be described equally
validly in common conscious and discursive language, the most
they will do is float upon the top of the poem (in so far as it is
otherwise a poem). They cannot become part of a poem till they
have been broken down by the enzymes of the poet's unconscious
associations. All concepts, and this is true also of the Christian
and Classical conceptions of Man, are thus liable, from the point
of view of poetry, to be pre-conceptions. Even those poets who
have joined themselves consciously to the neo-scholastic, neo-
classical conception may find that they can only go to church or
the temple on Sundays. Their poetic working-week, if it is a
repaying one, is spent being humanistic, concerned with the
habits of man on his planet. This is true even of Mr. Eliot, though
as a kind of literary deacon he may have to attend more lip-
services in his poems. I am not saying that religion cannot be a
whole way of apperception. Indeed, where it exists, it must and
ought to be so. I do say that this for poets has nothing to do with
orthodoxy as such. It is, as always, a question of the personal
attempt to discern truth.

I have been trying in this chapter to do two related things:
to establish a connection between poetry and what we ought
to call 'truth', that is, verifiable apperception, and also to
show how the poets who are, although so roughly, classified
as Romantic may be said to have revived and developed

an exploratory character of poetry which is its real nature.

I must now explain more fully my use of the word 'representative', which is somewhat specialised and has occurred in various contexts.

The poet when he is not engaged upon a poem becomes, as Wordsworth said, "an ordinary man again". His mind, relaxed from the special concentration of writing a poem, is occupied with a variety of words and images, sometimes disconnected, sometimes in process of arranging themselves, with the aid of another kind of concentration, for discursive speech or writing. Potential discourse always implies an audience in some form or another, and is therefore in close touch with an objective external reality, something, that is, which can at once be realised as common by a number of persons, and which is thus at a high level of consciousness. Certainly there are unconscious formulations in words, since people talk in their sleep and under anæsthetics, but by the time that any given human being is ready to record the words which are passing through his mind we can hardly doubt that he is conscious in a way which we recognise as referring at least in part to the ordinary world of sense around us all.

From his general behaviour we may or may not be able to infer that very much more is going on in his mind than his words alone account for, but every individual person, and the poet too, while he is being an 'ordinary man' can be aware of many other characteristics of his ordinary passive mind. He knows that thoughts and images trail off into infinity like a crowd along a dusty road; that he can spend hours in mental immobility or absence, while his hands or feet can be busily employed—and then receive some relatively clear formulation in words which proves to him that he has all along been occupied in a mute and even perhaps imageless kind of *thinking*. Or his own actions may reveal this to him, although by the time that is possible they will do so in some verbal formulation. In the course of his life, if he becomes mature, he will also recognise, fleetingly or unmistakeably, that there is a pattern in his experience and behaviour which makes him resemble everybody he knows, but which at the same time is peculiar to himself. He may also come to see that this pattern is deposited from the circuit of judgments which runs endlessly between the mute and the verbal, giving our human behaviour its special potentialities for subtlety and error. I have used these rather laboured substitutes for the terms 'conscious' and 'unconscious' because Freud and his followers have made these too topographical and I wish to describe a normal mind in its circumscribed but sea-like restlessness.

There seems no reason to doubt the contemporary psychological view that the normal mind is continually at work. When I have used the word 'passive' I have still referred to this normal activity which is automatic and continues when the mind is detached from concentration on the self or on some object. What then is this normal and continual activity? I have said that the mind lives on, or rather *is*, a circuit of experience which runs from the outer world (extending from a given immediacy to a wider and wider abstraction) to an inner world, individually private but never, probably even in insanity, totally disorganised. There is always some pattern which can be, even if fleetingly, recognised in overt conduct, some fragment of a law to be observed. Indeed I think we can say that this 'unconscious' behaviour, whether it is also verbal or not, is much more wholly law-bound, more circumscribed, more predictable than the very wide range of behaviours which we call conscious.

By these I mean those which are in the closest relation to the objective world and which we can most readily subject to classification. Those behaviours may seem in some cases—for example, the more exact sciences—to be circumscribed only by the objective conditions among which they move. It may appear that the scientist's mind, while he is being a scientist, no longer lives on the eternal circuit between outer and inner experience. To the extent that he is wholly concentrated on the object and on operations which are needed for its elucidation, that is a practical truth. But as soon as he passes more fully into theory, as soon as he begins visibly to relate his object to the rest of the world, even to the purely objective world, the rest of the circuit reveals that it is at work. This automatic mental process is the means by which, throughout his lifetime, he has learnt his very spontaneity from interpretation of other people's behaviour and of their precepts, and if it has done nothing else it has conditioned the choice and emphasis of his interest. He is an extreme and specialised example of the normal mental activity which continues all the time in everyone at all levels of intellect, consciousness and sanity. This activity is a continual interpretation of what appears to be given both from inside and from outside. We shall see more clearly how it compares with other more deliberate or more specialised mental activities if we call it a kind of myth-making.

The Concise Oxford Dictionary defines myth as 'purely fictitious narrative describing supernatural personages and embodying popular ideas on natural phenomena, etc.' The most revealing part of this definition is the second half. For myth-making is an attempt at interpretation of *given* experience, and, like all such interpretation, it is also an attempt to hold the experience in some recognisable pattern for future use: in the case of primitive myth, for the chief use of all, for continuing to live. It is therefore implicit theorisation. Primitive myth-making, continually interpreting the outer and forming the inner world, is clearly a way of living on the circuit of continual mental activity which I have described as characteristically human. From the most primitive level upwards, a human mind is all the time at work on this dual and reflexive organisation of its inner and outer worlds. The inner criterion is satisfaction (that is, the reduction of the tensions of anxiety); the outer criterion is survival. There is no form of judgment which is wholly objective, which is an immediate unconditioned response to an external impression. It is not possible for me to say 'That is a cat' or 'a tree' or 'a man', in pure detachment from my own emotional matrix. That is represented, at the very least, by some final conditioning of my interest or the direction of my attention. As a human being, it is my profoundest emotional need to be satisfied about the nature of my given world. As I become only gradually acquainted with the external and its complications, the more inwardly-orientated emotional criterion of satisfaction lasts me a long time, throughout my early formative years. But the criterion of satisfaction must pass over into that of survival. We confuse ourselves about this and sometimes talk about 'mere' survival as though that were the cruder, more primitive and baser aim, simply because we forget that during the defenceless dream-life of our infancy our surviving is done for us by other people. Growing up means assuming individual responsibility for our own survival and therefore learning to put a greater emphasis upon it than upon mere satisfaction. To put it another way, each individual, as he becomes aware of the growth of his own powers and of the objective conditions of continuing to develop them, re-defines survival for himself. To survive as an individual, which means with harmony between the inner and outer worlds, becomes a more and more complex and co-operative endeavour. In my immaturity I have to become satisfied about the existence of my human powers, and in my growth and ripeness about the nature of the outer world on which they operate.

We can see this, for example, in the case of emotional drives conditioning choice of profession. A girl may live without harm as the heroine of her own inward drama, but if she decides to go on the stage, she must sooner or later learn to act. If she does not she will fail to survive. Even if she marries into the peerage, as a whole and continuous personality she will have failed to survive. In adult life the inner criterion of satisfaction can only be met by mastering the conditions of survival. Mastering the conditions of survival, in this case and others, may mean learning for oneself exactly why the original demand for satisfaction was an impossible one. This in the chorus girl's case might well be the realistic fruit of trying to learn to act. This would probably work by clarifying the original demand for satisfaction, which may have been merely confused, not wholly fantastic.

However, it would have been impossible for the chorus girl to make her choice of entrance into common and outer experience if she had not lived first in this world of fore-evaluation, if she had not first constructed her interpretative myth.

The mental circuit, if left to work automatically, is roughly self-corrective. As far as our interpretations of the world, referring to its possible fulfilment of our own needs, are concerned, Freud's reality-principle works for us over a great range of them, rather like the cat's cuff on the ear for her kittens. Where the criterion of survival, moreover, is immediately dominant for us, words are much less necessary and the possibilities of error and deception are thus reduced. Where there are words, there must be, if not lies, at least always inadequacies. Perhaps more than any other single factor, words are responsible for the successes and the failures of the human being as compared with the rest of animal kind. Words are always abstractions from experience, abstraction is progressive and is always on the way to hypostasis, which, when we follow this course of its development, reveals itself as a disease.

I said that the individual myth-maker, the human being who from the earliest times has been trying to give himself some pictured account of the external world which shall result in mental satisfaction, cannot do much harm to anyone, even himself, unless he feels compelled to test his vision and the vision proves unacceptably false.

A myth begins generally at a very low level of abstraction. It is a name or an image which is an attempt at precision, at making one's percept clear so that it can be held in the mind. But myths, of all things, tempt the organisers of power; and there is always a priestcraft waiting for man the myth-maker.

Where the criterion of satisfaction is dominant in the continual human circuit of interpretation, and where therefore the test of experience is not immediate, the priests who are, at any time in history, any organisers of abstraction for the purposes of power, can always take charge with their hypostatical magic.

For it is in the hypostatical dictionary that myth is split from science. It is the hypostatising definers who claim that we are living in a purely scientific age (and ought to be ashamed of it); that science is the great killer of myth, poetry and religion; or alternatively that dogmatic and/or mystical religion is the psychological counter-force which heals the wounds caused by a killing science. But in fact it is not religion, but myth or poetry, which is the necessary pole to science. We continue to need myth just as much as science and the poet at least as much as the scientist, because myth is part of science and the scientist exists potentially in the poet. Just because the criterion *is* progressively one of survival, because all human labours of any kind become more and more divided and co-operative, we need to know more and more about the source of our satisfactions and why and how they create a human world, and themselves survive, not by protecting and fixating themselves but by developing and spreading their range and subtlety. This we shall discover rather by looking into ourselves and at each other than at the sky or into the dusty works of the Church Fathers, or even into the sibylline leaves of Mr. Eliot.

Both poet and scientist are specialists. The poet was the primitive physicist and later the primitive psychologist. But the fact that both physics and psychology became more objective, exact and generalised does not mean that poetry and science have split and have no further use or need for each other. They represent the poles of the natural mental circuit. The poet or myth-maker discovers or receives the given material of experience, charged with its natural interest; the scientist examines and relates it to all other experience. Both poet and scientist are potentialities of the same creative outlook.

Both are primarily concerned with how and why we live on this planet, and, for survival, the adult criterion, the scientist must protect the poet from the priests and the poet must protect the scientist from the politicians. In the perversion of language, one of our most necessary tools of survival, priest and politician are not very different from one another.

The poet has been historically the discoverer of the myths, of the intuitive interpretations of reality which are later analysed and expanded in the particular sciences. What then is the poet's speciality in polar relation to that of the scientist?

I have said already in this chapter that far more poets have been humanistic in their choice of subject than otherwise. I will go further and suggest that the natural choice of poetic theme is something to do with love or death. The poet may pick his images from here, there and everywhere, and indeed may write a great deal of verse which is strictly 'occasional', but what is spontaneously poetic in his work, what is *given*, will be in some way about the natural biological drama implied by these central themes. He lives on the normal circuit of mental activity, he is always, like everyone else, interpreting his experience at one level or another. On the poetic level he is always particularly engaged in discovering a pattern of experience which, while keeping them in indissoluble connection, will take his inner world and his outer world, respectively, as deep and as wide as his perception and expression allow. The inner world of imagery and rhythm is, not private, but very much his own, individualised in the continual restless circulation of mental life and, in his case, unusually available to consciousness, partly as the result of practice. He remains the individual myth-maker whose meanings, in so far as he is a poet, are never organised for him passively by priests, professors or pressmen. As a myth-maker his job is the organisation of his own multiple meanings—this is where mythopœia and poetry coincide. In this respect we can say that poetry is a development of language as the eye is a development of the skin. It is a higher degree of organisation of the original creative and synthesising activity of language. In poetry this mythopœia, this primitive synthesising capacity, may reveal itself in a variety of ways of using language which have this in common, that they are all a form of what I have called 'representation'.

This quality of the poetic is one which distinguishes it from prose expression, the intention of which is to say everything, to exhaust meaning and arrive at a conclusion, but to do so by referring or alluding to experience, rather than by recreating it or creating some equivalent for it. (On this basis, imaginative prose cannot be sharply distinguished from poetry.) The poet, on the other hand, in his poem, always remains standing on the circuit of his experience between the inner and outer worlds of apperception, he remains in the presence of his total relevant experience and continually, in the poem, demonstrates it to us. His poem is not an abstract but a concentration of experience. Moreover this concentration is not at all a disadvantage, it is not a *faute de mieux*, it is inherent in the nature of the poem. As I said earlier, I use the word 'representation' in something like an electoral sense, meaning that the technique or method of employing words represents, stands for, or does duty for a number of other possible uses or meanings. These 'representatives' can be, for example: a single word (although usually in a specialised context)—'incarnadine', 'Forlorn, the very word is like a bell', etc.; the image or symbol; what used to be called *wit*; verbal music, which represents ranges of implicit experience; and, importantly, story or action.

The value of a dramatic or narrative action is not merely that it holds one's attention, but that by selection of events (a form of representation) it universalises experience. The drama or narrative is revealed as a unity within the unity of experience and as an example of that awareness of law or pattern which is the most necessary condition for poetic receptivity. That the action is a mythopœic and representative element in my use of the term is illustrated by the fact that we don't really need a story to be new and surprising, in fact the most enduring dramatic poets have certainly borrowed their stories, whatever they may have done about their philosophies. Aristotle was right when he spoke of the importance of 'recognition'. The more surprising, the further from the normal mental circuit with its dip into the symbolising organisation of the unconscious, the further then from poetry— and the nearer to farce, which has been the historic degeneration of the drama. In fact, the real value of the 'surprise ending', when it comes, is seen to be that, surprisingly, it reveals itself, after the whole of the work, as inevitably implied. This is an example of the way in which action, one representative element, stands in relation to experiential reality, to the verifiable. We may take the farcical as the example of a disease which affects and atrophies poetic comedy. Similarly, with the other examples of representation, we can diagnose their corresponding diseases. With the

Georgians there was hypertrophy of the single word (e.g. 'opalescent'); with the religious Metaphysicals especially, a divorce of wit and metaphor from apperception which certainly meant that the poet too often was not living on the circuit of experience; while the disease of audilism is what smites verbal music, as with much of Swinburne and in Mr. Eliot's incantatory passages. They are all examples of a dislike of meanings, and they are analogous to hypostasis in philosophy.

The poets who are called by the neo-classicists Romantic, as if that were necessarily a term of abuse, may certainly be subject to this hypostatical disease, particularly Shelley, and Wordsworth too, when his voice is that of the old half-witted sheep. But when these, or when Keats, Coleridge and Blake, stayed on the circuit of the given, when their meanings retained normal contact with the verifiable, however indirect, and when they did not, as business men, politicians and idealistic philosophers do, organise their words, consciously or unconsciously, for an interested use of power, the poetry they wrote was as pure as any that has been written before or since. The important condition for this was freedom or release so that the poet could look at the object with his own eye, one which had grown from the habit of such looking, which was radically individual but which also, since at every stage it had been true to given experience, was also human and universal. That was the real Romantic contribution.

Cleanth Brooks* thinks that the Romantic (as he defines Romanticism) weakened poetry by trying to limit its choice of subject to the 'high serious' or the 'specifically poetic'. I think he was right when he insisted that poetry ought to be able to digest any theme. But I should also say that the quest for the 'high serious', when it produces bad poetry, reveals itself as only another example of the hypostatic disease to which all uses and all kinds of language are liable. I see no reason why the Christian and orthodox spectacles which Mr. Eliot must want to put on the poet's nose should not make him see only another and worse set

*Modern Poetry and the Tradition.

of distortions. Poetry, on the other hand, whatever its choice of techniques of expression, is naturally tragic; concerned, that is, with the laws of life as they are given in the poet's experience. He does not have to look for the 'high serious' as if his job were a self-persuasion that life is strange and terrible, but at the same time rhythmical, symbolic and significant. He is naturally and intimately concerned with love and death, the basic biological themes.

CHAPTER IX

Lord Peter Views the Soul

THIS book is an attempt to isolate and criticise a philosophical tendency which is common to a number of contemporary writers. Most of them are poets or critics of poetry.
They are concerned with what is generally called creative writing
and they are laymen in theology as well as science. As a rule, they
do not attack science directly, only the humanism to which science
lends, by implication, support. They may even have a temperate
respect for what they call 'exact' science, by which too often they
mean a science which keeps to the limited place they have prescribed for it. This is true even of T. E. Hulme, whose 'exact'
science had to toe a line clear of the 'muddy mixed zone' of the
sociological sciences. This terrain he wished to preserve for later
development by his equally 'exact' theology.

The overt attempt of these writers, unlike, for instance, Maritain,
has not been to restore theology to its medieval status as 'Queen
of the Sciences'. They aim rather at a royal equivalence like that
of William and Mary. For the purposes of discussion they have in
general been content with expressing or implying the doctrine of
the Two Truths, the view that the fields of Science and of Theology
are distinct and that each is paramount within its own field. Since
they are commonly motivated by a moral and eschatological
anxiety which the results of scientific method certainly do nothing
to relieve, they behave as if the reticences of science were
admissions of invincible ignorance, and were also an implicit
support of their own Dual System. Thus they refrain from

asking some of the more obvious questions, for instance: How can one admit the primacy of science even in its own specialised fields, since theology, if it is independent of ordinary observational method, must claim to include all original causation and the whole ground of knowledge, everything that philosophers have called the self-subsistent? They deal with this only by a verbal usage which implies that all science is quantitative; by ignoring that science is a method of concrete investigation, not a framework of abstract generalisation; and by abstracting everything which they call 'value' and putting that under the primary of religion.

The two writers whom I wish to consider here are in a rather different class. C. S. Lewis and Dorothy Sayers are both lay theologians; but, giving the term a specialised slant, they may both be described as fundamentalists, and this distinguishes them from most of the other writers I have mentioned. By this I mean that they do not dodge any of the theological issues, but are ready to give all the answers. If we wish we may regard this as courageous and therefore creditable, but I am not sure that it is in fact so. In both may be discerned again and again a wish to discredit scientific thinking which springs from a profounder wish to make theology paramount again. They are both writers and broadcasters with considerable popular appeal; and if, as I hope to show, their apparent willingness to probe the most fundamental intellectual issues merely masks this underlying wish, their distractive performances serve to put objective and verifiable thought in greater popular danger than it generally is in. They both serve themselves and their cause by a variety of tricks. One which is employed by Dorothy Sayers I will mention here as an example. She refers in one of her *Unpopular Essays* to a discussion between a scientist and a theologian, in which the scientist seemed to be quite unaware that the word 'substance' had a special technical meaning in theology, and she implies that the discussion from the scientist's angle was by this ignorance rendered null and void. Now one may say without exaggeration that all and every discussion which may go on between theologians and adherents of a scientific discipline is basically about the question whether any meaning can be attributed to the theological usage of such terms as 'substance'. The underlying argument is precisely about the right of theologians to regard theology as a special discipline with an existent subject-matter and therefore about their right to coin special technical terms or to use terms with a special definition in order to classify this subject-matter. The truth is that a philosophy which bases itself on scientific thinking must challenge this right.

Mr. Lewis, while no less thorough-paced in his determination and his efforts to re-establish the intellectual sovereignty of theology, is in general less blunt and less detailed in his attacks on 'science' than Miss Sayers, who sounds, when standing up to Fred Hoyle, as if she were lecturing him through spiritual pince-nez. Her equipment and armament is often more up-to-date than Lewis's; he is generally content, on the positive side, with sneers at science and scientists, and rarely specifies their kind. He relies on the negative approach in this respect, for instance, in the example already given of the spectacle of armed men fighting in the sky which was 'commonly seen' during the sixteenth century. His comment, "I have not seen them myself," is not an admission but a disingenuous insinuation, whose purpose is to maintain anti-scientific emotion.

Though both may be described as 'literary', they have approached the theology which now governs and organises their whole output from very different careers. This, with the difference of sex, may account for the differences, if not oppositions, in some of the practical applications which they favour. Lewis, more Pauline perhaps, who is continually troubled about something which he calls Hierarchy [which means in practice the submission of the female to the male] thinks it would be better if these two sexes had respectively more babies and more beards. Miss Sayers, who often still disarms one with her common sense, never, to my knowledge, hypostatises the wearing of trousers, and thinks that women may in some circumstances wear slacks.

Though Mr. Lewis, like Mr. Willey, is academic, there are some

respects in which his literary status may be compared to that of
Miss Sayers rather than to that of any of the other writers whom I
have discussed. They are both of course interested in what is
generally thought of as creative writing and have written about it
and evolved theories about it. Whether Mr. Lewis regards
himself as a serious creative writer I do not know. Miss Sayers
certainly so regards herself; and this not only on the basis of her
religious plays, but also of her detective fiction which, as I have
earlier pointed out, she uses as the material of her æsthetic theory,
with insufficient attention (though in this field alone) to the other
creative productions of mankind. She seems to be well versed in
the *Divine Comedy*; and if she had chosen this work, let us say,
instead of her own novel *Gaudy Night* as the material for her
analysis of the creative process (e.g. in *The Mind of the Maker*)
such objectivity might have saved her from the great risk of
confusing the introspective and the creative, which always besets
the writer of projected fantasies. Mr. Lewis writes, quite well, a
kind of scientifiction. There is no·reason why he should not;
just as there is no reason why Miss Sayers should not write
detective fiction. There is a legitimate market for competent
entertainment. But since there is no doubt that Miss Sayers at
least takes her Wimsey phase rather too seriously, we have some
ground for suspecting that the preference of both these writers for
abstraction is significant. Their later theological development
illuminates an incapacity or a dislike for analysing and com-
prehending concrete individual human character, which was
always characteristic of them. I do not say that all poets and
novelists who substitute the theological generalisations for a
sound psychology will be led absolutely away from wisdom and
knowledge of the human heart, although to my mind there is
evidence in the later work of Graham Greene that he is beginning to substitute generalised case-histories and the lives of the
saints for observed people. This is only an illustrative disquisition
on the actual literary and critical status of two writers who
certainly do what Mr. Eliot tells all writers and readers to do—that
is, subject literary creation and criticism to theological standards.

Their importance for this book is, however, something quite different: that they are *popularisers* of kinds of glaringly fallacious thinking which more subtle creators often have the good sense to avoid, and that they reproduce all the stock arguments in an unusually explicit form. Through them the B.B.C. in particular has given the Two Truths theory a kind of real presence. They are allowed to criticise the theories of scientists—particularly Miss Sayers—as if on the same level of *expertise*. On the other hand, while the B.B.C. allows a certain amount of free discussion as between Bertrand Russell and Father Coplestone, it is very niggardly in the time it allows to convinced and competent scientific agnostics who may wish to present a considered attack on theological pretensions. There is a distinction here which it is important to notice. The philosophical conclusions of a specialised scientist such as Fred Hoyle are seldom a direct attack on religion or even on theology. Yet how often they are given an 'answer' from the theological angle from speakers such as Mr. Lewis and Miss Sayers who are not even of comparable standing in their own field, and how seldom they are encouraged to initiate any positive statement of their own views unless these are directed towards harmonising religion and science. As far as most of the organs of publicity in this country are concerned, the lay public can easily escape noting that agnosticism is a positive belief about the universe, and may well conclude that it is just an unreasoned or even accidental lack of religion.

As a result of this state of public discussion, Mr. Lewis and Miss Sayers have been allowed to appear in the common mind as interpreters of something which is supposed to be, more than anything, intellectually and technically difficult. Their implication is that, if understood, it would, while retaining its original authority of sanctity, be also as convincing as scientific demonstration.

Finally I have chosen these two because of their general emotional tone. They both have that knowing quality of elected-ness historically common to those communities of saints which have been preoccupied with sin rather than with charity. Often their proposals of salvation look more like a threat than a promise. Mr. Lewis in particular has a bias of interest towards the devil, as readers of his *Screwtape Letters* will realise. I do not mean that he approves of the devil's existence except for other people. Nor do I suppose that he has ever 'seen' the cleft foot and the tail any more than he has 'seen' the armed men fighting in the sky. This is only interesting here as an illustration of his bold fundamentalism and of his method.

Since this book is a discussion of the philosophical validity of the revived scholasticism which is being used to provide an intellectual structure for much contemporary literature, we can now go straight to the unusually explicit statements which these two have given of their theoretical beliefs.

In Mr. Lewis's case, we find this in a book called *Miracles*, 'on which Mr. Lewis has been engaged for several years' and which is 'a study preliminary to any historical inquiry into the actual occurrence of miracles'. He proposes to discover whether miracles are or are not 'intrinsically probable', and claims that most historians decide against the probability of miracles unconsciously before they begin their investigations into evidence.

Mr. Lewis's basic argument is contained in the following propositions:

The word 'Miracle' means an interference with Nature by supernatural power. There is a distinction between the meanings attached to the word *Nature* by those (the Supernaturalists) who believe that something else exists, and by those (the Naturalists) who believe that nothing else exists. For the latter, Nature is a great process of 'becoming', which exists on its own in space and time, and in which all events are interlocked. For the former, Nature is something dependent, a mere filling to the framework of space and time, which has been produced by some One Thing else which alone is self-subsistent. For the Supernaturalist, there is no difficulty in believing that miracles are possible, since there is no reason why the Something Else, which exists for him 'outside Nature', should not interfere with the Nature that depends upon it. On the other hand, if it can be shown to the

Naturalist that Nature is not, as he claims, a totally closed system, the 'whole show', but that we have experience of phenomena which in principle are independent, which cannot be totally explained in terms of the whole interlocking system, then we have to abandon Naturalism.

Such an independent phenomenon Mr. Lewis finds in rational thought. All possible knowledge depends on the validity of reasoning or thought (he uses these words interchangeably). No thought is valid if it can be explained fully as the result of irrational causes.

A rational belief, says Mr. Lewis, is caused by argument from observed facts. So far so good, but we shall see that Mr. Lewis at once begins to abstract from his own definition and to put all the practical stress on causation and argument, leaving the contribution of observed facts in the air. We shall also see that the idea of causation, in his usage, is narrowly mechanistic. For irrational belief, on the other hand, he gives a variety of causes, for example, association of ideas (causing, for instance, fear of black dogs), a bad liver, a complex or one's class-situation, lunacy, or a bit of bone pressing on one's brain: or more importantly, the Total System or Nature. What these have in common is that they do not argue or infer. Whatever does not argue or infer is, not merely other than rational, it is irrational, and the irrational cannot cause the rational. "A train of thought," he says, "loses all rational credentials, as soon as it can be shown to be *wholly* the result of irrational causes."

Accepting, though only for the moment, Mr. Lewis's account of Nature, just given, as irrational, we must suppose that this statement means that a logical or rational train of thought cannot arise from the mere contemplation of Nature. It is clear that Mr. Lewis, although he claims to be a Monist, is troubled enough by the old difficulty of Cartesian dualism—a question which has been sharply worded by Professor Ryle:* How does the Ghost actually work the Machine?—to sheer away from re-examining it. He deals with this by expressly stating that he is not discussing

*The Concept of Mind.

consciousness or mental life as a whole. Of many of our mental effects, he says: "No absurdity would follow from regarding them as parts of Nature. The distinction we have to make is not one between 'Mind' and 'Matter' . . . but between Reason and Nature." It should be clear that he has made an arbitrary abstraction of something which he calls Reason, and thus put himself in a position of extreme dualism where natural causation, as he implicitly defines it, certainly cannot operate. For causation, to Mr. Lewis, is *either* mechanical (natural and irrational), it consists of shunting operations by which a train of behaviour is pushed into some depot, *or* it is rational, it is a train of thought which is not at any point, either beginning or end, composed of mechanical contiguities. One would like to know more of its provenance and destination—what, in fact, any such train of thought is *about*. Mr. Lewis says categorically that rational thought means valid inference or the capacity for valid inference. He also says that to be thus valid it must give us a genuine insight into realities beyond our own minds. But in practice he has completely lost sight of the real structure of a valid inference. One cannot see how Mr. Lewis's 'Rational Causation' could cause anything at all. It seems that he must follow Berkeley and believe that our ideas are rational because and if they are directly implanted in our minds by God, but this in Lewis's case is certainly to beg the question at issue in his book. On his definition and in his usage, Reason could not have any causal connection with the rest of mental life, whether rational or irrational, it could not have any connection with observed facts at all. In practice, Mr. Lewis ought to confine rational argument, Reason therefore, to the illustrative syllogisms in the text-books of classical logic, which certainly in themselves do not give us 'genuine insight into realities beyond' our own minds. It is only when the realities can be accepted as first existing, as 'given', that a syllogism or any other piece of formal logic will provide us with new knowledge, that we can use them for valid inference.

We might concede that Mr. Lewis does mean just this, that he is referring to the syllogism or to our ability to make and instantly comprehend other more mathematical abstractions; that he means that it is the human capacity for purely formal abstraction, without necessary or particular concrete content, which is uniquely independent of all other phenomena, mental or physical. But this view could only be maintained if the human formal capacity could be shown to be directly implanted in us in a final shape and if it were not in fact always found inextricably entwined with our other mental capacities, and these at very different levels of development.

On the contrary we can say that the formal or abstracting capacity is present in some degree in all mentalities, even those below the adult human. It can be observed to grow; and even mathematics has a history from primitive counting and from land surveying and astronomy. And if we are talking of individual mental development, the higher forms of abstraction are not absolutely distinct from the lowest. For instance the attaching of denotative names, which we witness in infancy, is a form of abstraction or formalisation. In this bare form it is of course association of ideas, which Lewis wrongly describes as irrational. Finally, our formal capacity *is* abstraction, and that word by itself implies that something (Nature, the observable, etc.) is abstracted from, and is an essential part of, the operation.

Lewis says that we can describe an inference or an argument as valid only if it does not arise from wholly irrational (by which he means *natural*) causes. This is putting the cart before the horse. For can Lewis or anyone else show us an argument or inference which arises from wholly 'rational' causes? I have suggested that for purposes of discussion he might use some of the more abstract generalisations of higher mathematics, especially in those branches which have so far found no practical application. He does not appear to claim this possible advantage. The language of mathematics, however, exemplifies our abstracting or formalising capacity at its highest level, it is our most rational variety of thought and, in its later developments particularly, it can be considered as independent of immediate experience. But mathematics in fact is only the perception of logical relations. Since moreover Mr. Lewis has been talking all along about origins, how our capacity for rational thought gets into the universe, we are entitled to point out that, as a mental capacity mathematics is not distinct from all the other forms of abstraction by which we do all our thinking. The fact that the higher developments of abstraction can take place without immediate empirical reference does not mean that they have arisen in total independence of experience, either the experience of the human race or of the individual. We *are* abstracters, perceivers of relations and oppositions. That we can abstract at higher and higher levels tells us nothing about the source of Human Reason, it only tells us that as animals we have characteristics which by practice become accomplishments. 'Reason' of course is not found in the universe, only people behaving or thinking rationally. Even mathematics, in its most detached formulations, arises in a human (natural) context, the body of a mathematician and a special learning or environment. Such 'gifts' are all greater or more specialised refinements of relation-perceiving.

But we can see that valid inference of the sort we continually use in leading our lives on the level of speech or below it, is attached to experience at both ends. There is no such thing as a valid inference in complete abstraction from anybody's experience. Inference is an arc which is *afferent* from Nature (Mr. Lewis's 'irrational') and efferent to Nature again. Nature is the given and observable which provides our inferences and arguments with a final court of validity. Many of our most rational arguments do begin in some form of association of ideas (classified by Lewis as irrational); for instance, those of the astronomer which result in logical predictions but which would never have originated at all if someone somewhere in history had not noted a constant association of two or more natural events. To say this is not to ignore the role of hypothesis, including intuition or even hunch, in the work of scientific observers. But a hypothesis which leads to a significant perception of new relations arises in a context of trained experience. Einstein may have felt convinced of the validity of the theory of relativity without waiting for the experiments of Michelson and Morley, but the thought of Newton, among other experiences, had taught him where to look, even if after looking he discovered a different set of relations. At any level of consciousness, we hardly ever observe an isolated fact, there is nearly always some beginning of theory. But no hypothesis ever came right out of the blue. Because the layman finds it difficult to follow scientific process in its totality and complexity, he should not think that it does not exist, immensely co-operative, and inextricable, at its roots, from all human experience. In short, he should not be misled by Mr. Lewis and others into hypostatising Reason. This may lead him into thinking of The Scientist as an embodiment of Rationality, and inevitably hating this figment of his own imagination.

For the validity and the rationality of an inference are *shown* at the point where the efferent arc arises, upon its return, that is, to the Nature of observed and observable facts, which Mr. Lewis stigmatises as 'irrational', and which does often consist for us in the more or less passive observation of associated ideas. Some associations of ideas, like that of danger and the black dog which once bit us in childhood, given as an example by Mr. Lewis, would be called irrational by most of us, but not by any means all associations of ideas which occur without logical argument result in invalid inference. I do not believe that Mr. Lewis would say that a real dog, black or otherwise, argues rationally. Such a claim would certainly involve him in trouble with the Church Fathers and their views on the soul. But he must admit that when the dog hears the dinner-bell and runs straight to a piece of real meat, it may truly be said to have inferred correctly. With all of us the actual bringing home of the bacon is the only *test* of our rationality or irrationality.

It should not be difficult to see that Mr. Lewis is, no doubt unconsciously, playing on the meanings of the words 'rational' and 'irrational'. He is confusing the two commonest meanings of the words 'rational'—that which can either reason or results from reasoning, and that which can be reasoned about. Hence, I suppose, it is possible for him to say:

"This (the belief that God created Nature), and perhaps this alone, fits in with the fact that Nature, although not apparently intelligent, is intelligible—that events in the remotest parts of space appear to obey the laws of rational thought."

The confusion is responsible for most of the other unconscious puns in that sentence. Nature does not 'obey' any 'laws' of rational thought or otherwise. The laws are the ways in which we are obliged to perceive nature because they are the given structure of nature. It is no wonder therefore that nature is intelligible. This trick, one of the common forms of hypostasis, is characteristic of Mr. Lewis's thought. There is an interesting and instructive illustration in his Preface to Milton. Mr. Lewis, as I said, is much concerned with the notion of an hierarchic order in the universe. It is true that this notion was also interesting to Milton and his contemporaries. According to Mr. Lewis, Milton looks on his characters as obeying or disobeying the 'rules of the game' and it is clear in the context that Mr. Lewis has an emotional and abstractive attitude towards the word 'rules' as he has towards 'Laws'. He has not understood that rules in a game are matters of pure organisation, not of degree or dominance and that even leadership is the spearhead of structure.

As far as the word 'irrational' is concerned, Mr. Lewis has converted a mere negative into a positive. If, as he does, we mean by 'rational', capable of arguing or inferring, all that we can justifiably say about Nature is that Nature is non-rational. A rational (logical) inference is based on our observation of the regularity of our experience, of the statistical laws of nature: all men are mortal, Socrates was a man, therefore Socrates was mortal. The fact that we do observe these regularities, that nature is intelligible, gives us no ground for supposing that nature is influenced by any abstract rational procedure, our own or that of some Higher Reason. The word 'irrational' has however a positive and valid meaning. It refers when meaningfully used to behaviour which cannot be brought under a law of observation objectively discovered. The irrationality of the conclusion about the dangerousness of black dogs used by Lewis as an illustration, is due to the fact that the sufferer is unable to observe the actual behaviour of real black dogs. He is not looking at real black dogs but at a private mental image of a black dog. That his reaction is based, not on logical argument, but on association of ideas, is irrelevant. If he were able to attend to his actual experience that most black dogs wag their tails at him, he would, without thinking consciously at all, most probably pat their heads. He would generally infer, though not necessarily consciously, on the basis of associating the ideas of black dogs and friendliness.

Another part of Mr. Lewis's mental furniture is the image of Nature as the mute slave attending the rational will of her Lord, not only of God, but even of Man as far as he is rational. Common language is liable to mislead all of us here, and does so with Mr. Lewis when he tries to make Nature's intelligibility depend on her 'obedience' to law. Nature, he says, is colonised by Reason. "When Nature . . . attempts to do things to Rational Thoughts, she only succeeds in killing them . . . but . . . every object you see before you at the moment—the walls, ceiling . . . your own washed hands and cut finger-nails, bears witness to the colonisation of Nature by Reason . . ."

How far the various skills by which we make use of or, in some cases, interfere with the normal operation of the 'laws of Nature', the 'going-on of Nature on its own', result from or employ logical argument or conscious reasoning, may be a little difficult to determine. But it is certain that a great many skills, even those which are complex, operate by copying a pattern or by obeying an authority. A number of our biggest and most striking interferences with Nature, let us say the Forth Bridge or a Comet aircraft, are the work of a community of detail-operatives who may have no clear comprehension of the whole nor therefore of what Mr. Lewis would call its rationality. Mr. Lewis would say that the whole is the fruit of the rational calculations of the engineer who planned the work. If we adopted Mr. Lewis's use of the word 'rational', or what seems to be the commonest of these uses, we might say that this is true, but in fact the engineer works by finding out about, or by being instructed in, stresses and strains, the laws of his given material, of observed and regular Nature. He masters Nature (or 'colonises' her) by first obeying her. This is no more than to say that we are all living beings with a capacity for learning and for creating in a material.

Mr. Lewis has expressly stated that he is not trying to tell us anything about the mental or the conscious as a whole. But I do not see what meaning we can give to the word Reason, as he uses it, if we try to dissociate it from the concepts of mentality or consciousness as a whole. I do not see what other basis Mr. Lewis can use—if and when he examines the communal operations by which we change the face of Nature—to distinguish between the learned and later reflex skills, and the planning and analysing operations of Reason. The fact is of course that I do things of greatly varying complexity, from cutting my finger-nails to playing the piano, without being conscious that I am using my reason at all, if indeed it can be supposed that I am actually doing so. If I continue consciously to 'use my reason' after reaching a certain degree of learning or proficiency in these accomplishments, I shall have to give them up because I shall become inhibited from performance. Certainly in the intervals of performance I can think about more efficient ways of doing them, but this 'use of my reason' is necessarily conscious. In short, everything that is not conscious abstract thought must, on Lewis's definition, be indistinguishable from 'Nature'. He may seem to have covered himself by saying that 'No harm' would come from regarding certain aspects of the mind, for instance emotion or mental images, as 'parts of Nature', but it is obvious that this limits reason to *conscious* ideas or abstractions which are either about physical Nature or about our remaining mental operations.

It is in fact very difficult to find a definition of the ideas of reason which distinguishes them from what Mr. Lewis defines as Nature, other than our consciousness that we have them. Our capacity for valid inference is not sufficiently exclusive in itself to fit what Mr. Lewis apparently means. And this leaves his argument in a very unsatisfactory state. For if the rest of consciousness may 'without harm' be regarded as part of Nature, this must mean that it is not necessary that reason, which we are to regard as totally distinct from Nature, should be dependent on consciousness. And indeed it is true that we can 'act reasonably' in the conscious judgment of others, without being ourselves conscious that we are doing so. But in that case how does Mr. Lewis draw any distinction between our reason and our learned skills, which may be unconscious; or between the animal and the human; or indeed between the animal and the automatic machine? Whether he means to or not, he seems to be making too much of the fact that we can think—and of course talk—about ourselves, unlike the 'mute' creation awaiting the will of her Lord.

Colonised Nature, the objective world of manufactured or cultivated objects, gives us no precise information about the parts played respectively by reason and Nature in their production. The product, whether it is regarded from the angle of the one who designs or of the one who copies the design, results from a learned skill. Again we can say that Mr. Lewis has erected an impassable Cartesian barrier between his 'reason' and his Nature, and might have saved himself the trouble, and even perhaps the trouble of writing his book, if he had noticed that he was doing so. When we 'reason', what do we reason about? If by 'reason' and 'being Rational' we really mean nothing but the capacity to make valid inferences, then reason cannot arise without Nature. Nature, from this point of view, is the sum of things we reason about. The trouble is that by reason and the rational Mr. Lewis means too many other things as well, many of them mutually exclusive.

We can now produce machines which will make valid inferences of high complexity. To be consistent, Mr. Lewis would surely have to admit that the inferences of the grocer's adding machine, which result in a correct price-ticket, are valid and therefore rational. There seems to be no particular point in describing even the original design of the machine as a colonisation of Nature by reason, since it was not produced by someone who sat down and took his conscious abstract thought out of the blue. It can only be understood as the result of the whole development of mathematics; and mathematics began as one of the tools stumbled upon by a tool-making animal in the course of his trials and errors.

The ectypal machines are certainly the products of particular skills, not of repeated inferences. But the grocer's machine, once it has been manufactured, and as long as it is in working order, goes on making valid inferences without any assistance from our reason or even the grocer's; while it is highly improbable that the original designer will be asked to come down and make it behave rationally. We trust it because it comes from a reputable firm and because it does not in practice add up to our disadvantage, as the grocer has been known to do. We would much prefer that the grocer kept out of the situation. Here we may borrow Mr. Lewis's phrase and say that, in relation to the Nature represented by the till, the grocer's reason could only 'raid to kill'.

If the machine goes wrong and its inferences become invalid, that is never because the grocer's reason or ours or anybody's has been withdrawn from it, but because it has somehow fallen to pieces and reverted, not to chaos, not to the irrational, but to the laws of the raw materials of which it is composed. Intelligence or rational thought or reason (or any such term which you prefer, to describe the conscious application of a learned skill) can understand or repair it only by obeying those laws, which are a description of the way that Nature has been found to behave.

In Mr. Lewis's use of the word 'rational' there are implied two other common meanings which he repeatedly confuses—the 'mental' and the 'trustworthy'. It is only by thus confusing them that he can arrive at his conclusions about the relation or opposition between Reason and Nature.

Reason does not 'colonise' Nature—maybe it is Mr. Lewis's passionate wish to discern hierarchy in the universe which makes him use this expression—but we continually succeed in changing Nature, not merely by thinking out what we should like and telling her to get on with it, but by a hardly separable process of thinking out what we should like *and* by discovering what we can actually achieve within the framework of existing natural law.

The two processes are perhaps always present, but as thought only produces an object or a change by submitting to a material which regularly produces objects and changes of its own, whether we are there to interfere or not, we must conclude that, of the two, it is Reason rather than Nature, in so far as we can validly distinguish them, which is in the expectant and subservient role.

The opposition which Mr. Lewis makes between Reason and 'irrational' Nature, is not only the basis of his whole argument, it also leads him, as I have said at the beginning of this chapter, to a position which is much more extreme than that of the other literary philosophers whom this book discusses. He certainly does not operate from the Two Truths theory, and he claims to be a Monist. That means here that he regards the rational, the mental, the ideal, as the real and primary, and the physical, the mechanical, the 'irrational', as secondary and dependent. This does not mean that he has solved the awkward form of dualism in which Descartes involved philosophy, only that he has evaded it. The only solution of the difficulty which we might take him as suggesting, the only account he gives of the way in which the Ghost really does 'operate the machine', depends on a double use of the expression the 'Laws of Nature', which is nothing but the old hypostatical trick in one of its commoner disguises. To this I shall shortly refer.

His uncompromising view of the primacy of reason, which leads to a depreciation of 'Nature' and so of experiment and observation, is responsible for statements that "We may be nearer the end of the Scientific Age than we think," and that scientists have already surrendered the claim that science is true. We may ask which of them have in fact surrendered this claim; and I think we shall find that these are speaking, not as scientists engaged in their special investigations, but as amateur philosophers often influenced by more personal considerations, and surrendering for the moment the methods by which they otherwise obtain true results. This last statement of Lewis's is in the context of a reference to the Heisenberg Uncertainty Principle, which he does not understand. The Heisenberg principle, whose misinterpretations are already of philosophical ill-repute, is so constantly misused by literary philosophers trying to make out a case against scientific law that I refer to it here at length, in a footnote.*

The statements I have just given from Lewis are useful as examples of the extreme right-wing position which he takes up in the controversy about the nature of knowledge, and also as conveying his emotional tone. For myself, I can believe that we might be at the end of the first great Scientific Age, but I do not find that an occasion for rejoicing, since the end would be brought on by historical and political events whose operation would destroy the only principles which have given us any genuine understanding and enlargement of our human condition. Mr. Lewis however shows signs of rejoicing.

Before leaving the basic verbalism on which Mr. Lewis erects this extreme attitude, to discuss some of his secondary misuses of language, I shall quote the type of argument, as commonplace and even journalistic as it is misleading, by which he illustrates it. The

---

Human Conduct and the Uncertainty Principle.

1. There are persistent attempts to smuggle a Cartesian 'mind' into a Cartesian 'machine' through the Uncertainty Principle of Heisenberg. Behind these attempts is the urge to prove 'free will' as a necessary step to having 'a soul to save'.

2. (a) In one way the whole controversy is outdated, for we now see that an infinitely predictable universe—even in its non-living parts—is not the goal of science.

(b) In another way the controversy is unscientific, or—what is equivalent—dishonest in scientific terms, for it consists of an obstinate attempt to bring back the landlady's ornaments.

(c) The persistence of the landlady's mentality leads one to suspect her when she comes in dressed in laboratory overalls, produces the objects and says diffidently "Now let's just *see* if there's room for them."

(d) Nevertheless, human actions of the sort important for 'saving one's soul' are, if nothing else, massive and sudden enough to warrant their enclosure in the frame of a scientific theory. It is therefore pertinent to ask whether a twelve-stone man will walk into a brothel or a mission-hall, depending on unpredictable variations in the configuration of his brain having the order of magnitude of Planck's Quantum of Action.

3. First it must be admitted that contemporary knowledge is far from any such statement of the causes and effects of change in the human brain, regarded entirely as a part of Nature, as would determine whether a given human action was predictable or inexplicable by scientific theory. Dr. Grey Walters has constructed some animal-like artefacts, his 'tortoises', which have the simplest powers of observation, learning and action. These have

basic statement, a verbalism as I have shown, was that Reason, including the human capacity for logical inference, cannot arise from Nature, since rational thought cannot arise from causes which are wholly irrational.

To illustrate this he quotes the popular and superficial accounts, which he accepts, of the Marxian and Freudian theories. The Marxian, according to Mr. Lewis, says that all thoughts arise from class-conditioning, the Freudian that all thoughts are merely due to complexes. Confronted with this popular abstraction, Mr. Lewis very pertinently asks: How then could either Marx or Freud attribute any rational validity whatsoever to their own theories? The answer is, fortunately, fairly simple. It is a factual denial. The Freudian and the Marxian, in so far as they understand the theories thus called, do not say what Mr. Lewis (and the daily press) attribute to them. They do not say that all thoughts are caused by 'irrational' causes. They say that men's thoughts, by which they mean the interests and pre-occupations which men

---

no soul, no free will; yet the pattern of behaviour of two of them in a room full of obstacles is too complex to predict. Thus there is no need at this stage to look for atomic phenomena in the study of human behaviour.

4. (a) Besides the random behaviour of particles within the frame of the Uncertainty Principle there is another cause of *practical* randomness: the shaking and chattering of all material at the temperature of our planet, the vibrations of heat. When these appear as noise in the physicist's delicate amplifiers, or as a slow swing in the galvanometer with which he measures the energy of a muscle fibre, he calls them 'random' and finds it inconvenient to examine them further. But in detail such thermal motions are subject to exact study and verification; they are separable in principle from the 'uncertainty' of the quantum theory. They are even expressed in a different unit of measure.

(b) Nevertheless, it is difficult to devise or postulate mechanisms which, at normal temperatures, show *mass effects* due to the Uncertainty Principle variations which are not totally masked by thermal randomness. The Uncertainty Principle typically comes into the open with mass effects, at the temperature of liquid helium, seventy times colder, on the absolute scale, than any animal brain can function. To bring out the effects of the Uncertainty Principle to a significant degree, we appear to need an artefact.

5. Therefore if 'a soul to save' is equated with free will, and both are postulated as the magnified effects of variations within the limits of the Uncertainty Principle, one can answer—"*Perhaps* human beings may have a soul to save, but at present the evidence seems against it. However, I can certainly make *robots* with free will, if that's what you want.'

will select to think about and the emphasis they will give to them, are conditioned by their complexes or their class-position. The complexes and the class-position exert pressure on thought. The point for both of them is that the internal stimulating causes of thinking may be *unconscious*—whether they are irrational or not is beside the point. We see however that Mr. Lewis has slipped in a new meaning for 'irrational'. Also whether intentionally or not, Mr. Lewis has attributed his own usual misuse of the word 'irrational' to followers of Marx and Freud. This is one sense in which they do *not* use it. Since both, in very different ways, are concerned with what has gone wrong with human society (Lewis's 'colonised Nature'), it is highly unlikely that either party would conceive of Nature as *irrational*. It may be true that parts of the unconscious complexes are irrational in a meaningful sense, that they partially relate to forgotten fantasies, for instance, the black dog, and not to past or present realities. But it is doubtful whether a Marxist would regard the automatic service of one's class-interests as 'irrational'.

We may not agree with either the Marxist or the Freudian in their conclusions as to what the preoccupations of a fully and correctly developed consciousness should be and the kinds of action and co-operation which would follow from these. But we may reasonably agree in principle that it is possible, even if difficult, to apply our consciousness to the examination and correction of our automatic assumptions, so that rational thought may begin to operate. The efferent direction of the arc towards external reality can be discovered or resumed. It is precisely on this possibility, and on no other, that both Marx and Freud base their treatments, the one of society and the other of the individual. In whatever mistakes and practical misapplications of their own theories both Marx and Freud may have involved themselves, there is no question that both of them thought that the initial step towards the changes which they advocated was an attempt at extension of consciousness. To both of them, people's thoughts, as well as the observable facts of physical nature, were among the given phenomena of which we had to become more conscious.

When Mr. Lewis chooses to call these given phenomena 'irrational' he is merely opposing them to others which he has already chosen to classify as 'rational'. Strictly, it is only our behaviour which can be judged finally as rational or irrational. The thoughts, images or ideas which drift through my mind at a lower or higher intensity of consciousness cannot be said to be rational or irrational before I have begun to communicate them. By the time they have reached the degree of consciousness at which I am able to communicate them, even to myself, I have already begun to act. For to state that they exist at all, even to myself, and even more to attach any emotion to them, *a fortiori* to judge them as rational or irrational, is initial action, in which it is fair to include refraining from action. No action at all, however trivial or reflex, appears without some preceding train of inferences, whether they are valid or invalid. And whether they are valid or invalid is shown by their relation to external circumstances. My previous examples of the Pavlovian dog and of the employment of learned skills will illustrate this. Moreover, inferences always result in some degree of action, some involvement of myself in the general activity of people and things outside myself, of the given and observable, some general conditioning of my behaviour, however slight. If images of pink elephants pass through my mind, this is in itself neither rational nor irrational. Countless images of all kinds pass through my mind, to which I attach hardly any emotion, to which I in fact pay no particular attention, and from which no action results. This is mindstuff, part of the given (what Mr. Lewis likes to call Nature). As soon as I do pay the slightest attention, even from curiosity, I have begun to judge and therefore to act. I have begun implicitly to decide what sort of person I am, and therefore, in some degree, what is my relation to the rest of humanity, and of the given world. It is here that the question of rationality or irrationality arises.

This becomes obvious if I am indeed haunted or obsessed by ideas of pink elephants. The degree of activity which may result is not relevant. It does not matter if I run up the garden or climb the curtains or just quietly take to drink without mentioning, or asking anyone else to investigate, my inconvenient retinue. The point is that to be 'haunted' or obsessed by an idea or image is to have begun to judge, to have drawn conclusions about the status of this idea in the general world of phenomena and thus necessarily to have conditioned my own course of action. I may look at the world from the top of a tree, with the false serenity of an imaginary mahout. Whether this behaviour is rational or irrational, its meaning, in short, can be judged only in relation to those who climb or sit for more visible or communicable reasons, by myself perhaps in lucid intervals, or by my next-door neighbours when they have had time to witness several repeated performances. It is only as a phenomenon, as part of the observable, that I can be found rational or irrational.

I have already referred to the subsidiary verbalisms by which Mr. Lewis supports his illusions about the nature and relations of the rational and irrational. Perhaps the most important of these can be detected in his use of the terms 'producing', 'causing' or 'arising from'.

The most useful example of Mr. Lewis's handling of this concept of causation or of 'production' which I can find is the following:

"There is no conceivable means whereby what is abstract and general could itself produce concrete reality."

This is part of an argument to show that God, if he exists, must be concrete and individual, but it is also basic and general for the whole of Mr. Lewis's case.

As stated it is hardly more than a truism. Since abstraction is essentially an operation by which we classify, compare and make concrete judgments about the concrete phenomena given to us in experience, we should hardly expect it to produce them, to cause them. This statement then is Mr. Lewis's way of saying that God is not any kind of pure abstraction, such as pure Rationality or the Immanent Infinite or the Superpersonal, and it is necessary, I suppose, because otherwise Mr. Lewis would not have been able to go on with explaining how God could have been the actual Creator, how he could be said to have caused or 'produced' anything. The difficulty of explaining *how* he has in fact done so still remains, because it is Mr. Lewis's own unresolved and unconscious dualistic difficulty to which I have already referred. Mr. Lewis has himself so sharply sundered the 'rational' and the 'irrational' or 'Natural' that he can hardly be expected to conceive of any means other than divine intervention by which they can be joined together again. Indeed on his view it is difficult to see how any causation or production, rational or natural, can go on at all; or any change, continuity or creation—for all of these are implied in his concept of 'production'. His God is 'out' of the machine, with a vengeance. His concrete individual God is a question-begging mechanism, and the statement 'There is no conceivable means by which an abstraction can produce concrete reality' is simply the converse of the statement in the first chapter that the Rational cannot arise from, cannot be produced by the Irrational (or Natural).

In order to be able to use his own definition of miracle as a supernatural intervention with ordinary Nature (something coming in from the 'outside') Mr. Lewis has had to adopt, perhaps unconsciously, a view of causation which is mechanistic in a surprisingly crude sense. It is much more mechanistic than the view held by many philosophers who were far from being idealists, for instance Hume, or than that which is used or implied by the modern scientist, who has long ago scrapped the pushing tactics of billiard-ball atoms. Mr. Lewis says rightly that it is impossible to avoid metaphor; language—natural language at least—*is* metaphor, living, decomposing or dead. But it is possible to avoid confusing metaphor with argument. Thinkers who work on the basis of the observed unity and regularity of natural change are those who learn most readily to think behind their own symbols to the observations for which these stand. The idealist or the dualist, on the other hand, usually have far greater difficulty in thinking in any other terms than those of spatial contiguities and gaps. If we hypostatise at all, if we attribute Substance to the totally unobservable, we are liable in referring to Nature, to the physical universe, to suffer from a crude and primitive form of mechanism which betrays us as inverted animists. We have unconsciously abstracted all the life, all that is also spontaneous and given, from what goes on around us, and put it up on some great Shelf which we call God or Spirit. No wonder that what remains is conceived of as a Machine, even the parts of a machine, of not much more use than a car which no one can start. To the Spiritualist, or the Supernaturalist as Lewis calls him, the mechanical, even if he has to use it or to rely on it for some philosophical and practical purposes, can only be thought of as a kind of insult. Hence perhaps the extreme Manichæan idea of the flesh as essentially evil. The 'orthodox' view differs only in degree from this heresy.

Whether Mr. Lewis himself is or is not unconsciously influenced by metaphors of birth and begetting when he talks of 'production', or causation, whether or not he really means 'reproduction', it is certain that he uses the terms metaphorically and has fairly distinct images of spatial contiguities in his mind. This is well illustrated in Chapter VII ('Miracles and the Laws of Nature'). His aim here is to assure or reassure the reader that miracles do not break the laws of nature. But the assurance turns out to be based on nothing more truly reassuring than a verbal confusion of that abstract and concrete which Mr. Lewis has himself already divorced. The "laws of nature," he says, are one such abstraction "made by the human mind and human operations." As he justly says, they do not "cause anything to be," they state the pattern of events. On the next page, however, he goes on to talk of them as though they were indeed part of the causal chain, the sequence of concrete events, of things which shove and are themselves shoved—as though Nature were one great hold-up in the trams.

"It is . . . inaccurate," he says, "to define a miracle as something which breaks the laws of nature. It doesn't. If I knock out my pipe, I alter the position of a great many atoms—in the long run and to an infinitesimal degree, of all the atoms there are. *Nature digests* or assimilates this event with perfect ease, and harmonises it in a twinkling with all the other events. It is one more bit of raw material for the laws (of nature) to apply to, and they apply."

Now it is no wonder that 'Nature digests' or assimilates not only Mr. Lewis's pipe-knocking, but all his other activities, including the writing of his book about miracles, and the causes for doing so, no doubt classified by himself as rigidly 'rational' in his own restricted use of the term. 'Nature' in the context means the same as the laws of nature. In using the expression 'The laws of nature are an abstraction' we must be careful not to imagine that this means that the laws of nature are anybody's airy abstraction. It is true that they are our classification of regularities observed in concrete phenomena. But even if we adopt the extreme Eddingtonian view that they are finally indistinguishable from the laws of human perception, we must still remember that they are the way in which, after due information, we are compelled to perceive. There is no way of thinking behind the laws of nature to something we can call 'Nature'. Mr. Lewis, still doing the splits between the Rational and the Irrational, sometimes treats the laws of nature as if they were just this type of human mental abstraction. But when it suits his argument he treats them as if they were in fact part of observed (and 'irrational') Nature. The pipe-knocking is "One more bit of raw material for the laws to apply to, and they apply" or 'take over'.

Mr. Lewis now proceeds to list some miraculous items which once they have made their appearance, are 'taken over' by the laws of nature. At Nazareth the miraculous spermatozoon impregnates, and at Cana the miraculous wine intoxicates. Does Mr. Lewis mean that a miracle ceases to be a miracle as soon as it has happened? What does a miracle mean except an event which the laws of nature cannot 'take over' (cannot account for or explain, if we may use language which while still necessarily metaphorical, has become more disinfected of anthropomorphism that Mr. Lewis's Christian muscularity of speech?) If a phenomenon arises which appears to be unaccountable but which, after due and competent investigation, can be regarded as 'taken over' in any meaningful sense by the laws of nature, then the phenomenon was after all a natural one and not miraculous. If the spermatazoon really impregnates, if the wine really intoxicates, they were not miraculous. Since it is not possible to apply the appropriate physical tests to those who participated at Nazareth and Cana, this statement means that we have elected the party of those who regard miracles, on the basis of general human experience, as intrinsically improbable. But it was only by classifying the 'Rational' as distinct from the 'Natural' that Mr. Lewis was able to find an analogy for miraculous interference, and that argument has been disposed of.

Therefore we must turn to his views on the nature of probability in general, to which he has devoted a chapter. This chapter is mostly about David Hume, whose sceptical conclusions on 'probable' or inferential knowledge have, according to Russell, never been adequately refuted, and do not seem to have been refuted even now by Mr. Lewis. There is the main body of Hume's work to be considered (*The Treatise of Human Nature*, and *The Enquiry Concerning Human Understanding*), and there is also the *Essay on Miracles* (which was a later inclusion in the collection known as the Enquiry). Mr. Lewis gives nearly all his attention to this last essay. That would have been both natural and correct, if its basic propositions were not in fact inconsistent with those of the sceptical views on probability expressed in the main body of Hume's work.

"The odd thing," says Mr. Lewis himself . . . "is that . . . his (Hume's) *Essay on Miracles* is quite inconsistent with the more radical and honourable scepticism of his main work." But here the odd thing is that, having noticed that Hume is in effect corrected by Hume himself, Mr. Lewis finds it necessary to go on arguing with the minor and inconsistent view. Flogging a dead horse, as here, may be more than an academic exercise. It may stop people putting their money on one which may still win philosophic races. Certainly Russell regards Hume as quite a live horse.

Hume's theory in the *Essay on Miracles*, to which Lewis gives all his attention, is described as follows:

"Probability rests on what may be called the majority vote of our past experiences. The more often a thing has been known to happen, the more probable it is that it should happen again; and the less often the less probable. Now the regularity of Nature's course, says Hume, is supported by something better than the majority vote of past experiences: it is supported by their unanimous vote, or . . . 'by firm and unalterable experience'. There is in fact 'uniform experience against Miracle'; otherwise, says Hume, it would not be Miracle. A Miracle is therefore the most improbable of all events. 'It is always more probable that the witnesses are lying or mistaken than that a Miracle occurred.' "

Now there are good reasons for saying that this view is incorrect, although they are not necessarily the ones which Mr. Lewis gives, and there are better reasons for saying that it is also inconsistent with the main body of Hume's work. Probability cannot be adequately or even correctly described as it is here described. The scientific conception of probability can be found in the text-books. But it is not true to say that probability depends on a majority vote, nor is it by any means always true that the frequency with which a thing has been known to happen has any bearing, one way or the other, on the frequency with which it will happen again. If out of fifty tossings of a coin we get fifty heads, that tells us strictly nothing about the number of times we shall get tails in the course of the next fifty tosses. Similarly "the majority vote of our past experiences" is meaningless unless we know more about the kind and bearing of the experiences. Probability, in short, is meaningless without reference to the complexity and context of the events which are or are not probable.

Further, Hume was mistaken and inconsistent in abstracting an absolute or unanimous vote of experience in relation to the Uniformity of Nature and suggesting that that was philosophically in a different class from other probable experiences. Our belief in the uniformity of Nature does not depend for its validity on any kind of party-membership. If we allow ourselves to adopt Mr. Lewis's loose and misleading expression, which, incidentally, is not Hume's, we can only say that the 'majority vote' must be the verdict of an informed majority, who are capable of observing, recording and understanding the real complexity of those things which are classified as events, and also as scientific generalisations. On more and more subjects scientists give us short cuts. We may hope that, when all the facts are assembled and available, the Village will not indefinitely Vote that the Earth is Flat. But Mr. Lewis's individualistic non-conformism alone would be enough to prevent us having any confident assumptions on that point.

Even if Hume was mistaken in setting up an absolute of experience which he called the regularity or uniformity of Nature, we do not have to agree with Mr. Lewis that he had made up his mind about the improbability of miracle on an *a priori* basis. When he appealed to more common or immediate experience, he said something with which most of us are bound to agree—that it is always more probable that witnesses are mistaken or lying. It is not necessary on this basis to consider miracles in a special class. With the most ordinary events, even those with the lowest emotional interest, the majority of witnesses are inaccurate (mistaken). Where there is any emotional bias (there mostly is) the majority of witnesses are concerned to tell a story or give an impression rather than the bare facts (are lying).

There are, however, good reasons why Mr. Lewis chooses to analyse the *Essay on Miracles* rather than Hume's main work. In the *Treatise of Human Nature*, Hume analyses the causal connections on which our probable or inferential knowledge is based. The result of the analysis, as we have seen, was a complete philosophical scepticism. Since Hume it has really been clear that whatever causal connections may be, they cannot meaningfully be described in terms of shoving and being shoved. Nor should it now be possible for any mind's ear to hear, as Mr. Lewis's still does, the brisk click of atoms as they cannon off each other. According to Hume, when events of the kind A are found in conjunction with events of the kind B, A leads us to infer B, by which he means that the sight of A causes the expectation of B and so leads us to believe that there is a necessary connection between them. 'Perhaps the necessary connection depends on the inference' and not vice versa. He says that the inference is not determined by Reason, since that would require us to assume the uniformity of nature, which itself is not necessary but only inferred from experience. This last statement, while inconsistent with the view quoted by Mr. Lewis from the *Essay on Miracles*, is strictly in accordance with Hume's sceptical empiricism. Mr. Lewis himself says that Hume 'knew better'. Surely then it is disingenuous to spend time in demolishing a view which the consistent expression of the philosopher's mind contradicts? If we are concerned with truth, we normally seek the best and most considered enlightenment and information an expert can give us, and argue only with his approximations to that truth. We are interested to know whether an astronomer has or has not discovered a new star. We do not wait to ask him till he is drunk and we can be sure that he is pointing the telescope the wrong way. In the *Essay*, Hume was perhaps a little eager to confute miracles, a philosophical blindness in him—just as Mr. Lewis is a little eager to see them, a braver and more Nelsonian gesture.

If in the *Essay* Hume had used the sceptical arguments of the *Treatise*, the case against miracles would have been covered. For if all our probable knowledge can only be described in terms of the constant associations of experience, and not at all in terms of any absolute connection or form of substance (such as Reason), then though we have no certain ground for supposing that the sun will rise tomorrow, we have even less for supposing that there will ever be a miracle. A miracle is by definition (Mr. Lewis's definition too) the rarest of all events. But it is not intrinsically excluded from the investigations of probability. It is only at an extreme degree of improbability compared with the rest of history or report, because it especially resists the techniques by which probability is normally established. We must repeat that the probability of anything is not 'normally' established by a majority verdict, but by a verdict of those qualified to judge in what the actual event consists. Miracles especially resist investigation by being too long or too far away from objective-minded experts. The consistent view which is based on Hume is that all knowledge can only be described in terms of probabilities, and this is true of events which will be almost exactly repeated and events which have vanished irrevocably into the past.

It seems to me doubtful that Mr. Lewis really knows what he means when he refers to 'intrinsic probability' and therefore when he says that Hume has been followed by most historians in regarding miracles as 'intrinsically improbable'. To be sceptical as Hume was, in his main work, means to agree that you cannot decide, of any event, miraculous or otherwise, that it is intrinsically probable. The modern historian tries to make his probabilities approximate more and more to the concept used by the other scientists. It is the special difficulty of writing history that important parts of its data are irrecoverably lost. On the other hand more and more data are continually discovered by the other sciences and made available for the historian.

Even if miracles do occur, the instinct of the historian to prefer any 'natural' explanation', anything that is based on a wider and more detailed, recorded classification of human behaviour, is sound, since improbability ought to be the criterion of historical science. We ought in fact to reflect that modern psychological investigation and discovery about crowd-behaviour, mass-hallucination, and the effect of unconscious wishes upon sense-perception in general are an important part of the growing body of scientific data which are continually fed into the historical sense and technique.

As Lewis himself says: "Most stories about miraculous events are probably false: if it comes to that, most stories about *natural* events are false. Lies, exaggeration, misunderstandings and hearsay make up perhaps more than half of all that is said and written in the world."

The historian's job is precisely to be sceptical, to start from the basis that nothing is *intrinsically probable*. In so far as he is dealing with the unrepeated, that which cannot be made subject to control, his method, like that of Sherlock Holmes, is elimination. He is like a judge trying to root out evidence from opinion. The better the historian, the less he will allow opinion, including his own opinions, to obtrude upon his work.

Even an extreme rationalist like Gibbon, with the weakness of enjoying satirical emotion, tries to let the facts give an account of themselves. But though we may never cease to enjoy him, or the opinionated Macaulay, as literature, we turn, if we are looking for precise knowledge of the past, more and more to drier and more co-operative, that is, less individualistic, documentation, and to monographs where the material is more limited and more microscopic, and the scope for whimsy and opinion is less. Lewis confuses the philosopher who appeals to historical evidence with the historian whose job it is to bring it to light.

Even in spite of his admission that most of the 'evidence' circulating in the world is false and that only those stories (of the miraculous) are to be accepted for which the historical evidence is sufficiently good, Lewis will not be parted from his conception of 'intrinsic probability'.

By limiting his study of Hume's views on probability to the *Essay on Miracles*, he falsifies, as we have seen, Hume's main position. According to Lewis, Hume made the whole idea of probability depend on the uniformity (or regularity) of Nature. This is misleading. In the chapter in the *Enquiry Concerning Human Understanding* which he devotes to the study of probability, Hume makes it clear that by uniformity of Nature he understands causes or laws which have 'hitherto admitted of no exception'. To Hume therefore, in his main work, the uniformity of Nature is not a 'necessary connection', not a principle which can be abstracted to provide a certain basis of prediction about the future; it is a description of what has been found to happen in experience, it is the sum of the most reliable accounts of the past. Probability, in this sense, is to be distinguished from numerical or calculable probability, it is simply a natural assumption, a state of normal expectation. Numerical or mathematical probability, on the other hand, which is less subjective, is also less individualised, but can tell us something which approximates to extreme precision about what is likely to happen with various classes of events. We cannot forecast with any certainty that John Smith will enter an A.B.C. in the middle of next June and sit down and eat an ice-cream, but we can work out with surprising accuracy how many people in the whole of London will enter A.B.C.s on that day to eat ice-cream, according to the number of degrees upon the thermometer.

But both these conceptions of probability are apparently different from Lewis's criterion of 'intrinsic probability'. This, on the one hand, obliges us to believe in the general uniformity or regularity of nature, but also permits us to think it possible that that uniformity will from time to time be broken by miracle (that rarest of all events, as Mr. Lewis agrees).

The ground of this belief must be something quite different from anything Hume meant or the mathematicians mean. It is simply, as Mr. Lewis puts it, our 'sense of the fitness of things'. But the further logical ground for this view is our belief in the rationality of the Creator. This belief, in turn, is based on our own rationality which the Creator, according to Mr. Lewis, must have implanted in us, otherwise we can find no explanation of how it got into us. The argument, we see, has come full circle.

The illustration and elaboration which he gives, however, of the general operation of our 'sense of fitness' gives us a little more insight into the fundamental nature of this argument, which is interesting because it is also the dominant type employed by Lewis's fellow-thinker, Miss Dorothy Sayers. He says that it is not only 'we', the lay public, whose quest for regularity or uniformity in nature is based on this sense of fitness, but also the scientists. Scientists too, when faced, like all the rest of us, with a mass of irregularities in their experience of Nature, cannot rest till they have found a new regularity, that is, a new hypothesis which appears to reduce the irregularities to order. According to Mr. Lewis, this means that we are all 'already enlisted on the side of uniformity *in advance of experience*'. But a glance at the history of the race or at the history of our own individual mental history will show that this statement is nonsense. Primitive mankind did not expect uniformity or regularity. Neither do infants. They both start off with a strong presumption in favour of arbitrary power or magical interference with their own affairs and those of 'Nature'. The notion of regularity is gradually impressed upon us by experience; our own, in the case of our more obvious and limited affairs, and that of trained observers and recorders, in the case of more universal events.

What Mr. Lewis finally comes down to, therefore, in his explanation of the 'sense of fitness' is a purely analogical argument which he has already borrowed with acknowledgements and handsome compliments, from Miss Dorothy Sayers. This æsthetic view is the real substance of their contention in both cases. I have alluded to it briefly in an earlier chapter, but since this is a book about a certain misalliance which has taken place between philosophy and the literary mind, and since the argument is really a description of what one literary mind, Miss Sayers's, viewing its own operations, supposes to be the process of Creation as a whole, it is worth considering here.

In her introduction to *The Mind of the Maker* Miss Sayers tells us that she does not intend to discuss the truth of the Christian theological dogmas, which depends on historical evidence outside her scope. Nor does she intend to discuss her own opinion on this question. Her object in this book is to select certain doctrines, in particular that of the Trinity, which claim to be statements of fact about the nature of God, and to show that these are, indeed, exact statements about the only kind of creativity known to us, that of the human mind. She mentions parenthetically that, according to orthodox Christian belief, it is not only the mind of man, in its creative aspects, which shows a Trinitarian structure, but this is also the structure of the universe as a whole. Whether this view of the universe is objectively true or merely anthropomorphic is a theme which in her introduction she sets aside as irrelevant. And the essential part of the book which follows is indeed simply an account of the process of creating a book as Miss Sayers conceives it to go on in her own mind.

Whether the account of creative process, given either by Miss Sayers or the Church Fathers, is accurate or not, we are obliged to begin by asking if the anthropomorphic view can indeed be irrelevant. Is it possible to make statements of fact about the nature of anything at all unless we have ground for supposing that it exists? It seems to me obvious that if those who drew up the doctrine of the Trinity claimed to be making statements of fact about the nature of God, they were also claiming that God exists. We can afford however to do as Miss Sayers wishes, and leave this question aside. But then the whole book is seen to be solely a discussion of human mental creation which, like any other æsthetic treatise may be considered on its merits, but which, like any other æsthetic treatise, has no bearing on theology. According to Miss Sayers, her purpose is only to illuminate theological dogmas by integrating them with a normal human experience. But unless her analogy from human experience is also intended to be in some way a proof of the validity of theological dogmas, she cannot be said to have illuminated them at all. Unless we can start with the doctrine of the Trinity and show that it is a true and essential description of the structure of the whole universe without which human creativity, with all other processes, is unintelligible, the two subjects, theology and æsthetics, remain in departmental obscurity, until we can illuminate them by some more scientific examination.

Miss Sayers is not likely to be frightened by the suggestion that she is arguing from analogy. Her view of language, that it not only always is metaphorical but ought to remain so, for all purposes, is integral to her whole discussion. Her attack on the scientists for trying to control the metaphorical twists of language and to use within their special fields a language of greater precision than common speech, must be discussed separately. Her conception of this is purely negative. She does not seem to understand that a striving for the utmost precision may be a duty, and a positive one in scientific work. To the non-mathematical, the use of a mathematical language often looks like sheer perversity, if not the deliberate wickedness of the old black magic. Mathematics is of course a foreign language to those who have not learnt it, and all foreigners are wicked. My justification for these remarks is that Miss Sayers uses the strongly emotive expression, the scientists' 'flight into formulæ'. Let us leave the scientists out of the question. Miss Sayers tells us again and again that she is a creative writer. Did any creative writer worthy of the name ever think that the metaphorical force of language should be allowed to overwhelm us? Surely even poets do not wallow in metaphor. They use metaphor for greater precision, and they regard language as a horse to be ridden, a force to be disciplined for their special and immediate purposes.

We must, as I said, look upon Miss Sayers's book as an æsthetic treatise, an attempt to give some account of human psychology in its creative aspect. Miss Sayers has debarred herself from really illuminating the theological dogma of the Trinity. The question remains whether or not the Trinity really illuminates her understanding of the artistic process, or ours. In my opinion it does not. It is very easy to see trinities or multiples of trinities all over the place, and it is even characteristic of some forms of mental pathology to do so. Poets like doing it. Dante did it with great effect in the *Vita Nuova* and elsewhere. It was for Dante reasonable and not even anti-scientific to do so. But he would probably have found it agreeable in any case. What I mean is that Miss Sayers uses the Trinity as a metaphor of human creative process. But surely what she meant to do was precisely the opposite.

She tells us that her whole book is an expansion of the speech of St. Michael in her own play, *The Zeal of Thy House*. This speech is an account of creative activity as symbolised by the doctrine of the Trinity. The three relations of the Trinity can be expressed, she says, as Creative Idea, Creative Energy, or Activity, and Creative Power. As I understand her, the Creative Idea means the original conception or intimation of the work, the Creative Energy or Activity means the actual working out or materialisation of the Idea, its expression in concrete form with all the labour and implicit criticism which that involves. The Creative Power is, to me at least, the most difficult of the three relations. It shares the obscurity and the transcendental quality which characterises the Third Person of the theological Trinity. I wonder if the reason for that may not possibly be that Miss Sayers is too determinedly Trinitarian and that this section of her pattern is simply *ad hoc.* The Creative Power is described by Miss Sayers as the readers' response to the book, which includes their awareness of the book as existing in all the concrete detail of its particular kind and also at one and the same time as an æsthetic whole. It is normal for æsthetic theories to make some attempt at accounting for the possibility of communication. Moreover Miss Sayers expressly allows for the case when the author is the sole reader of his book and communicates it only to himself. But, for Miss Sayers, the three relations or manifestations, like the persons of the Trinity, are inseparable, are all implied in each other. We must have all three of them or none. When we find further that the book does not actually have to be written but may remain entirely in what Miss Sayers calls the heaven of the imagination, we are hard put to it to assign any meaning at all to the Creative Power. An æsthetic theory which bases itself on the examination of particular works may very well try to tell us what an ideal reader's reaction ought to be, what possibilities of communication therefore we can find in a book after it has come into existence. But the author conceiving and writing his book can certainly have no fore-knowledge on this point, otherwise the world would not be so full of works which have failed to please or have pleased the wrong people for the wrong reasons, wrong at least from the author's point of view. An æsthetic theory, moreover, which does try to account for the phenomenon of communication may be and often is wrong. Communication, readers' response, Creative Power or whatever you like to call it, is something which we discover and judge in experience. It is not something which can be immanent in the Idea of a book, written or unwritten. We are obliged there-fore to lop off the third member of Miss Sayers's Trinity. It looks as if the trinitarian structure which she has discovered in her own mind has refused to reveal either its own mystery or that of the theological dogma.

If we simply peel off the theological metaphor, we discover that those parts of Miss Sayers's æsthetic which at all resemble genuine psychological description have been stated before, rather more simply, by Shelley and others. Shelley, for instance, commenting on the unconscious character of inspiration, says that "Milton conceived the *Paradise Lost* as a whole before he executed it in portions."

It is not unnatural that Shelley's conception of inspiration should be in keeping with his Platonic outlook; but on the other hand in his frequent and interested references to the operations of the mind in composing poetry there is much that is in harmony with modern psychological theories, and nothing, as far as I know, which is opposed to them. In his own practice, Shelley was well aware of the role of unconscious mental activity in the composition of poetry. Miss Sayers's choice of terms for the three phases of her creative process suggests to me that she is insufficiently aware of it. For Shelley the "mind in creation is as a fading coal . . . the most glorious poetry that has ever been communicated to the world is probably a feeble shadow of the original conceptions of the poet". I do not say this is a strictly scientific account, I only say that it gives us a truthful glimpse of the dynamic and dædal nature of unconscious process, on which most psychologists are agreed. For Shelley, the 'Idea' of the book is certainly not without parts and passions, it is not 'known to the writer as a complete and timeless whole' which 'is not changed or affected by the toils and troubles of composition', as it is for Miss Sayers. Since Miss Sayers says that the writer cannot know his Idea except by the working of the Energy or Activity which formulates it to himself, how does she know that it exists as a timeless whole? Indeed she asks this question herself, but answers it by saying that the Energy is in fact conscious of referring its acts to this existing and complete whole. I do not see how the Energy is conscious if the writer does not know how he is conscious. Both Shelley and Miss Sayers are Platonic, but Shelley does not let his Platonism interfere unduly with his observational description of his own activity.

If we wish to see a triadic relation in the creative process we can do so without harm by adopting the classification of M. Ernest Dimnet and others. This is a description of what does actually appear to go on in an author's mind: that there is a period of intimation, a period of gestation when the work simmers in the unconscious, and a period of production. The work establishes a reaction and a re-adjustment between the author's experience and his individual mental capacities. One advantage of this view is that it agrees with the introspective observation of most writers and does not involve us with any near-mystical implications about pre-existing wholes nor with the unpredictable responses of readers. It also agrees with observation about all kinds of mental activity, the process of learning and even moral learning or changing one's character included.

Elsewhere (*Creed or Chaos*), in discussing Original Sin, Miss Sayers allows that the biologists and the psychologists may have something worth listening to, to say on this subject (and therefore, one must assume, on all matters connected with the human mind, including creative processes). But she allows these sciences only an ancillary status. Their job will be to 'restate' the doctrine in terms which the ordinary modern man can understand. For in her view what these sciences have done is a considerable work of exposure of the nature and mechanism of 'man's inner *dislocation*' —by which she means Sin. Their reward ought to be that they should become 'powerful weapons in the hands of the Church'. Many psycho-therapists, probably the majority, see their functions differently. They think they have also done something to expose the *origins* of 'man's inner dislocation'. They do not accept the concept of a pre-existent and inherent sinfulness, and therefore do not use it as a basis for their work. They see that the notion of sin is at least as inseparable from the notion of punishment as it is from that of forgiveness, and they do not think that punishment is remedial. In other words, they do not want to be weapons in the hands of anyone. If we wish to find out how knots have been tied, we try to untie them, we do not use a sword.

Miss Sayers can maintain her somewhat patronising attitude towards psychology because the field of its inquiry coincides with that which was formerly occupied by theological concepts. But (and this is typical of her attitude to all the sciences) she does not seem to understand that there is nothing arbitrary about the psychological attempt to find a new terminology. Any science changes its language under the pressure of real changing observation. Psychology does not merely have to speak to modern man in language which he can understand. In so far as he wants to know anything about himself, it provides him with a language, new only because it embodies genuinely new concepts, which he has to learn. Every new science has to invent a new language, and it is not necessarily a jargon because it appears alien and cumbersome. Jargon is an attitude of mind even more than a habit of speech. In psychological matters it chiefly characterises those who are trying to turn the new terms into metaphors of old and insufficient concepts. These people, whatever their relation to religion, are generally dominated, though often unconsciously, by a view of human experience which is at least derived from theology. The linguistic result is jargon at the newspaper level. We may even agree with Miss Sayers that, *at one time*, some of the theological dogmas were an attempt at framing precise definitions of the facts of human feeling and behaviour. This does not mean that we should agree with the jargoneers, unconsciously dominated by theology, that Libido is only old Lust writ large; nor even that the idea is worth discussing. But a similar attempt is often made with other pairs of terms—to equate, for instance, Sin with the Freudian concept of basic aggression, or with egocentrism. Many psychologists do in fact take what the theologians would call a much more Pelagian view of human character than Freud's. They believe that aggression, the impulse towards hate and destruction, is not innate but acquired. But it is not on theological grounds that they argue with Freud. And for the theologian it does not much matter who turns out to be right, because all psychologists admit that even in early infancy there is an observable phenomenon which is at present better described by the term 'aggression' than by any other. No psycho-therapist can allow himself to be influenced, in his *practice*, by a concept such as Sin. It would not only undermine his relation with his patient, and therefore his treatment, but invalidate any claim that the treatment was scientific.

The two terms, in fact, Sin and Aggression, provide us with one of the most instructive and practical proofs of the fundamental importance of terminology. Before Freud began his observations and treatment of the insane at La Salpetrière, which provided the basis for many of his later theories, lunatics were still generally regarded as wicked, and were often punished by being chained and ill-treated. The treatment of mental illness was, in short, still subject to the theological dogma of Sin. Since that time there has been progress in the treatment even of severe psychoses. Whether this has been achieved by methods akin to Freud's or by physical methods does not matter. The point is that in one field theology was exchanged for science, the concept of blameworthiness for that of mental illness. For Sin is a theological notion, related to God at one end, but of course to punishment at the other. If Freud had not been able to see behind Sin to observable and often automatic reactions such as aggression and its repression, it is doubtful that our undeniable progress in the understanding and treatment of insanity would have yet begun. One very obvious practical reason is that it may always be necessary to use some force in the handling of violent madmen. Unless we understand the meaning and the actual necessity of force we always come to associate it with blame for the victim. Dogma of any kind never helps us to disentangle and limit this necessity of civilisation.

The psychology of the unconscious is a relatively young science. For that reason its basic concepts are still wide open to discussion and even to conflict among informed opinions; and the meaning of its terms inevitably fluctuates according to experience. This condition makes it possible for Miss Sayers, I have said, to award the science a status ancillary to theology. Her mode of attack on the more quantitative sciences has to be rather different. Her view is like Mr. Eliot's, that the present importance of a return to Christianity, by which she means the dogmas of the Church, is not so much that Christianity is ethically helpful or pleasant, but that it is *true*. The dogmas tell us the observational facts about human nature. Between two sentences referring to these dogmatic statements about our nature, our sinfulness and our inability to progress, she inserts a rhetorical question asking whether the increase of scientific knowledge has made us any happier, a question expecting the answer No. The question is not only in itself misleading but is also in its context significantly irrelevant. She is talking about truth and she expressly asserts that the aim of the dogmas is truth, not happiness. Most people would agree that the same can be said about scientific inquiry. If Miss Sayers blames the scientists, as by imputation she does, for the fact that the pursuit of truth does not directly and inevitably lead to happiness, she should logically also blame the theologians. There is a sense in which we can reasonably hold that the knowledge of truth does lead us, though slowly and painfully, to the only happiness of which we are capable. The statements of Christ were in general sound observational truths. Their overriding motive was the reduction of anxiety by love. Therefore we can say that they were concerned with the actual conditions of happiness. But the dogmatic theologians ever since have paid less attention to the subject. In this context Miss Sayers is not really concerned with it at all. Recognising the necessary opposition between scientific inquiry and dogma, what she means is that if dogma leads to the truth, then science does not.

What she further implies—and this is the essence of her whole discussion—is that the sciences in their necessary attempt to evolve precise languages and to avoid metaphor and analogy are in fact struggling to escape from our necessary conditions of truthful expression. If scientists do take 'flight into formulæ' they must also be fleeing *from* something. What can Miss Sayers mean by this except a flight from the truth, since she holds that language is always and necessarily analogical or metaphorical? She tells us that we must think by analogy or refrain from thinking at all, and that thinking about God is merely no exception to this rule. To sceptics who complain that man has made God in his own image, she answers that man has made all existence in his own image. If we can be charged with anthropomorphism in our thoughts about God, we are equally guilty of it in our thoughts about 'light, oysters and battleships'. But of course what sceptics complain of in anthropomorphism is not the personal qualities which men attribute to God—they would not mind if he had a long white beard or not—but men's attribution of existence based only on their experience of their own. On the other hand we experience the existence of light and oysters as at least something given, while we are even partially responsible for the existence of battleships. At the back of this particular section of Miss Sayers's metaphors lurks the ontological proof of the existence of God, demolished by Kant and not even greatly favoured by Aquinas.

However, Miss Sayers assures us that even the physicist:

"struggling to interpret the alien structure of the atom, finds himself obliged to consider it sometimes as a 'wave' and sometimes as a 'particle'. He knows very well that both these terms are analogical . . . and, as pictures, they are incompatible and mutually contradictory. But he need not on that account refrain from using them for what they are worth. If he were to wait till he could have immediate experience of the atom, he would have to wait until he was set free from the structure of the universe."

But, in fact, the physicist was obliged to consider the structure of the atom in this opposing, unsatisfactory and metaphorical fashion only while he was developing the mathematics which enabled him to communicate this experience precisely, to those of the same level of training. And though his experience of the atom may be rather less immediate than that of eating an apple, it is about as immediate as his experience of a flying bullet (one which does not hit him), or rather more so. He can see its path and he can see a single object such as an oil-drop being knocked aside by an electron.

Miss Sayers's statement that the difficulty of communication which confronts the scientists is the result of their failure to understand or to accept the analogical nature of language, inverts the actual situation and is aimed at discouraging the rest of us from thinking observationally, impartially and precisely. We can accept the usefulness of metaphor. But we must not believe that the two terms of the metaphor are necessarily on the same level of reality or that analogy is in any way identity. Behind both common and scientific experience, which we are trying to communicate in signs or metaphors, there is always something which we are talking *about*. Or there should be. Otherwise there is no satisfactory way of choosing between metaphors. It is certainly natural and proper to use metaphors to maintain life and interest in our statements, but when we are trying to maintain or disentangle truth, we have for long periods, common man, artist and scientist alike, to avoid metaphor, especially those metaphors or signs which have been used by our forebears in very different applications. A new metaphor probably always lights something up. An old one often draws a veil or even brings down a thick fog.

My new metaphor is my attempt to say precisely what I mean about something which is a new experience and may therefore, as yet, not be totally clear to me. But to make new metaphor I generally have to break with the old. Thus we are all trying to escape from metaphor as well as to create it, every time we try to be faithful in description of some object, external or internal.

Miss Sayers expressly states, and it is essential to her case, that the theological dogmas are truths or statements of fact; they were drawn up as defences against heresy. But by heresy she does not mean opinions which were merely objectionable to a vested body of speculative belief. The dogmas "would never have been drawn up at all but for the urgent practical necessity of finding a formula to define experienced truth under pressure of misapprehension and criticism". The expression 'and criticism' can hardly be pleonastic with 'misapprehension'. Thought that is concerned only with truth and is confident of its capacity for verification, for instance a scientific theory soundly based on investigation of observable facts, looks on criticism as an aid to development, a welcome corrective. In the Albigensian Crusades and in the Inquisition, the Church, we lament to recall, 'defended' its dogmas only too vigorously. No genuinely scientific theory ever did or could maintain its *truth* by force. The truth prevails because it is great, or inherently powerful, not because it has developed the biceps of a secular arm.

Ecclesiastical Christianity, however, becomes muscular in this sense whenever our liberalism and humanism are weak enough to give it a chance. They are so today. As a faith and a way of living they have allowed themselves to be defeated by totalitarianism, no matter who won the last war and no matter how much the western nations square up to Russia. They are weak because they have allowed themselves to become nothing much more than a political and therefore abstract philosophy. In other words, they are the literary thinker's substitute for going to church. The liberal and the humanistic too often forget that their business, which should occupy them all the days of the week, is precisely personal relations, that if they are to do any good, they must do it in the minute particulars of everyday living. This hopeful, but naturally imperfect and small-scale, activity is based on the genuine experience of human possibility, which is their common stock with the teaching of Christ, and also with any other form of religion and philosophy which has faithfully and realistically concerned itself with the business of living on this planet. We are continually told, especially by the advocates of theological dogmatism, that the liberal and the humanistic in Europe are very small and rather decayed *rentiers* living on the dividends accumulated for them by Christianity. But this is totally misleading. No one can say that 'the Church' as a whole has ever stood for truth and charity (which are the essentials of the teaching of Christ, of liberalism and humanism when they are a practical way of living), for the very good reason that the Church has never been a whole. Throughout the last two thousand years, various sections of the Church, more or less powerful, have had to be reminded, more or less forcibly, by other sections, of truth and charity, of essential Christianity, liberalism and humanism. Generally other motives beside truth and charity precipitated the reminder.

Thus faced today with the threat of bigger and more successful forms of totalitarianism, the Churches have united so far as to claim that they are and always have been the guardian of the sacredness of human personality. But that is not the evidence of history. As a successful organisation, no longer in opposition, no Church has cared for human personality. The aim of Churches is and always has been to become successful organisations and to perpetuate themselves as such. Human personality, on the other hand, is a phenomenon which we only begin to observe when we are trying to approach our immediate and concrete relations with truth and charity. And charity depends on truth or knowledge. This fact is the common stock which makes a joint tradition of the teaching of Christ, of liberalism and humanism.

But if truth is the way to charity, if our ability to care for other personalities depends on our understanding of ourselves and of them, we can say that scientific inquiry, moving steadily if slowly into the field of human relations, is the heir of the essential and valuable in Christian teaching. It is our real tradition. One cannot say whether 'Science' considered as an abstraction has 'made us any happier' or not. But very few serious scientists seem to be unhappy men, whereas the floundering and fantastic among the literary who prefer, with the Churches, to maintain the essential 'mystery' of human nature too often exemplify that ignorance is misery.

We must indeed ask ourselves why the literary revivalists, including Mr. Lewis and Miss Sayers, put so little stress on the joys of salvation (a state of blessedness which has certainly been experienced, by those who claim it, as immediate and not deferred) and so much on the despairing doctrines of our fallen state and inescapable sinfulness. I do not think that this fact is sufficiently accounted for by the doctrinal compensations of the Incarnation or of Grace; nor as a reaction to the mistaken (and dogmatic) notion of inevitable progress, a partial eupepsia with which the

Victorians consoled their frequent gloom; nor even by the horrors and confusion of the present world.

The noteworthy fact is that the writers whom I have discussed in this book really dislike science and its developing tradition (which is behind all genuine liberalism and humanism) more than they dislike any form of totalitarianism. The worst enemy of dogmatism is, not another dogmatism, which can be physically attacked and with luck overthrown, but open-minded inquiry. If one's nature demands authority, one cannot live with hypothesis. These writers pay the price for the kind of emotional security they prefer in their obvious preoccupation with Sin and their more obscure eschatological preoccupation with various forms of punishment—they call it anything from damnation to eternal values. But there is no reason why the rest of us should foot the bill.

CHAPTER X

Augustinian Novelists

FROM the *Screwtape Letters* as well as from references in other works, we can see that Mr. Lewis, for one, has at least as much interest in the Devil as in God. Perhaps it is difficult for those who believe in an absolute Original Sin to abstain indefinitely from this final personification, and it may not be long before they try to commit us to the belief that the Devil also is what Mr. Eliot calls Original Sin, 'a very real and terrible thing'. Although Mr. Eliot discounts the theatricality in Baudelaire's Satanism, he seems also to have a certain nostalgia for it:

"Satanism itself, so far as not merely an affectation, was an attempt to get into Christianity by the back door."

"The possibility of damnation is so immense a relief in a world of electoral reform, plebiscites, sex reform and dress reform, that damnation itself is an immediate form of salvation—of salvation from the ennui of modern life, because it at least gives some significance to living."

The *fin-de-siècle* frivolity of this view is due, I think, to the fact that Mr. Eliot is here living in a world of words which have displeasing emotional associations for him. I am not sure that any of his ideas about damnation are orthodox. Indeed I believe that he and most of his fellow lay-theologians whom I have discussed in this book would be hard put to it to state clearly in what their orthodoxy consists. There is, as I have said, the basic question of the schism between the Churches. Most of the writers I have discussed are not Roman Catholics. If they were, the issue would be clarified. On the major dogmas such as the Virgin Birth and the Incarnation, apart from Hell and Damnation and the Miracles, the Church of England is by now officially flexible, if not vague. Those with an ideological imagination, such as Mr. Lewis and Miss Sayers, can produce a theological cosmos which is as far from theological orthodoxy, if that now exists, as the fiction of Jules Verne is from observational science. All the other more subtle *litterateurs* are, wisely, very vague. The only test which they would all impose, as far as I can see, is belief in Original Sin and the Fall. The belief in the Devil is an extrapolation from this with which the sado-masochistic imagination may like to toy. What we must all believe is that human nature is originally and essentially bad.

I have tried in this book to analyse and to illustrate this conception. In this chapter I want to touch on its spread into a more secular form which is markedly affecting the novel and the contemporary criticism of it. I shall suggest that, in this form particularly, it is a disguised emotional reaction which can best be understood in relation to the Anglo-Saxon literary prudery of the nineteenth century.

We remember, to begin with, that we have always found it very difficult to come across a clear statement of what exactly was (and is) the Original Sin. Though we are often given to understand, by those who will commit themselves at all, that the evil state of this world results from being cut off from the presence of God, and that Original Sin arises from our having been born into this evil, we are still not told with final clarity what it is that, either historically or spiritually, actually did so cut us off. I have never met anyone over the age of ten who thought it was actually due to eating an apple and have not met anyone else of that age or over who seems quite certain what the apple symbolises. We are still left with the half-hearted understanding that the sin by which Adam fell, and in which we are all born, is either sexuality or curiosity.

Moving now into the world of the novel and of the criticism of the novel, we find that the still mostly secular reviewers often try to purvey a new literary value which is based on the conception of an absolute Good and Evil. Henry James had this sense of an absolute Good and Evil, and Graham Greene has it pre-eminently. A few sentences from Mr. Walter Allen will delimit this theme:

"It would be generally agreed, I think, by his fellow-writers, that Graham Greene is the leading male novelist of his generation, and the purpose of this essay is to attempt to isolate and examine certain aspects of his art. Of these the first and most important is his deep-rooted and profound sense of evil, which is unique among contemporary novelists in this country.

"Broadly it seems there are two possible attitudes towards evil . . . Augustinianism and Pelagianism, after St. Augustine and the Irish monk Pelagius, who was his contemporary and opponent."

In Chapter II I made some attempt to distinguish between these two attitudes and some allusion to the modern critical attitudes which may be said broadly to represent them. Hulme was one of the first who equated Romanticism in art with Pelagianism in theology or ethics. The neo-scholastics in literature and criticism who have succeeded him could perhaps be both more deeply and more widely defined as Augustinians. What exactly this Augustinian belief in an Absolute Evil amounts to in the practical literary field still remains to be determined. It seems, in our own day at least, to be a virtue, since Mr. Greene, according even to secular admirers such as Walter Allen, owes his distinction to it. Good and Evil are distinct from Right and Wrong ("Mr. Howard Spring," says Allen . . . "did not see any difference between good and evil on the one hand and right and wrong on the other", when he reviewed *Brighton Rock*).

I cannot understand why Mr. Allen does not tell us what the difference is. He is a secular critic, therefore he is unlikely to be referring merely to the theologically orthodox view. But his main duty as a critic is to discuss common experience which can be imaginatively conceived. To accept, without examining, this cliché-dichotomy into Good-Evil on the one hand and Right-Wrong on the other, is to impute an overriding value to one kind of imaginative experience, the religious, and therefore to beg the question of the particular value of Mr. Greene's work. Conceivably an 'orthodox' critic may evaluate works of literature by 'precise theological standards', as Mr. Eliot wishes him to do. But then he cannot care very precisely about the literature itself. To evaluate by imprecise, because unexamined, theological standards, as Mr. Allen is doing, makes the worst of both worlds.

'Good' and 'Evil', as practically everyone now refers to them in literary contexts, seem to have no analysable content and nothing much that you can say about them except that they are Absolute. But both in life and literature we meet what is called good and evil in men and women and their actions and intentions—doing and thinking what, in a certain social or imaginative context, we judge to be right or wrong.

I do not deny that, in their imaginative self-deployment, those writers who, like Greene, are orthodox, or, like Henry James, are haunted, powerfully and often beautifully, in one wing of their minds, do provide a content for this Absolute. But then, as soon as it appears upon their pages, it is at least an implied judgment about what they think ought to have been done or not done, in the given circumstances, about right and wrong. By examining their works then we can hope to find, not—what we never will—what is Absolute Evil, but what they feel that people ought or ought not to do, what they judge to be relative evil.

We shall find that, though they may deal with a variety of 'crimes' and misdemeanours, what provides their feeling with the Absolute in the Evil, what makes them guilty men who in describing and projecting their guilt feel that they have described essential humanity, is basically the sensual, the sense of the flesh. It feels evil to them because it feels absolute and it feels absolute because it is ineluctable and it feels ineluctable because it is a natural, given, human impulse which cannot be totally defeated but can only be understood. F. O. Matthiessen clearly thinks that Henry

James's story *The Turn of the Screw* cannot be described in 'merely Freudian' terms. I am not sure how far it is necessary to bring Freud into it. The sense of the Absolute or supernatural Evil in this story seems to spring rather obviously from James's characteristic unwillingness to accept the particular facts of the life of the flesh, whether infantile or not, which is especially noticeable in his later work, and which can be observed by any reader who troubles to compare James's attitude with that of his French contemporaries.

The guilt of the flesh is not at all new in Anglo-Saxon literature. The interest for this study, of writers who have this flair for Absolute Evil and so have been enrolled in this odd order of merit, consists in the fact that they have simply inherited, in whatever mutation, a disease which infected the whole of English nineteenth-century fiction. This was the unconscious belief that women had no bodies at all below the neck, and men none, except for the athletic use of the legs, below the waist; and therefore, a natural consequence, that bodily enjoyment between men and women was out of the question. When this belief broke down, as we are often told that it did, with Hardy, and still further, and to an extreme, with Lawrence, it broke no further than the Augustinian phase of consciousness. Men and women actually got into bed, and Lawrence tells us so in considerable detail. But that any of Lawrence's characters ever enjoyed themselves, I gravely doubt. The results were still, in however disguised a form, sin and punishment.

I do not think we should cease to remark how absolutely astonishing this all is. If we look back, not merely at Boccaccio and the continent, but at Chaucer and most of the Elizabethans, we can easily remind ourselves that it is so. It is not sufficient to repeat that the Puritans did this to us. Most of us have gone on doing it to ourselves ever since. They made morality miserable, no doubt. The answer continually given by many, even at the worst of times, was to evade their morality. Their victory consisted in making misery moral. In the case of the novel, English or continental, I am not referring to the wider aspects of the sexual relation, psychological or social, which must often provide us with studies of pain and maladjustment. I am simply stating that physical sexual relations normally cause intense enjoyment and that no person, otherwise ignorant, would learn this fact from the works of our most influential novelists from the early nineteenth century to the present day. I do not suggest that writers ought to dwell on this mere fact. I only say that it is strange that none of them know how to imply its immense significance in the matrix of their work.* There seem to be still in general only two possible attitudes towards the fact of enjoyment, which both reflect its relegation to the pornographic. One has been revealingly, if not sensitively, described by Mr. Eliot as the Kruschen salts attitude. The other is the pursuit of damnation à la Baudelaire. We may agree with Eliot that damnation is the more dignified. Perhaps dignity is of interest to writers. It may be historically and socially more graceful to write about something which you associate with damnation than something which puts you in mind of a purge. It still seems strange that writers of normal critical liveliness can rest in either fantasy.

For a paragraph or more I must go into the question of the disguised Augustinians. They include some who on other ideological or æsthetic grounds might scorn one another's company.

The important distinction between the Augustinians and the Pelagians, referred to by Mr. Walter Allen, lies in the attitude towards Original Sin. The terms are useful for a broad classification only, and it should not be assumed that those who are not Augustinians, believers, that is, in the inherent damnableness of human nature, must necessarily be Pelagians in the strict theological sense. Those who are not Augustinians may simply hold a purely secular view that the efforts of men and women to understand and influence their own bents may have meaning and use. On the other hand, even strict theological followers of St. Augustine can hardly deny that his theory of human nature and

*To this Mr. Joyce Cary, who in his Jimson novels is trying to re-establish the tradition of Defoe, is an important and honourable exception.

its capacities was affected by his own prolonged struggle with his sensual impulses, nor indeed that the theological view of sin in general has been coloured by this strongly personal experience. To say that it was personal certainly does not mean that it was unique or even uncommon.

None of the Christian bodies gives the same express importance to sensuality in their theory of sin as it received by implication in St. Augustine's account of his own religious experiences. On the other hand, as we have constantly seen, they are not precise about the nature of Original Sin, in the life of the individual or in the history of mankind. One therefore has to deduce its real nature from a convergence of the theoretical implications and of the actual possibilities. The actual possibilities are not so many, by the time we get down to observation of the human infant in its cradle, and its relative feebleness and immobility. Faults, apart from being mostly potential, are necessarily classifiable in few, broad classes—multiple sensuality and disobedience to discipline or authority; or, to put it into the most elementary description, rage against the ill-comprehended will of the parent. In effect, the infant, squalling or cooing, if we take a moral view of his situation, is occupied with what Arnold called 'faults of sensuality and faults of temper'.

Let us leave aside, just for the moment, the name 'Sin' and also those emotional implications which we call 'sinfulness' or the sense of sin, and it becomes much easier for all of us to see Augustine's picture of original instinctive behaviour, and also to see Freud's, and to notice that as direct observation they have even much in common. If again one could rely on leaving out the emotional implications, one might, for the purposes of discussion, adopt Augustine's term 'concupiscence' as describing both the lust of the flesh and the lust of the world, or for power. Freud's terms were infantile sexuality and aggression.

As we might expect, when we remember the attempts that have been made in this century to enlist the Uncertainty of the physicists to the cause of the theological concept of freedom, Freud's psychology has also been adduced as evidence of Original Sin. It is quite possible that Freud had unconscious roots in the older philosophy which he did not sufficiently examine; but this has no important bearing on the value and meaning of his work, the whole conscious direction of which was towards releasing human beings from the burden of childish and fantastic guilt and anxiety. Even though Freud did apparently consider sensuality (which he perhaps misleadingly calls sexuality) and aggression to be instinctively basic in human mental life, this gives us no ground for equating aggression, as we can observe it in the human infant, with wickedness. The infant comes into the world equipped to seize the nipple and thereby to get food and sensual satisfaction. This in its direct form could be described as gusto. We can call it aggression if we please, provided that we remember that it is morally as neutral as digging the garden, blowing the ground up to build a road, or playing tennis for health and pleasure. What we in practice find shocking is thwarted instinctive aggression, which manifests itself in hate, guilt and fear. The incidence of the thwarting, and who instigates it, and why, is what we have to consider if we wish to regress to 'origins'.

The only question then which holds any real interest is: 'What is the sinfulness of sin?' I think it will be agreed by most theologians that Sin is a purely religious concept, it has no meaning without God, and therefore, whatever else it may or may not imply, it is inherently disobedience to God's will. On the other hand, the difficulty of knowing God's will in particular circumstances and especially before the age of reason does not seem to be met in any theology. The more clearly defined and agreed the body of theological rules, the greater the emphasis on the sinfulness of disobedience; as in the Roman Catholic Church, and as we might expect. The greater the emphasis on private judgment, on the individual conscience, the greater also the emphasis on puritanism, on the sinfulness of sensuality. God and Sin alike are more public in the Roman Church and more private in the various Protestant Churches. The Roman Catholic Church allows for sensuality; the unallowable *sin* is defiance of the Church's authority.

It was Augustine who drew our attention, in discussing Original Sin, to the observable origins of sin in infancy. It is therefore logical that we should also seek to observe the origins of the *sense of sin*. But the observable sense of sin is a feeling and we have, in degree, many irrational feelings. Even theologians have been known to rebuke penitents for over-niceness of conscience.

Now whether in adult life we are more troubled about our sensuality or about our general disobedience, our resistance to God's will, our preference of our power to his, the observable fact is that in infancy we were thwarted both in our sensuality and in our lust for power by our human parents. It seems certain that this human thwarting must still colour our imaginations and be responsible for at least some part of our sense of sin. We need not discuss how far we can learn to decide what is rational and what is irrational in this feeling which most of us experience. I do not indeed wish to labour this merely psychological explanation of sinfulness, of the subjective sense of sin, because of the useless emotional reaction this provokes in those who resist all psychological explanations whatever. I use it to illustrate that the emotional quality we attribute to the concept Sin does vary with time and place, and therefore presumably with different educations and disciplines. On this basis we can draw an instructive comparison between the novel in some European countries, particularly in France, and in Anglo-Saxon countries, particularly in England, as it developed throughout the nineteenth century, and can also refer to its newest manifestations. This may lead us to ask whether the recent theological development which has affected this form of literature is really new or whether it is not really a different disguise for an old psychological pattern.

Let us take Alphonse Daudet's *Sapho* as an illustration. This book was published in French in 1895, and later in an English translation. In France the book was received as an important work of literature. In England it made its way, via the Curiosa sections of the catalogues, to the Art Bookshops of the Charing Cross Road. It was generally understood to be a pornographic work. Those who read the book further understood that it was pornographic about heterosexual relations; those, the majority, who were so unfortunate as to be able to read only the title thought that it was pornographic about homosexual relations.

There is nothing surprising about this. I refer to this one book because its fate illustrates the diverging development of French and English literary and psychological history, during the nineteenth century. Briefly, the French remained adult in their understanding and treatment of the relations between the sexes, while the English (and the Anglo-Saxons generally) had become infantile. French fiction in general started from the basis of acceptance of sexuality and the French novelist therefore was able to use his sensibility within a framework of reality. Daudet said that the book was meant for the benefit of his son, when the boy became a man. It is of course not an immoral book, but the contrary. But it is a moral book simply because it is an adult and true book. It was dedicated to his son, not as a warning but as an education. It does not seem possible for us, in our present conditions in England, to reach this common adult attitude. Guarded scientific discussion is allowed to the public, and plays and books may be produced about the more unusual kinds of sexual behaviour, provided that such behaviour is always treated as a problem, provided, that is, that the morality and the public attitude which should have been criticised by the writer before he began to write are really taken for granted. Our general education is certainly not yet anywhere near the point when children can receive the facts of sexual behaviour at the same level of acceptability as other facts. The facts of life are still taught as if expecting the answer No. So the unusual becomes classified as the abnormal and hence excluded from general comprehension. But in an adult community, authority, either of Church or State, would have no say in public discussions of the whole range of these themes or indeed in any verbal statements about them.

None of the great English Victorian novelists achieved an adult attitude in this respect. Acceptance of sensuality was impossible for them. Basically they treated sex through the antithetical and abstract symbols of marriage and illegitimacy. Illegitimacy was the cruder symbol of the illicit. Some of the great women writers, and also more 'feminine' writers such as Henry James, achieved a faithful emotional exploration of the sexual relationship, but only through the same curious elliptical peep-hole.

In the twentieth century some English writers, notably D. H. Lawrence, apparently realised that English fiction was not moving in an adult world. But the plant in this case must grow again from the seed. In literature we have seen no reflection of real progress in understanding, only a variety of reactions. Lawrence and others were able in part to diagnose their own and the contemporary problem, but they could not in their single life-times both compensate for their own mal-education and lay the foundation of acceptance on which other novelists could make free use of their sensibility. By different routes, Lawrence and Huxley both went psychologically back to square nought.

Their most influential successors, both in poetry and fiction, have often gone back even further and in a disguised form have compounded with the nineteenth-century view. The framework of absolute Catholic theory employed by Greene, for instance, in his serious novels, really implies that sexuality is sinful and is not more than condoned by marriage. When Greene is writing about a real psychological situation he writes powerfully and movingly. Such a situation may well be one in which the particular actions of a character result from the reaction between a certain type of education and his concrete circumstances. This applies to the priest in *The Power and the Glory*. Compared with this the psychological situations of the policeman in *The Heart of the Matter*, and the novelist in *The End of the Affair*, seem factitious, even *ad hoc*.

To be artistically satisfying the situation must be objectively described. The author must not imply that, for esoteric reasons, he knows more about the answers to the problem than the characters do. You can write a human book about a Catholic if you do not at the same time write a book about Catholic theories of human nature.

The Power and the Glory is about the effect of Catholic belief and dogma on someone for whom that belief affords his whole *raison d'être*. We are allowed to concentrate our attention on the priest as a suffering human being. In *The Heart of the Matter* and *The End of the Affair*, which are about sexual and marital relations, the problems, while they are not less specialised and also peculiar to those who have had a Catholic education, are not resolved in their own terms, that is, also, in human and therefore artistic terms. The priest, a minor character in each of these two later books, is yet of major importance to Greene. He is a *deus ex machina*. He supplies the answers, dogmatic ones, not artistic.

The End of the Affair, for instance, is a book about sexual sin and about a superstitious bargain to evade punishment. The main 'answer' seems to be 'Catholicism is right, for look what happened' (some of it very odd). One of the concrete forms of the answer is that superstition is a good idea because anything is better than trying to resolve one's problems in rational terms. This is the answer given to the main character, who seems to be impressed by it, although not himself a Catholic.

Greene never shows the effects of Catholicism on the temperamentally cheerful and balanced, yet some of these people must surely exist without being too insensitive to merit either attention or salvation. In his books, moreover, the refined agonies of conscience which Catholicism may induce in the more sensitive do not bear impressive fruit of charity or even greater understanding of fellow-sufferers and fellow-sinners. For pathological types like Pinky in *Brighton Rock*, it only provides a certain security of vaingloriousness and self-satisfaction which is deeply offensive to a merely humane and ethical conscience.

When Evelyn Waugh writes as a Catholic, e.g. in *Brideshead Revisited* and *Helena*, he also writes about Catholic theory. His satirical novels are artistically successful because they are written outside the scope of Catholic dogmatism. It seems to be much easier for Catholic writers who are born Catholic, for instance Mauriac, to stick to psychological truth than it is for converts. This may be because it is much easier to ignore Catholic theory when it is acquired below the age of reason. Anglo-Saxon writers probably have a special disadvantage in this respect. Certainly continental writers more usually and readily retain warmth and kindliness in relation to the flesh than those who are continually obliged to maintain intellectual assent to dogma which merely rationalises their own sense of guilt about normal human impulse.

CHAPTER XI

The New Philistinism

THIS book might be regarded by some people as a defence of liberal and humanistic philosophy and faith, against the attempt to involve us in a return to dogmatic orthodoxy. But that has not been its special purpose. Certainly I have tried to contradict, wherever I have met it in discussion, the neo-scholastic claim that humanism is dead. I have done this to counter the view that humanism was always in error and has therefore merely died for its sins. This view implies that the true cultural tradition of Europe was based on the philosophy of dogmatic theology; that round about the seventeenth century this tradition fell victim to an unfortunate accident, the rapid development of the physical and mathematical sciences; that, granted a sudden and unexpected enhancement of his practical powers, Man became inflated with pride; and that humanism, a man-centred philosophy, is simply the expression of this pride, this *hubris*.

More or less directly, it has been to this pride that the dissociation of sensibility which befell imaginative literature has been attributed by those critics who have discussed the subject. In their conception, the imagination or heart made a forced surrender of its 'felt truth' to the intellect—which was proud, apparently, because its own truths could be demonstrated in material objects by means of measuring-rods.

I have accepted the fact of a 'dissociation of sensibility' but I have tried to show that the interpretation of the fact has been mistaken. Faced with an apparent opposition between thinking and feeling, we are often strongly tempted to try and give up one or the other. This to a mind which remains sane is not only un-necessary, it is impossible. If the 'thoughts', the intellectual conclusions, the working abstractions which we are obliged to make, in any case, so that we can understand, organise and communicate our experiences, happen to come in conflict with our present feelings and wishes, we do not in practice give up any attempt to 'think', to abstract and generalise. But we often do look round for another and substitute set of abstractions, another kind of intellectual framework, one which also appears to account for the observed phenomena and therefore to have a like validity of law, but which has the advantage of *not* conflicting too gravely with our present wishes and feelings.

This is what we are being asked to do today: to give up the philosophy, or the general conclusions, which are based on the observational techniques of scientific method, and to revert to the abstractions of dogmatism. For example, the necessary abstractions or generalisations of psychology, especially the psychology of the unconscious, do not present us with an im-mediately or totally agreeable picture of human wishes and behaviour. But these abstractions are based on observation of concrete and individual cases and if we fairly examine the data it is very difficult not to be convinced of the working truth of the main generalisations.

The abstractions of dogmatism also claim to tell us the truth, not less unpleasant, about the human mind and behaviour. But these abstractions are at a further remove from observation. They are essentially involved with another abstraction, the concept of Sin. This concept is not, as I have said, obviously agreeable. But it is inseparably associated with the consoling idea of an all-wise and all-powerful Father, an authority which, though it may certainly punish, can also forgive, and it is therefore a profound security.

I accept that a divorce or opposition between poetry and science, or, more widely, between imagination and intelligence, has vexed us during the past two and a half centuries; but I believe that the opposition is factitious. We can understand that some poets lose their nerve if they are continually told, as they were during the seventeenth century, that their subject-matter is mainly fictional, when this is taken to mean that imagination is no help towards understanding our real conditions. But this is not and cannot be the view of genuine working scientists. This particular attempt to put poets in their place put poets in the wrong place, and was made chiefly by those who philosophised falsely and in a hurry, about the nature of scientific method—by those, in short, who made bad abstractions, ones based on insufficient evidence. The trouble was, as usual, not too much science, but too little. Too little was known, before our own day, about the laws of mental operation and the functioning of imaginative and creative power.

I must not for one moment be understood as saying that this particular extension of scientific investigation has made or will make it possible for us to produce 'better' poetry and art. I only say that it will do something to extend our knowledge of the way in which we do actually understand reality, and perhaps to convince us finally that there is no real split between 'imagination' and 'intellect'. The faculties which we have been used to describing by these names stand in a different relation to the objects of experience, or they relate to different objects of experience. But to experience they do both relate, since experience is all that we have; and they are both employed in any production either of scientific or artistic thinking.

We certainly need to reunify our sensibility. But we can do this only by understanding our sensibility, by finding out and obeying its laws, by discovering what is psychologically possible for us and what is not; in other words, by an extension of scientific method. By this I indeed mean that poets must come to terms with science. But I do not mean that 'Science is wonderful'. In general when people speak of Science they are speaking of an abstraction, and we should not worship abstractions. All I mean is that what we call scientific method is the way we discover reality; that discovering reality is our most important business as human beings; and that poets will write bad poetry if they neglect or misconstrue our most important business.

That is the limit of my present interest in humanism. Humanism and liberalism are valuable and lasting attitudes in so far as they are erected on the belief in intellectual freedom, on the idea of our right and duty to find out about our internal and external conditions upon this planet; in so far as they are in harmony with the methods of science.

I have laid emphasis on the 'unification of sensibility', and I have limited my attack in this book to those who produce literature, especially poetry, and those who criticise it; and I have done this for one and the same reason. The reason is that it is peculiarly disgraceful that those whose professed concern is with the purity and precision of language should be doing so much to misuse it, by making statements and building theses which have no relation to reality. This lack of concern with what they are talking about is, I should say, more characteristic of the literary nowadays than of any other group which claims to have a disinterested intellectual standing. Out of this meaninglessness comes the main attack on scientific work and thinking. There is in fact a new Philistinism abroad in the intellectual world whose typical manifestations would be piquant if they were not shocking. Since the twenties, the old literary Philistines have been on the retreat, cowed by Mr. Eliot's obvious learning and respectability, if not by his poetry, and badly mauled by those wicked defensive animals, the Sitwells. Very few critics dare to admit that they do not understand a poem. Obscurity is not now made a major charge against poets except by those who obviously do not read any poetry at all. But the literary are now beginning to accuse the scientists of obscurantism. (Miss Sayers's expression, 'a flight into formulæ,' which I discussed in an earlier chapter contains this implication of a wilful obscurity.) In the discussions of the new Philistinism, it is not so much poetry or art, as Science, which is 'this modern stuff' which 'I don't understand' and (hardly *sotto voce*) 'don't want to'. No one need be ashamed of an ignorance which he admits and is trying to master; but the level of scientific and philosophical understanding and appreciation is at present disgracefully low among the literary, while literary discussions parade this ignorance and in their tone one can too often detect the inflexions of pride. The fact that a subject is 'above one's head' does not automatically imply that one speaks of it, with purer knowledge, from the heart. Mr. Eliot, among others, has sighed for the time when a man might have universal learning—before the opposition between science and the humanities appeared. But of course, knowledge, universal or short of universal, is only obtained by pursuing the one method by which we do in fact achieve knowledge.

Until about the time of Milton a major poet would certainly expect to be making progress towards universal learning, and intellectual curiosity was certainly a requisite poetic virtue. Admittedly knowledge is too extensive and too specialised today for the most gifted amateur to master, but with the poet it is the attitude which counts. Intellectual curiosity is still an essential poetic virtue. Moreover it is not impossibly difficult for poets to have a good working conception of the new knowledge which has been produced by methodical and patient investigators about 'the human heart'.

Dealing with the subject of obscurity in poetry, Mr. Eliot has justly observed that we should be glad that the obscure poet has 'been able to express himself at all'. This attitude of charity should be extended to the scientists. Not all scientific knowledge can be made popularly accessible, at least at present. We should not accuse the scientists of wilful obscurity. Rather we should improve the teaching of mathematics in schools. The 'flight into formulæ' is an emotional imputation. The 'flight into dogmatism', alas, describes a real fugue. Scientists use mathematical formulæ, not to be hierophantic, but to make themselves clear to those who have also taken the trouble to learn a precise language. This is really obvious, and so is the fact that no one should complain at being asked to take just so much trouble to obtain a piece of precise knowledge as that piece of knowledge does really take to obtain. The suggestion of wilful obscurity is linked with another common accusation that scientists are mainly motivated by love of power. Analysis of the depth psychology of most scientists would almost certainly reveal fantasies of power. So would the depth psychology of artists, priests and all other human beings. But impersonal sublimation with submission to the domination of experience is probably the least harmful use we can make of the power-drive.

The question of a precise language, whether mathematical or not, is, however, real and significant. It is partly because psychology and anthropology do not express themselves in mathematics, that some dogmatic thinkers believe and hope that they can come to terms, their own terms, with these sciences. They claim that psychologists are often saying the same things as themselves, in the language of a different technique. This, as I have tried to show, is a profound illusion. Where the psychologists are talking sense, they are talking about something quite different from the dogmatic concepts of human nature— about different concepts and different observations.

But lack of precision and lack of agreement in terminology is certainly one of the gravest weaknesses of contemporary psychology. The vagueness of many of its concepts and their liability to misinterpretation can often be traced to the fact that the psychologist's language is still overshadowed by unconscious theological assumptions. The opposition which Freud makes between a reality-principle and a pleasure-principle is a case in point. One cannot miss the implication that Reality is somehow right, and Pleasure is somehow wrong—that Freud has not quite eradicated from his own mind the theological notion that our instinctive drives are sinful. The point is that not all our instinctive drives are directly pleasure-seeking. Freud's pleasure-principle, to my mind, has put an obstacle in the way of accounting for the actual suffering which characterises all psycho-neurotic situations. It is far more significant and obvious that the neurotic is punishing himself and sacrificing his pleasure than that he is obtaining indirect satisfaction by his sufferings—although this is probably also true. Fear and propitiation by sacrifice is what is always most observable in his conduct. In short, by infantile, fantastic and useless means, he is trying to preserve himself, not please himself.

The psychologists too have not been careful enough to avoid a topographical terminology. This is another weakness which favours the dogmatic offer of a united front. If the psychologists had not allowed us to go on thinking of 'The Unconscious' as a receptacle, it would have been easier for us to avoid the association of the bottomless pit. I give these examples only to illustrate my view that psychology and dogmatism should not come to terms—there is a real opposition between them, as between dogmatism and all science. The risk of infiltration is, however, grave, and psychologists should do all they can to purify the language of their tribe from theological associations, conscious and unconscious.

Scientists, including Eddington, who have written works of popular exposition are not altogether blameless for another mis-interpretation which has given comfort to the new Philistines. This is the 'æsthetic' view of science and mathematics. In one sense what Dr. Lewis says may be true—that the scientist decides by his 'sense of fitness'; or it may be true that faced with alternative proofs of equal validity, the mathematician chooses the most pleasing. But we must remember that neither in art or science is the æsthetic to be identified with the arbitrary or even with individual taste. The 'sense of fitness' decides by *what fits*, by what is *most* fit. In other words, there exists something given to fit into. Many correct estimates are based on a total body of experience and do not require and cannot even make use of measuring-rods. In these cases your guess, however, is not as good as mine, if I am the scientist or the mathematician and you are not.

However, this 'æsthetic' view is so valuable, because so easily misunderstood, to the new Philistines that one may soon expect to hear some of them saying of the unsettled hypotheses of contemporary biology, psychology and physics—'I don't know anything about it, *but I know what I like.*' This statement, however, in any context, probably does not mean what it says. Really to know what one likes is not distinct in kind from really knowing anything else. Its main clause contains the truth, a truth which invalidates the subsidiary. In matters of poetry and art, it is usually painfully clear that those who merely claim to 'know what they like' are not only extremely ill-informed about the main body of the subject, they do not want to know about it. Further, they in general cannot or will not grasp that the subject is one about which any genuine knowledge can be had.

Behind all such attitudes, when they are erected into any kind of philosophy, lurks what I have called the Two Truths theory. This the majority of the literary dogmatics, uneasily aware that they are only ridiculous if they do not come to some sort of *modus vivendi* with the scientific approach to experience, have made their base. They will allow scientists to experiment and measure, even to observe and record, to analyse and to write things up in notebooks and on graph-paper. In exchange, they make, though often tacitly, an astonishing claim to what is in fact the whole field of the non-measurable, on behalf of some authority, the Church, inherited wisdom, tradition, whatever they please to call it. Most of them appear dominated by a fantasy, perhaps unconscious, of 'Science' interfering with material bodies with more or less sharp instruments; and of Scientists as directly motivated by ideas of inevitable progress and by an arrogant Pelagian belief in the essential goodness of all men and especially of themselves.

The point that they miss is that the scientific is a mode of perception and our fundamental one. 'Science' is not an isolated nor essentially a specialised activity. It cannot be confined to special fields of inquiry. Whenever we approach our experience with the intention of trying to understand it, we are acting scientifically. Understanding our experience always involves us in relating it to other fields of experience. The methods of science and theology can never converge. Theology might conceivably be called a science if it erected its generalisations upon the experience of mystics. But this it is not able to do. In fact theologians treat mystical experience as nothing more than an interesting commentary upon revelation and authority. Conversely, scientific method can treat mystical experience only as a department of psychological experience.

The literary neo-scholastics, led by Mr. Eliot, are greatly concerned with the idea of a western Christian tradition and with the importance of a return to it. Mr. Eliot, in particular, in all his works, has drawn attention to the necessary connection between culture and tradition, and in *Notes Towards the Definition of Culture*, he makes it clear that the essential kind of tradition which he has in mind is a religious one. No one ought to under-estimate the part which ecclesiastical Christianity has played for good and bad, in developing our European tradition. What is striking is that one can read the whole of Mr. Eliot's works, including the *Notes Towards the Definition of Culture*, without finding any indication that he understands that scientific method and activity have had anything positive to do with the development of European culture or with the tradition which has nourished it. In the works of the literary scholastics I have not yet found any conception of the fact that science *is* a tradition. Yet the tradition of science is as old as any form of religion, and modern European science comes from sources which are as wide as, if not wider than, Christianity.

Mr. Eliot gives lists of cultural activities, including the barque-construction of the Dyaks, and others characteristic of the contemporary British—for instance Derby Day, the dog races, Wensleydale cheese, nineteenth-century Gothic churches and the music of Elgar. From this list he goes straight to the statement that what is part of our culture is also part of our lived religion. He makes it clear that the moral, social and æsthetic values in his list are deliberately mixed and that therefore he wishes to avoid the suggestion that a nominally orthodox religious attitude will necessarily provide us with cultural objects and activities of a high value. This exonerates one, on the other hand, from any impulse to prove that the part which scientific activity has played in the development of culture and tradition has been or ought to have been wholly desirable or estimable. What is profoundly interesting is that Mr. Eliot does not think it worth mentioning that in all the cultural activities, and objects, desirable or undesirable, which he enumerates, the role of what is basically a scientific activity is very much more immediately obvious than that of a religious one. All the practical and useful arts belong to the same human tradition which stems from the first flint-makers and inventors of wheels. Any craft, however rudimentary, implies that the craftsman has discovered and submitted to the rules of his material sufficiently to body them forth in an object which works. And this attitude contains the essence of science.

That is fairly obvious in the case of most of the objects and activities of Mr. Eliot's cultural list. Music is one of the more interesting examples. No one would trouble to deny that the religious tradition of Europe has had a profound and stimulating effect on European music, on its themes, on its opportunities for performance and on its communal value. But those communal opportunities have generally been quite as important to the composer as the orthodox significance of the themes he has used. On the other hand, no one who has anything to say about the subject of culture and tradition in Europe can ignore the connection between the singular development of western music and that of various crafts and techniques.

A strong feature of Elgar's music is his use of horns: necessarily valve-horns, not hand-stopped horns. The valve-horn was invented and produced by those who profited from acoustic theory, and from the availability of accurate lathes and boring-tools. To say this is not to advance the absurd theory that Elgar's music is in 'a scientific tradition' (nor even that it is in any exclusive tradition). Tradition is manifold. But if we are considering all the arts, fine and useful, which we include in our conception of culture, and which reflect traditions, the one tradition which we cannot afford to neglect is that of science and technology. For it is in the matrix of this tradition that the most striking and irreversible changes in these arts have been produced.

Mr. Eliot has tried to cover himself by suggesting that though all cultural activities are lived religion, the religion which they live may be debased or primitive, that is, not purely Christian. "We must not think of our culture as completely unified—my list . . . was designed to avoid that suggestion". This statement implies, nevertheless, that some of the listed activities do express Christianity. Which, one wonders? There is no visible source of arbitration except Mr. Eliot's own personal taste—I believe that he approves of Wensleydale cheese; I surmise that he does not approve of boiled cabbage, cut into sections or not. But *Notes Towards the Definition of Culture* is surely an attempt to further the task adumbrated in *After Strange Gods* where the identification of æsthetic and orthodox evaluation was first proposed. If this is so, it is difficult to believe that Mr. Eliot's list deliberately reflects his personal tastes or distastes.

"To judge a work of art by artistic or religious standards, to judge a religion by religious or artistic standards should come in the end to the same thing: though it is an end at which no individual can arrive."

As Mr. Eliot revealingly says: "The way of looking at culture and religion which I have been trying to adumbrate is so difficult that I am not sure I grasp it myself except in flashes, or that I comprehend all its implications."

I suggest to him that he has made understanding more difficult for himself than it need be, by neglecting the real basis of the tradition in which æsthetic objects and activities bud and flourish. In Mr. Eliot's vague sense, all cultural objects and activities may express religious values. But practically all of them—one can say *all* of them, if one thinks of the entelechy of poetry as the drama— are inextricably involved with the laws of material nature, living or inorganic. Our oldest tradition on this planet is the endeavour to understand the conditions for our continuing to live on it. This may blossom into religion and art. It must develop into science.

If one is concentrating on religion and poetry, one may, if one likes, continue to say that a tradition was broken in the seventeenth century. But if one is talking of human psychological history in general, it is much more reasonable and informative to say that the tradition of science, of obtaining real knowledge, was rediscovered in the seventeenth century. We might also reverse Miss Sayers's statement that the dogmas were framed to rescue Christian truth from heretical misstatement and misinterpretation. The attempt to formulate the inductive method, and many of the statements of particular scientists, were made to rescue knowledge from dogmatic and orthodox misrepresentation.

Mr. Eliot and many of his school are all for the teaching of the Classics. They not only allow the immense literary and artistic influence of the Greeks but even demand that it should be perpetuated and over-emphasised at the cost of the natural development of education. But they have nothing to say about Greek science, for instance, Greek astronomy, which was based on ages of observational work among the Babylonians and Egyptians and which also, in important respects, anticipated the discoveries of the Renaissance. It is worth remembering that the work of Aristarchus of Samos, who actually put forward the main hypothesis which we attribute to Copernicus, was deprived of its due historical effect by contemporary religious prejudice.

Science can be regarded as our fundamental human tradition, because any genuine attempt to describe and classify experience is the germ of a scientific attitude. The confusions and errors of dogmatism arise when we try, as we repeatedly do, to hypostatise the language of description into prophecy and prescription. Aristotle in the *Poetics* was being scientific. He was describing, classifying and analysing the actual works of the Greek poets and dramatists. His 'Rules' were laws in the scientific sense, they were descriptions of what had worked in the past, not authoritarian prescriptions for future performances. An important part of literary history is concerned with a natural but probably wasteful rebellion against the dogmatism which was promptly built on the rediscovered Aristotle.

I believe that our contemporary dogmatics are doing something similar, and of course much more dangerous, with the teaching of Christ, the bulk of which consists of remarkably exact and vivid statements about human psychological laws and human relations.

Most of them reveal their meaning and use only when regarded in this way, and not as commands or prophecies. 'Thou shalt love thy neighbour as thyself' is a statement of the discovered law of survival. It tells us what is not only possible but necessary if we are to continue to live on this planet. It contains an implied observation which by now we are used, or we should be used, to seeing in the longhand of contemporary psychology—that we cannot love our neighbours if we hate ourselves. But when we subscribe to the obstinate dogmatic insistence on the concept of Sin, we are hating ourselves. We oppose another abstraction to the abstraction which centuries of theological dogmatism have taught us to make out of the idea of Love, and forget that we take the first and essential step towards charity only when we clarify our understanding of our own needs and possibilities.

ACKNOWLEDGEMENTS

The author acknowledges, with thanks, permission to quote from the undermentioned works, which has been granted by the following publishers:

George Allen and Unwin Ltd. (Bertrand Russell: *History of Western Philosophy*, *Human Knowledge* and *The Scientific Outlook*).

Geoffrey Bles (C. S. Lewis: *Miracles*).

Cambridge University Press (Eddington: *Nature of the Physical World*, and *New Pathways in Science*).

S.C.M. Press (Norman Nicholson: *Man and Literature*).

Chatto and Windus (Basil Willey: *The Seventeenth Century Background*).

Eyre and Spottiswoode (D. S. Savage: *The Withered Branch*).

Faber and Faber (T. S. Eliot: *Four Quartets, After Strange Gods, Essays Ancient and Modern, Selected Essays, The Idea of a Christian Society, Notes Towards the Definition of Culture, Points of View*).

Heinemann Ltd. (J. Bronowski: *The Common Sense of Science*).

Journal of the Philosophy of Science, Vol. II, No. 6 (Herbert Dingle: 'The Scientific Outlook in 1851 and in 1951').

The New Statesman and Nation and Mr. Walter Allen, June 9th, 1951 (Review of *The Common Sense of Science* by J. Bronowski).

Phœnix House, Ltd. (Walter Allen: *Reading a Novel*).

Poetry London (Cleanth Brooks: *Modern Poetry and the Tradition*).

Routledge and Kegan Paul (T. E. Hulme: *Speculations*).

The Times Literary Supplement, June 8th, 1951 (Review of a book by John Nef, *War and Human Progress*).

INDEX

Works are listed under their authors' names.

When a reference occurs on a series of pages, the first of these is given in italics.

ALBIGENSES, Crusade against, 25
Allen, Walter, *18*, 23, 301
Anceschi, Luciano, 187
Anti-Pelagianism (*see* Pelagian heresy)
Aquinas, Thomas, 46, 188, 195, 236, 294
Archimedes, 86
Aristotle, 78, 180, 224, 236, 250, 323
Arnold, Matthew, 26, 29, 36, *40*, 109, 122
  Culture and Anarchy, 56
  God and the Bible, 30, 33, 36
  Literature and Dogma, 30, 33, 36, 42
Augustine, St. (Augustinism), 69, 107, *304*
Augustinians, 23, 299
Austen, Jane, 115, 227
Ayer, A. J., 49

BABBITT, Irving, 36, 109, 123
Bacon, 59, 142, 149, 168
Banville, Théodore de, 151, 187
Baudelaire, 109, 231
Being, 148
Bergson, 11, 20, *75*
Bible, 34, 35, 40, 115, 182
  Old Testament, 34, 39, 41, 176, 178
  New Testament, 34, 176, 178
Blake, William, 33, 170, 237
Bradley, F. H., 34, 109
  Ethical Studies, 36, *41*
Bradshaw, 89
Bramhall, 119
Bronowski, Dr. J. (*The Common Sense of Science*), *18*
Brooks, Cleanth, 59, 161, 164, 166, 168, 251
Browne, Sir Thomas, 57, 142
Browning, Robert, 187

CARY, Joyce, 304
Causality, 63, 65

Christ, 24, 50, 52, 54, *177*, 293, 323
Churchill, Sir Winston (then Mr.), 24
Classicism, 57, 74, 220, *232*
Clausewitz, 25
Coleridge, S. T., 237
Copernicus, 145, *156*
Coplestone, Fr., 257

DANTE, 109, 168, 188, *190*, *197*, *208*
Daudet, Alphonse, *307*
Dawson, Christopher, 146, 149, 226
Defoe, Daniel, 304
Demant, Canon, 59
Descartes (Cartesianism), *44*, *98*, 160, 259, 267, *269*
Dimnet, Ernest, 290
Dingle, Professor Herbert, *64*
Dogma, dogmatism, 6 *passim*
Donne, John, 53, 194, 217

EDDINGTON, Sir Arthur, 12, 15, 58, 318
  Hypothetico - observational method, *15*, 21, 58, 59, 62, 155
  New Pathways in Science, 63
Einstein, Albert, 24
Elephants, pink (rats, ditto), 273, (66)
Elgar, Sir Edward, *320*
Eliot, George, 29, 34, 38, 116
Eliot, T. S., *passim*
  After Strange Gods, 6, 9, 33, 107, 117, 223
  Ash Wednesday, 7, 219, 235
  Cocktail Party, The, 53, 153, 154
  Essays Ancient and Modern, 7
  For Lancelot Andrewes, 7, 109, 220
  Four Quartets, 53, 219
  Idea of a Christian Society, 31, 117, *125*
  Notes towards the Definition of Culture, *55*, 125, 130, 135, 224, 228, *320*

Sacred Wood, The, 117
Selected Essays, 109
Sweeney Agonistes, 53
Tradition and the Individual Talent, 221
Waste Land, The, 53, 220
Existentialism, Existentialists, 19, 51, 79
Experimentalism, 5 *passim*
Explication, *80*

FAITH, *1*, 35
Fall, the, 47, *52*, 57, 69, 176, 208, 300
Fancy, 161, 167
France, Anatole, 88
Frazer, Sir J. G., 171
Free Will, *62*, 75, 83, 101, *270*
Freud, 48, 83, 84, 96, 158, 244, 247, 271, *291*, *305*

GALILEO, 16, 145
Galton, Francis, 81
Gladstone, W. E., 210
God, 16, 41, *45*, *274*, *294*
Goethe, 152
Graves, Robert, *151*
Gray, Thomas, *237*
Greene, Graham, 8, 108, 115, 153, 256, 301, *309*

HAMILTON, G. R., 234
Heisenberg (*see* Indeterminacy, Principle of)
Heresy, 7 *passim*
Hobbes, T., 119, 148, *160*, *168*, 180
Honour, Spanish conception of, 152, 232
Housman, A. E., 215
Hoyle, Fred, 255, 257
Horizon, 96
Hulme, T. E., *8*, 11, 41, *56*, 105, *141*, 146, 157, 167, 181, 215, 233, 238, 253
Human Nature, 75
Humanism, 4 *passim*
Hume, David, 3, 79, *278*
    Essay on Miracles, 279
Huxley, T. H., *79*
Hypostasis, 11 *passim*

IDEALISM, Idealists, 61, 65, 67, 85, 86
Imagists, 73

Incarnation, The, 32, 47, 57, 68, 101
Indeterminacy, Principle of, *17*, 62, 86, *269*
Induction, 77
Inference, 5, Ch. IX *passim*
Intellect, 80, Ch. III *passim*
Intuition, *82*

JAMES, Henry, 303, 309
Janet, 83
Jansenists, 71
Jeans, Sir James, 62, 155
Joyce, James, 9, 113
Judgment, 161
Jung, 96, 171

KAFKA, 218
Kant, 3, *42*, 78, 122, 294
Korzybski, Alfred, 203

LAWRENCE, D. H., 9, 58, 94, 96, 113, 226, 309
Leavis, F. R., 200, *206*
Lewis, C. S., 2, 8, 43, 48, 59, 68, 76, 106, *175*, 211, 231, *254*
    Miracles, 48, 258
    The Screwtape Letters, 258, *299*
Liberalism, 4, 21, 108, 126, *137*
Locke, John, 165
Lucretius, 78, 145, 198
Luddites (Luddism), 16, 225

MACAULAY, Rose, 29
Manifold, Extensive and Intensive, 82
Mann, Ida (*The Science of Seeing*), 100
Mansfield, Katherine, 9, 113
Maritain, 8, 59, 79, 146, 148, 253
Marx, Marxism, *271*
Materialism, 17, *59*, 65, 67
Mauriac, 8, 310
Meynell, Alice, 213
Milton, 70, 140, 159, 167, *169*, *172*, 264
Miracles (*see also Miracles under* Lewis, C. S.), 258

NAPIER, John, *23*
Nazis (Hitler), 2, 94, 134
Neo-scholastics, neo-scholasticism, *4*, *12*, 15, 21, 62 *passim*, 106
Nef, John (*War and Human Progress*), 23,

Newman, Cardinal, 32, 35
Newton, *23*, 62, 145
Nietzsche, 78
Nicholson, Norman, 62, 172
  Man and Literature, 59, 78

OGDEN, 45
Original Sin, 6, 22, *25*, 28, 48, *52*,
  55, 57, *68*, 74, 90, 104, 106, *176*,
  196, 208, *299*
Orthodoxy, 5 *passim*

PAUL, St., 177, 232
Pacifism, 24
Pelagian heresy (Pelagianism) 40,
  49, 57, 70, *230*, 291, 301
  Anti-Pelagianism, 22, 26, 50
Plato, Platonism, *89*, 201
Pope, The, 126, 152
Progress, 6, 22, 71, 150
Psycho-analysis, 60
Psychology, psychologists, *15*, 69,
  152
Punishment, *176*
Puritanism, 175, 179, 183

REASON, *1*
Renaissance, 72, 74, *147*, 157, 220,
  224, *232*
Rats, pink *see* Elephants, pink
Read, Sir Herbert, 72, 101
Russell, Bertrand, 15, 47, 62, 120,
  156, 169, 257
  Human Knowledge, 157
  The Scientific Outlook, 18
Ryle, Prof. Gilbert (*The Concept of
  Mind*), 259

SAURAT, Denis, 175
Savage, D. S., 114, 154
Sayers, Dorothy, 8, 43, 48, 59, 68,
  76, 106, *254*, *284*, 315

  Creed or Chaos, 290
  Gaudy Night, 256
  The Mind of the Maker, 48, 256,
    285
  The Zeal of Thy House, 287
Scholasticism, 57, 149
Science, *10*, *16*, 68, *150*, 159
Self: Superficial, Fundamental, *82*
Semantics, *56*
Sensibility, dissociation of, 9, 29,
  159
Shakespeare, 74, 78, 112, 170, 197,
  216, 241
Shaw, G. B., 55
Shelley, 167, 195, *236*, 251, 289
Sprat, Thomas, *170*
Stapledon, Sir George (*The Land*),
  225

TILLYARD, Dr., 141, 175
Theology, 5, 41 *passim*
Thomas, Dylan, 217
Times Literary Supplement, The, 23,
  25
Truman, Harry, 24
Two Clocks Theory, 99
Two Truths Theory, 58, 61, 64, 71,
  74, 88, 102, *181*, 253, 257, 319

UNCERTAINTY Principle (*see* Indeterminacy Principle)
Unconscious, The, 84, 224

VALÉRY, 201
Visualisation, 81

WAUGH, Evelyn, 310
Willey, Basil, 2, 11, 16, *141*, *159*,
  210
  *The Seventeenth Century Back-
    ground*, 2, 36, *141*, *159*
Wyatt, Sir Thomas, 213